Trade Threats, Trade Wars

For a complete list of books in the series, please visit
www.press.umich.edu/subjects/econ.html

Trade Threats, Trade Wars

Bargaining, Retaliation, and
American Coercive Diplomacy

Ka Zeng

THE UNIVERSITY OF MICHIGAN PRESS

Ann Arbor

Copyright © by the University of Michigan 2004
All rights reserved
Published in the United States of America by
The University of Michigan Press
Manufactured in the United States of America
⊚ Printed on acid-free paper

2007   2006   2005   2004   4   3   2   1

A CIP catalog record for this book is available from the British Library.

Library of Congress Cataloging-in-Publication Data

Zeng, Ka, 1973–
    Trade threats, trade wars : bargaining, retaliation, and American
coercive diplomacy / Ka Zeng.
        p.   cm. — (Studies in international economics)
    Includes bibliographical references and index.
    ISBN 0-472-11358-5 (cloth : alk. paper)
    1. Economic sanctions, American.   2. United States—Commercial
policy.   I. Title.   II. Studies in international economics (Ann Arbor,
Mich.)
    HF1413.5 .Z46   2004
    382'.0973051—dc21   2003010312

Contents

Figures

Tables

CHAPTER 1

Introduction

Increasing international interdependence has been accompanied by heightened commercial rivalry among nations. In the past two decades, trade conflicts between advanced industrial countries have intensified as these states have competed to maintain a vibrant domestic production base. Confronted with the possibility of eroding economic competitiveness and challenged by other developed nations, the United States has engaged in a never-ending series of trade conflicts with its European and Japanese competitors, particularly in those high-technology industries such as semiconductors and aircraft that directly affect the national economic and security interests. Some of these conflicts even led to trade wars.

As the United States was forced to adopt an increasingly aggressive trade strategy in dealing with its competitors in the industrialized world, it also had to cope with growing trade challenges from developing countries whose pursuit of mercantilist and protectionist policies for rapid economic catch-up put them on a collision course with the Americans. In the late 1970s and early 1980s, the United States increasingly began threatening trade sanctions to liberalize markets in newly industrializing countries such as Taiwan, South Korea, and Brazil.

More recently, China's remarkable economic growth has begun to pose another major challenge to American trade policy. Although total trade between the two nations grew from $4.8 billion in 1980 to $121.5 billion in 2001, making China the fourth largest U.S. trading partner, the U.S. trade deficit with the Chinese is also on the rise, reaching $83.8 billion in 2000 and $83.0 billion in 2001 (see fig. 1.1).[1] In 2000 China for the first time surpassed Japan as the country with the largest trade surplus with the United States.

It is not surprising that Washington and Beijing have found themselves embroiled in a wide range of trade conflicts over the past two

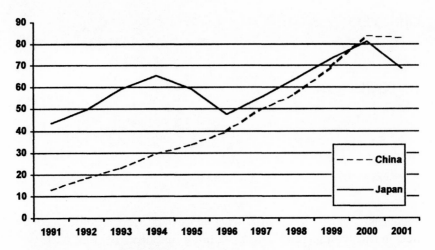

FIGURE 1.1.   U.S. trade deficits with Japan and China, 1991–2001 (in billions of dollars). (Data from U.S. Department of Commerce, International Trade Administration, *U.S. Foreign Trade Highlights,* various years.)

decades in such areas as intellectual property rights (IPR), textiles, market access, and China's Most-Favored-Nation (MFN) status. What is most surprising, in view of the disparity in bargaining power and resources between the two countries, is that America's sanction threats against China have succeeded in winning unilateral concessions in few of these conflicts. Prior to the 1999 U.S.–China agreement on terms of China's entry into the World Trade Organization (WTO), the Clinton administration encountered considerable difficulties in its effort to open up the Chinese market because the Chinese government, preoccupied with problems associated with its efforts to further reform the economy, demonstrated little willingness to dismantle trade barriers. Although recent moves by the United States to integrate China into the world trade body appear to have produced some genuine market-opening outcomes, Washington's attempt during most of the last decade to threaten China with trade sanctions for unilateral trade gains has by and large failed to induce Chinese concessions. It could be said that, for American trade dispute diplomacy, China has become the most challenging state, on a par with Japan in the 1990s.

The record of these commercial rivalries presents us with two puzzles. First, even though the United States has always been the country with greater aggregate power and bargaining resources in bilateral trade disputes, it has had uneven success in extracting concessions from its trading partners through the use of coercive strategies. As my survey in chapter 3 of Washington's attempt to unilaterally open foreign markets under Section 301 of U.S. trade law indicates, the degree to which the target countries yield to American demands often varies in ways that cannot be neatly explained by their dependence on the American export market. For instance, although Japan is less dependent on the American market for exports than many U.S. trading partners, it has given in most frequently to U.S. pressure.[2] Interestingly, countries that are more heavily dependent on the U.S. export market (such as China, Brazil, and India) have turned out to be more resistant to American demands.[3] Despite having fewer power resources, they have frequently been able to negotiate better dispute settlements than gross measures of power would predict. Clearly, traditional realist theory, with its emphasis on nations' underlying raw power balances, cannot explain why, on average, American coercive diplomacy works less well with countries whose raw material power should have put them in a more disadvantaged position vis-à-vis the United States. It seems necessary for us to look at factors other than raw power to understand the variations in the effectiveness of America's pressure tactics.

The second puzzle motivating this study is that the pattern of democratic peace that has been found to be a distinctive characteristic of international security conflicts does not seem to apply to trade conflicts. The empirical evidence presented in chapter 3 on the pattern of state involvement in the aggressive escalation of trade disputes leading to mutual retaliation suggests that trade conflicts between pairs that match democratic and authoritarian states have not more frequently escalated into trade wars than have conflicts between democratic trading partners. Indeed, statistical analyses of the determinants of trade retaliation indicate that states' regime type has no significant bearing, in either a positive or a negative direction, on the probability of aggressive escalation of trade disputes.

In a nutshell, the theory of democratic peace posits that democracies are significantly less likely to go to war with one another.[4] With a few exceptions, most of the recent democratic peace literature has focused on the effect of regime type on the probability of military wars. Relatively little effort has been made to assess the relationship between regime type and the likelihood of trade wars.[5] Nevertheless, as this chapter will later explain, the insights of the democratic peace theory should be applicable not only to analyses of military wars but also to analyses of trade wars. In particular, one version of the democratic peace theory, the theory of "democratic signaling" put forward by

James Fearon, provides a logic that suggests that democracies should be less likely to engage in trade wars with one another.[6]

However, as the empirical evidence presented in this study reveals, democracies are *not* less inclined to be involved in trade wars with one another than with authoritarian states. The record of America's involvement in trade conflicts under both Section 301 of U.S. trade law and the dispute settlement procedures of the General Agreement on Trade and Tariffs (GATT)/WTO suggests that, even if we take into consideration alternative explanations, the United States still has been involved in a large number of trade wars with its democratic trading partners, such as Japan and Europe, a pattern that clearly does not accord with the theory of democratic peace. These empirical irregularities raise an important research question: Is democracy indeed associated with an enhanced propensity to be involved in high-intensity conflict in trade, or is trade war driven by some more fundamental causal mechanism than regime type? Furthermore, if regime type has no association with the probability of trade war, what can we deduce about the "audience cost" rendition of the democratic peace in explaining the pattern of military wars? By studying trade conflicts, light is cast on this important theoretical question of whether democracies do indeed resolve disputes efficaciously, a question that continues to grapple scholars of international relations today.

In approaching the two puzzles described, I draw on the notion of "two-level games" to show how domestic and international politics interact to affect negotiation outcomes. The two-level game approach, which has gained prominence in recent years, argues that political leaders must play their hands in the domestic and international arenas simultaneously. Their behavior cannot be understood without taking into consideration the constraints and pressure they face in both arenas. The metaphor, by adding a new level of analysis to international relations, allows us to go beyond the unitary actor assumption to view central decision makers, legislatures, and domestic groups as independent actors in international politics.

However, although the two-level game concept provides a good starting point for organizing empirical studies, most of the literature inspired by it has fallen short of generating explicit hypotheses about the interaction between domestic and international politics. Moreover, the two-level game approach remains underdeveloped theoretically. Although a number of recent works address this problem by developing more rigorous treatment of the domestic game, and some even systematically investigate the possibility of democratic cooperation on trade,[7] few have explicitly utilized the two-level game concept to explain variations in threat effectiveness and the outbreak of trade wars. This study fills this gap in the literature by developing a systematic analysis of domestic interests and institutions and of their impact on international negotiations. It argues that a system-level variable, the *structure of trade* among nations (specifically, whether the bilateral trade relationship is complementary or competitive), affects threat effectiveness by influencing both the level of unity among domestic interest groups and the degree of divided government. The same factor also affects the propensity of trade conflicts to escalate into trade wars.

The structure of trade, as will be explained in more detail in the next chapter, refers to the degree to which two countries engage in the export of a similar range of products. If two countries produce a similar set of commodities and can easily replace imported commodities with similar products produced at home, then they have a primarily *competitive* trade structure. But if each of them specializes in a different set of products in which it has a comparative advantage, and trades them for commodities that it is incapable of producing at a reasonable cost, then they have a *complementary* trade relationship. To put it in another way, trade complementarity involves the mutually beneficial exchange of goods in areas where each is deficient. By looking into the structure of trade among nations and its impact on domestic politics and international negotiating outcomes, this work offers a plausible explanation for the two empirical puzzles previously summarized, and, in doing so, it aims to capture an important aspect of the dynamics of international trade negotiations.

Variations in Threat Effectiveness

The first puzzle of this study concerns variations in the degree to which U.S. economic coercion succeeds in achieving its intended objectives. Following the realist insight that bargaining outcomes reflect states' underlying power balance, one would expect the United States, which holds greater aggregate power vis-à-vis all of its trading partners, to be most successful in extracting concessions from its least powerful trading partners. Unfortunately, however, this theoretical expectation has insufficient empirical support. Previous studies of asymmetrical trade negotiations have uncovered many cases where powerful states failed to impose their demands on weaker ones.[8] Moreover, if we look at the record of all Section 301 cases concluded by 1995, we can see that the degree to which the United States has achieved its negotiation objectives varies in ways that cannot be readily explained by the realist theory.

For instance, although the European Union (EU) has the lowest ratio of asymmetrical export dependence on the United States (EU's export dependence on the United States, measured by EU's exports to the United States as a percentage of EU's GNP, averages only 0.96 times the U.S. export dependence on the EU between 1975 and 1995), it is among the U.S. trading partners that are more responsive to American pressure.[9] Similarly, although on average Japan is only 4.63 times more dependent on the American market than vice versa during the same period, it has yielded more often to American demands than nations that are much more dependent on U.S. export markets, such as China. In U.S. negotiations with Japan under Section 301 of the U.S. trade law, American pressure proved to be largely successful in achieving market-opening results in four out of a total of twelve cases, produced partial success four times, and resulted in nominal success in the remaining four cases.[10]

In contrast, the United States has had greater difficulty imposing its demands on nations whose raw material power should have put them in a relatively weak position vis-à-vis U.S. demands.[11] For example, China, which was on average 29.6 times more dependent on the American export market than the U.S. was on the Chinese market between 1975 and 1995, has yielded far less frequently than America's other trading partners. In recent trade negotiations with China, the United States has had considerable difficulty convincing the Chinese to conform to its demands. In the two Section 301 cases involving China in the early 1990s (IPR protection and market access), the United States was able to achieve only nominal success.[12] In these cases, although the United States managed to secure China's written consent, it rarely received substantial compliance with the terms of the agreement. When the Chinese government did agree to change its policies, it did not implement and enforce these policies completely either because of the lack of political will or because of domestic intransigence. If we apply the same criteria Bayard and Elliott used to evaluate the degree of negotiation success in two other major U.S.–China trade disputes (textiles and MFN) conducted outside of the framework of Section 301 of U.S. trade law, we can see that American pressure has been similarly ineffective. The Americans were only nominally successful in the textile case since the bilateral textile agreements were not implemented to U.S. satisfaction: Chinese sales of textiles to the U.S. market skyrocketed despite the quota restrictions mandated by the agreement; Chinese textile and garment producers also found ways to circumvent the quota restrictions by transshipping Chinese textiles to the United States via third countries.

The United States fared even worse in efforts to change China's trade and other domestic practices through threats to revoke China's MFN status. The Chinese side completely rejected most American demands and made few, if any, changes in its domestic policies. The MFN case thus represents almost a complete failure for American negotiating objectives. On the whole, it seems fair to say that U.S. coercive strategy has produced rather limited results in China: Beijing did not offer even minimal concessions to the United States in some cases. In those cases where Beijing did commit itself to written agreements, it was either unwilling or unable to implement the promised policies.

China's ability to resist American pressure is particularly puzzling in view of the fact that other similarly trade-dependent countries in Asia such as Japan, South Korea, and Taiwan have tended to be much quicker to offer concessions. This contrast suggests that raw power per se is inadequate to explain the variations in the outcomes of international trade negotiations. Factors other than raw material power need to be taken into consideration for us to better understand the dynamics of international bargaining.

Democracy and Trade War

There is another puzzling aspect of international trade conflicts: inconsistent with the predictions of democratic peace, it cannot be established that, in trade, democracies are less war prone with one another than with authoritarian states. Simply stated, the democratic peace thesis contends that, while democratic states are as war prone as other regimes, pairs of democracies are less likely to fight wars against each other.[13] Three strands of arguments have been offered to explain why democracies are less war prone in their relations with fellow democracies. The norms-based explanation, which focuses on the constraining effects of democratic norms and principles on democracies' external behavior,[14] is based on a logic that seems to be most relevant to international security conflicts—the only area in which empirical evidence has been marshalled to support the contention that there *is* a democratic peace. However, institutional explanations of the democratic peace and, most importantly, the audience cost argument, which extends the institutional explanation to highlight the role of domestic audience costs in constraining democracies' propensity to escalate their conflicts to the level of a "war," emphasize a causal mechanism that should logically yield solutions to both security *and* trade conflicts among democracies.

Norms-based explanations of democratic security peace regard the norms of self-determination, regulated political competition, compromise solutions to political conflicts, and peaceful transfer of power as powerful restraints on violence between democratic systems. According to Russett, "If people in a democracy perceive themselves as autonomous, self-governing people who share norms of live-and-let-live," they are likely to extend these norms to other national actors who are "also perceived as self-governing and therefore not easily led into aggressive external behavior by a self-serving elite."[15] In other words, democracies are constrained and perceive other democracies as constrained by the same set of structures and behaviors that limit aggression. The externalization of democratic rights and principles, it is argued, mitigates democracies' fears of being dominated by one another, thus preventing conflicts between democracies from escalating to the use of military force. But when a democracy comes into conflict with a nondemocracy, it will not expect the nondemocratic state, which does not abide by the norms of peaceful resolution of conflicts in its internal politics, to refrain from the use of force in its foreign relations. Out of fear that its moderation may be taken advantage of by the nondemocratic state, a democracy may resort to more forceful conduct to obtain a decisive outcome. In short, democratic principles and practices that denounce the threat or use of violence allow democracies to be more "dovish" in their foreign relations, fostering a "zone of peace" among democratic states.[16]

The norms-based explanation has been frequently invoked to explain the democratic peace in the realm of international security. The second explanation of the democratic security peace focuses on the role of structural and institutional constraints on the use of violence. While this explanation can most readily be applied to security issues, it has potential implications for understanding trade conflicts as well. From the institutional perspective, democracies are inhibited from going to war by the need to ensure broad popular support. The complexity and lengthiness of the mobilization process mean that leaders will be reluctant to take the country to war unless they can convince the public that victory can be achieved at a reasonable cost. Structural delays in the process of mobilization for war on both sides of the conflict should also provide greater scope for negotiation and other means of peaceful conflict resolution. By contrast, since leaders of nondemocracies are not as constrained as leaders of democracies, they can more easily and rapidly initiate the use of force. In short, "the constraints of checks and balances, division of power, and need for public debate to enlist widespread support" in democracies will slow decisions to use force and reduce the likelihood of war among democracies.[17]

Building on the structure-based account, the third theory developed to explain democratic peace, the audience cost argument, emphasizes how democratic states are better able to learn about an adversary's resolve in a crisis situation and is based on a logic that seems more likely to apply to economic as well as security conflicts. For example, Bueno de Mesquita and Lalman's work dealing with the informational properties of political institutions argues that, due to the presence of active domestic opposition, democratic leaders face generally higher costs in the event that they fight a losing or costly war. In other words, democratic institutions help to signal a state's true preferences by revealing that the government faces relatively high costs for using force, regardless of whether that government is making a conscious effort to signal its intentions.[18]

James Fearon builds on Bueno de Mesquita and Lalman's model and contends that democracies should be able to cope better with the security dilemma because they can signal their resolve to other states more credibly and clearly than can authoritarian states. According to his formal model, domestic audience costs, which refer to the reaction of domestic political audiences interested in the leadership's handling of foreign policy issues, allow states to learn about an opponent's willingness to use force in a dispute. Since democratically elected leaders face higher domestic audience costs for escalating and then backing down, they are less inclined to bluff than are leaders of nondemocracies. To the extent that a democratic leader does threaten war, the threat is rendered credible because the leader is able to generate *costly signals* by incurring audience costs that would be suffered if he or she backed away from the threat. These believable signals between democracies allow them to learn exactly where their bottom lines are in a dispute. Given the high costs entailed if war actually breaks out, two democracies then have the incentive to use this information to reach a mutually acceptable settlement. The signaling and committing value of a stronger domestic audience makes democratic pairs less likely to begin or to escalate conflicts, thus ameliorating the security dilemma between such states.[19]

Kenneth Schultz takes Fearon's argument and develops a more elaborate framework showing how domestic political competition can help democratic states overcome the problems associated with asymmetric information. In this view, a strategic opposition party enables democracies to send more informative signals about their true preferences by creating a second source of information. An opposition party can enhance the ability of the government to make threats by publicly supporting those threats in a crisis, or it can undermine the credibility of threats by publicly opposing them. In the latter case, the presence of a domestic competitor with political incentives to reveal its aversion to war makes it more likely that the rival state will resist the threat, leaving the home government with less opportunity to bluff or to misrepresent its preferences. Hence, institutions associated with democracy, by providing more credible information about a state's resolve, give democracies an enhanced capacity to resolve their disputes peacefully relative to states that do not permit open competition.[20]

The "democratic signaling" argument, although applied thus far only to the absence of security conflicts between democracies, is based on a logic that ought to extend to trade conflicts as well. In trade conflicts, as in security conflicts, democratic leaders face high domestic audience costs that enable them to reveal their true willingness to fight over the interests involved in the dispute. Thus, threats to impose economic sanctions should strengthen the target's belief that the threats actually will be carried out and provide the opponents with greater incentives to avoid trade wars and to arrive at negotiated settlements. Trade wars, like security conflicts, also impose high costs on nations that fail to come to negotiated settlements and allow disputes to escalate. For example, it is estimated that the trade war over agricultural subsidies in third markets between the United States and the European Community (EC) cost the two sides approximately $2.5 billion over three years. Therefore, democratic dyads should have as strong an incentive to use the information generated by their enhanced signaling capacity to avoid trade wars as to avoid military wars.

The argument that this democratic peace theory should apply to trade wars as well as to security conflicts is strengthened by Fearon's own claims that the two issue areas share a common "strategic structure." Fearon argues that "diverse international issue domains can be productively viewed as having a common strategic structure."[21] He contends that earlier cooperation theories that treat states as facing different strategic structures in different international issue domains are misleading. He believes that characterizing the strategic structures facing states as either coordination or collaboration games not only creates difficulties in assigning state preferences but also leads to the neglect of bargaining problems that are not captured by these simple game structures. Regardless of whether the issue involves arms control, trade talks, exchange rate coordination, or environmental regulation, he argues, states are invariably confronted with problems of dividing up new or potential benefits of agreements and of monitoring and enforcing cooperative agreements. In this sense, he writes, trade bargaining has essentially the same strategic structure as "international crisis bargaining in which one state threatens military action and war."[22] If different international issue domains share a common strategic structure, as Fearon posits, then the same theoretical mechanism that helps explain the observation that crises between democracies are less likely to escalate into wars in the security realm should apply to trade disputes as well.

Indeed, some recent studies have devoted greater attention to the relationship between states' regime type and their propensity to cooperate on trade issues. Based on a variety of theoretical premises, most of these studies conclude that democracies, whether alone or in pairs, should be less confrontational over trade issues. For example, Daniel Verdier concludes that democracies are more likely to pursue free trade policies because democratic elections enhance the power of voters with free trade inclinations vis-à-vis particularistic business interests with a protectionist slant.[23] Dixon and Moon focus on the effects of regime similarity on the likelihood of international cooperation. They assert that, since states with similar regime types ought to be more familiar with each other's business practices, they should experience less political conflict in bilateral economic exchanges and consequently have freer trade than mixed dyads.[24]

Mansfield, Milner, and Rosendorff contend that democratic pairs are more likely to conclude free trade agreements either because of the executive's need to obtain ratification from the legislature or because of the need to retain the political support of both voters and interest groups.[25] Leeds offers a similar hypothesis, arguing that democratic dyads should cooperate more with each other than should two states with dissimilar regimes because democracies face higher domestic audience costs for breaching international commitments.[26] Still another explanation for democracies' superior ability to settle trade conflicts cooperatively is offered by Dixon and Raymond, who emphasize the importance of democratic norms and principles in constraining democracies' tendency to conflict over trade. From this perspective, democratic principles such as "bounded competition" and the rule of law extend to both security and trade relations between democratic pairs. Despite the diversity of interests that characterizes democratic regimes, democracies should more frequently invoke these principles in their trade relations and bring their disputes to adjudication under international institutions governing trade such as the GATT/WTO. As a result, democracies are more likely to resolve their disputes more cooperatively.[27]

Of course, not all of this literature emphasizes properties of democracies that diminish the chances of trade conflicts. Some scholars also highlight those aspects of democratic regimes that enhance their risks to trade confrontation. For example, Verdier contends that trade type (i.e., whether trade is intra-industry or propelled by scale economies), rather than regime type, is a necessary condition for trade conflicts. According to Verdier, even if a democracy alone were more likely to be engaged in free trade than an autocracy, democratic pairs are more likely to experience an increase in protection because similar regimes tend to enhance the political power of the same class of producers.[28] Reinhardt, based on an empirical study of the determinants of GATT/ WTO trade dispute initiation, asserts that democracies are involved in a greater number of trade disputes. He reasons that, since democracies empower producers over consumers, democratic regimes are particularly susceptible to the demands of both import-competing and export-dependent producers to initiate trade disputes against foreign protectionist measures in order to obtain a "fair" trade outcome. Democracies' vulnerability to producer interests also lessens their ability to compromise and to settle disputes cooperatively.[29] For similar reasons, Sherman finds that democracies are more likely both to participate in GATT disputes and to be targeted under Section 301 of U.S. trade law.[30]

On the whole, these existing empirical studies have not yielded definitive conclusions about the effect of regime type on the likelihood of cooperation over trade issues. While some researchers find that democratic regimes cooperate more on economic issues, others disconfirm this view with contrary evidence.[31] The current literature on democracies' behavior in trade conflicts thus begs the question of whether the relationship between democracy and trade conflict is real. If the answer to this question is negative, then what might be the more fundamental causal process that drives state involvement in trade conflicts? What implications will these findings have for the debate over the relationship between regime type and trade cooperation, a debate that has only very recently unfolded? What can we infer from such a study of trade conflicts about the theoretical foundations of the democratic security peace?

This book provides a plausible answer to these questions by assessing the influence of regime type, among many other factors, on the probability that states will escalate their trade disputes to trade wars. An important objective of such an empirical analysis is to assess the conflict-prevention properties of democratic institutions as emphasized by scholars such as Fearon, Mansfield, Milner, and Rosendorff. As explained earlier, the audience cost argument proposed by Fearon posits that democratic institutions bestow democracies with superior signaling capacity that renders them less conflict prone than mixed pairs. Mansfield, Milner, and Rosendorff and Milner and Kubota share an optimism about democracies' ability to cooperate on trade issues, finding that democracies are more likely to undertake unilateral tariff reductions or to enter into preferential trade agreement due to greater voter control or the larger size of the winning coalition in democratic regimes.[32] These arguments highlighting the greater degree of institutional constraints in democracies ought to lead us to expect fewer trade wars between democracies than between mixed pairs. However, if the empirical evidence does not support this hypothesis, then we may need to explore alternative explanations for the pattern of aggressive escalation in trade conflicts and would consequently have reason to be skeptical of democratic institutions as the key to democracies' enhanced ability to cooperate on trade issues.

Before proceeding, it is necessary to define one of my key dependent variables: trade war. For purposes of clarity, I will follow Conybeare's definition and consider trade wars as sustained, protracted, and high-intensity international conflicts "where states interact, bargain, and retaliate primarily over economic objectives directly related to the traded goods or service sectors of their economies, and where the means used are restrictions on the free flow of goods and services."[33]

This definition allows us to distinguish trade wars from two other kinds of commercial conflicts: politically motivated trade sanctions and low-intensity trade conflicts with minor consequences. First, since trade wars mainly involve the use of economic means in the pursuit of economic objectives, they are distinct from other types of conflicts (such as trade embargoes imposed by countries involved in a military war) where economic means are used for political purposes. The following analysis will thus consider trade restrictions that have predominantly economic objectives. But it should also be noted that empirically "very few trade wars are sufficiently pure to be devoid of any political goals."[34] Many trade conflicts involve the pursuit of both political and economic goals. In the dispute over China's MFN status, for example, the United States sought to use the threat of MFN withdrawal to induce the Chinese to concede on human rights issues, in addition to the economic objective of forcing changes in China's trade policies. In such cases, political factors are treated as a form of the "linkage" policy; their inclusion into the analysis, where necessary, will be justified.

Second, a trade conflict needs to reach a sufficiently high level of intensity to be called a trade war. According to authors such as Conybeare, routine customs decisions on tariffs involve fairly low-intensity conflicts. But if a conflict moves out of the bureaucracy and reaches the executive level of government, it can lead to high-intensity conflict. An "escape clause" petition in the United States would be an example of such high-intensity conflict. Furthermore, trade wars should involve the active participation of both sides. This means that the actor targeted for economic sanctions will engage in at least one round of retaliation for a trade war to exist. Thus, the imposition of antidumping duties or other forms of trade sanctions constitute a trade war only if the target country retaliates. An element of tit-for-tat is essential to this definition of trade war.[35]

Judging from these criteria, trade wars, as far as those involving the United States are concerned, have taken place primarily between democratic trading partners. As the case summary in chapter 3 and the case studies in chapters 6 and 7 illustrate, the United States has been engaged in a series of trade battles with the EC over agricultural products, including the Chicken War in the 1960s, the Turkey War in the 1970s, the war in the early 1980s over agricultural export subsidies in third markets, the U.S. imposition of penalty duties on EC pasta in 1985 in retaliation for EC tariff preferences in favor of Mediterranean citrus fruits, and the EC enlargement case in the mid-1980s. In 1983, the United States imposed tariffs and quotas on specialty steel from the European Economic Community (EEC), prompting EEC counterretaliation against imports from the United States. In 1989, when the EC implemented its ban on beef from cattle treated with growth hormones, the United States responded with retaliatory tariffs on $100 million of EC products. Trade wars also took place between the United States and Canada regarding lumber products and over Canadian provincial restrictions on imports of U.S. beer.

In comparison with this long list of democratic trade wars, trade conflicts between democracies and nondemocratic regimes have not more often escalated into tit-for-tat retaliation. For example, the United States has threatened to impose economic sanctions against China numerous times but rarely has carried out its promised threat, instead reaching agreement with the Chinese on most issues. The only exception occurred in 1983, when the United States imposed a unilateral agreement on China restricting Chinese textile exports to the American market in response to pressure from the textile industry, after which China retaliated by suspending imports of American agricultural products. The United States also imposed sanctions on China in the aftermath of Tiananmen, but these sanctions were a unilateral reaction to a crisis situation whereby the U.S. government suspended investment and development programs in China. Since the United States was not trying to use sanction threats in negotiations to compel or deter Chinese actions, the Tiananmen sanctions were clearly quite different from normal bilateral trade disputes whereby the United States threatened to close its markets to Chinese exports should the latter fail to comply with its demands. All other Sino-American trade conflicts in the 1990s ended up with both sides making concessions and backing down from escalation. A near absence of trade wars has come to characterize U.S.–China trade relations. Since the literature on crisis bargaining predicts that misunderstandings leading to escalation are especially likely when the disputes involve at least one party that is nondemocratic, the contrasting pattern just described is particularly puzzling and will be a major focus of the following empirical analysis.

To reiterate, this study is interested in addressing two empirical puzzles associated with international trade conflicts. First, why has U.S. economic coercion been more successful in extracting concessions from some countries than from others? What explains the variations in American threat effectiveness? Second, why hasn't the United States engaged in more trade wars with authoritarian regimes than with its democratic trading partners? Through an exploration of these questions illustrated by specific cases of U.S. negotiations with its trading partners, this study aims to offer a better understanding of the conditions that limit or enhance the effectiveness of coercive diplomacy as well as those that facilitate or hinder the prospect for the peaceful settlement of international trade disputes.

The Argument in Brief

As mentioned earlier, the following analysis will draw on the concept of two-level games as the starting point of its analysis. But, in doing so, it also improves on the two-level game approach by laying out more clearly and systematically the linkages between the structure of domestic interests and preferences and international trade negotiations. In the first place, it develops a specific model for understanding when threats are likely to be supported by domestic interest groups. Second, it advances explicit propositions about the conditions under which domestic institutions will be more favorably disposed toward the use of coercive strategies.

Specifically, it will be argued that the structure of trade among nations (i.e., whether bilateral trade relations are competitive or complementary)[36] affects threat effectiveness by influencing both the level of unity among domestic interest groups and the level of divided government. The United States will find it more difficult to extract concessions from countries with which it has complementary trade relations than from those with which it has competitive ones due to the greater degree of domestic division in the former. This is because when trade is competitive, sanction threats will likely enjoy support from both export-seeking and import-competing interests in the nation issuing the threat as both groups gain from aggressive tactics that promise benefits whether the threat succeeds or fails. For instance, in the U.S.–Japan semiconductor trade dispute in the mid-1980s, American threats to impose sanctions on Japanese computers, television sets, and other electronics products unless Japan opened up its market to American semiconductor products enjoyed support not only from semiconductor manufacturers who were seeking expanded access to the Japanese market but also from industries targeted for trade sanctions (such as computer and electronics manufacturers) that faced stiff competition from Japanese imports themselves and hence would benefit from limitations on Japanese exports to the American market.

In contrast, when trade relations are complementary, domestic interests in the country issuing the threat will be divided in their policy preferences because of the division between export-seeking and import-using industries. Sanction threats in these cases will enjoy backing only from the export-seeking sectors, who only gain if the sanction threat succeeds. They will not enjoy support from the import-competing sector since such a sector will not exist in cases involving complementary trade relations. Instead, threats will encounter opposition from a large domestic constituency that makes use of imports from the target country. These divisions in domestic interests in the United States ought to substantially reduce American threat credibility. Trade between the United States and China, two countries with a highly complementary trade relationship, is a case in point. In U.S.–China trade disputes, active opposition from a large import-using constituency that has developed a considerable dependence on the labor-intensive products made in China (such as apparel, textiles, and toys), coupled with a virtually nonexistent import-competing sector in the United States, has rendered America's threat of trade retaliation far less credible and effective vis-à-vis the Chinese.

American threat credibility is further undermined by the greater degree of divided government in such cases. Since trade conflicts between countries with complementary trade relations will most likely involve noncompetitive, declining industries, the U.S. executive will be less inclined to respond to domestic protectionist pressure and to go along with the tougher approach advocated by the more hawkish legislature. Divisions in domestic interests and the wider gap between executive and legislative preferences should make U.S. threats of sanctions far less credible to the target.

It will be further argued that the same set of factors that account for the variable degree of threat credibility can also help us understand the lack of democratic peace in trade. This is because countries with highly competitive trade relations ought to face stronger pressure for brinkmanship in bilateral trade disputes due to the greater degree of unity among domestic interest groups. At the same time, the executive in the sender of threat should be more likely to approve of the need to impose sanctions in these cases if he or she perceives that domestic pressure for compensation is strong enough or that an industry vital to the future economic well-being of the nation is genuinely threatened by foreign competition. These factors tend to push countries with competitive trade ties toward more aggressive tactics with a heightened risk of escalation to trade war. Since the majority of democracies also happen to be advanced industrial countries with highly competitive trade, this explains why democracies are not necessarily less conflict prone in their trade relations. In other words, trade structure, rather than regime type, provides the more proximate explanation for the many trade wars we have observed between democracies.

Method

Two methodological approaches will be adopted to carry out the research. First, I will draw on the database of Section 301 cases and other data on international trade conflicts (primarily those taking place after 1980) to see whether the structure of trade is associated, as predicted, with threat effectiveness and the instances of trade wars. If it can be shown that a correlation exists between trade structure and the two dependent variables, we will then have increased confidence in the predictive value of the explanatory variable.

While such quantitative analyses may produce valuable results that shed light on my central theoretical questions, they may not provide all the necessary information that will allow us to draw valid causal inferences. Thus, to gather more evidence relevant to my causal inference, I conduct detailed case studies of U.S. trade disputes with China, Brazil, Japan, and Europe. By combining abstract quantitative models with qualitative research carried out on the basis of established rules of inquiry, I hope to generate valid and accurate descriptions of the underlying causal factors shaping states' interactions in international trade conflicts.

To produce well-formulated case studies, I undertake "structured-focused comparisons" as recommended by George and McKeown, supplemented by the "process-tracing" procedure intended to examine and trace "the decision process by which various initial conditions are translated into outcomes."[37] Structured-focused comparisons, which require collecting data on the same variables across units, ought to allow me to formulate "theoretically relevant general questions to guide the examination of each case."[38] The process-tracing procedure in turn places the process leading to the final outcomes at the center of the investigation and seeks to identify the factors that shape the actors' behavior and responses, including the effect of systemic, institutional, and societal factors on processes and outcomes. This strategy, by focusing on the motivations and perceptions of the actors involved in the decision-making process, allows us to account for the complicated bargaining process and to test whether the explanatory variable affects bargaining outcomes in the way predicted by the theory. In the context of this study, this strategy also enables us to see whether the structure of trade affects threat effectiveness and the instances of trade wars through the hypothesized mechanism, that is, by influencing the alignment of domestic interests and the level of divided government in the sender of threats.

To draw valid inferences from my focused comparative case studies, I select cases that could potentially yield new and interesting insights. In particular, I draw on standard criteria of case selection such as maximizing variation on the explanatory variable and controlling for alternative hypotheses. Selecting on the key causal explanatory variable does not introduce a bias into the research design, as the selection procedure has not ruled out any possible variation in the dependent variable.[39] Thus, in testing my hypotheses about the connection between trade structure and threat effectiveness, I concentrate on comparisons of negotiations between the United States and Japan, one of America's most competitive trading partners, with U.S. negotiations with China, a trading partner with one of the most complementary trade relations with the United States, to ascertain if divergent trade structure generates substantially different domestic dynamics. The expectation is that such contrasting trade structures ought to produce rather different patterns of interest group alignment and institutional support in the country issuing the threat, which, in turn, affect the degree of threat effectiveness. A similar procedure is followed in analyzing the sources of trade wars.

In addition to maximizing variations on the explanatory variable, I also take into consideration alternative explanations in choosing my cases. For example, in analyzing U.S.–Japan trade negotiations, I include both cases in which strategic trade concerns play an important role (such as semiconductors, supercomputers, and satellites) and those in which such concerns are absent (such as wood products) to control for the possibility that strategic trade considerations alone could have explained the success of U.S. pressure tactics against Japan. In a similar vein, in discussing how trade complementarity affects U.S.–China negotiations, I have supplemented the debate over China's MFN status with bilateral negotiations over market access to take account of the potential influence of geopolitics in the former case.

Using primarily the Sino-American trade relationship as an example of complementary trade, the empirical study will compare recent U.S.–China trade negotiations with American trade negotiations with Japan and the EU—two actors having highly competitive trade relations with the United States—to see how well its main arguments and hypotheses describe reality. In the first place, several episodes in U.S. trade negotiations with China and Japan will be detailed in order to explain the variations in U.S. threat effectiveness. These two trade relationships provide a good point for comparison not only because both are major Asian-Pacific trading states that have become the focus of American trade policy but also because the structure of trade between the United States and China differs significantly from that between the United States and Japan: the United States has a far more competitive trade relationship with Japan than with China. As mentioned earlier, this difference permits considerable variations in the explanatory variable and allows us to see whether trade structure does have the hypothesized effect on threat credibility.

Trade disputes between the United States and China over MFN status and market access will be compared with U.S.–Japan trade conflicts over semiconductors and the Super 301 investigations over satellites, supercomputers, and wood products. These cases are among the high-profile ones in the two bilateral trade relationships. Because of their high intensity, the forces pushing for or against trade sanctions in the United States are fairly transparent, better enabling the process-tracing procedure to identify the factors that shape negotiation outcomes. If the structure of trade does shape the domestic landscape in the United States in different ways, and if these differences, in turn, influence the degree of threat credibility, then we would have uncovered a crucial mechanism linking international and domestic politics.

In the MFN case, U.S. efforts to make the annual renewal of China's MFN status contingent on China's performance in the areas of trade, human rights, and nonproliferation have repeatedly been resisted by the Chinese. Any concessions by Beijing to the United States were merely token or symbolic. After three years of threatening to withdraw China's MFN status, most policymakers came to realize that the process had produced no tangible results for the United States. Recognizing the futility of using MFN as a weapon to influence Chinese behavior, President Clinton gave up the attempt in 1994. It is not an exaggeration to say that the MFN dispute represented a complete failure of U.S. negotiating objectives. A similar pattern existed in negotiations over market access. Although China signed a Memorandum of Understanding (MOU) with the United States promising to dismantle trade barriers, subsequent Chinese actions belied American expectations as American negotiators found that substantial nonimplementation of the agreement still existed. Washington again threatened sanctions against China just a few months after the agreement was signed. Thus both the MFN and market access negotiations highlight the difficulties the United States confronted in prying open the Chinese market.

Before proceeding, a few words about the selection of the MFN case are in order. It needs to be pointed out that, in contrast to the other cases examined in this book, the MFN negotiations were intended to address political (most notably human rights) concerns, in addition to trade barriers in China. But although this case is not purely about trade, it still can provide a suitable testing ground for my hypotheses for a number of reasons. First, critics may argue that America's demands on the human rights issues are more likely to touch upon Chinese sensitivities about their national sovereignty and, as a result, are more likely to encounter resistance from the Chinese than purely economic demands. However, precisely because human rights issues held such substantive meaning for the Chinese government, it is reasonable to expect Beijing to have been more willing to give in to the trade demands the United States made under the MFN threat to ameliorate the pressure on the human rights front. That linkage policy did not work to America's advantage and that the Chinese authorities did not cave in to trade demands even when they ought to have strong incentives to take the heat off the human rights issue suggest that there may exist other potential explanations for Beijing's unaccommodating behavior.

Second, since the objectives the United States sought to achieve under MFN pertained to both human rights and trade issues (such as market access and IPR), the MFN sanction threat did win the support of American exporters interested in gaining greater access to the Chinese market. In other words, besides human rights advocates, exporters faced with market impediments in China did enter into the debate in favor of the MFN threat, very much like what they did in other cases involving purely economic issues. Third, although the denial of MFN status would have produced far more extreme consequences than trade retaliation under Section 301, it was a step that was seriously considered by Congress and had caused much anxiety and nervousness for the Chinese government each year. Given the intense domestic pressure in favor of trade sanctions immediately following Tiananmen, the withdrawal of MFN status from the Chinese was a real possibility that could not be easily ruled out at the outset. In short, even though the MFN case involved the pursuit of both political and economic objectives, as distinct from other cases covered in this book, the existence of linkage and the presence of trade objectives on the negotiation agenda ought to ensure an appropriate test of my key hypothesis regarding the influence of trade structure.

To show that the coalitional consequences of complementary trade are not unique to a country such as China, which is both large in size and used to maintain tight restrictions on economic activities but rather can be generalized to other contexts, I supplement the China cases with a dispute between the United States and Brazil over informatics policy. In the U.S.–Brazil informatics dispute, persistent pressure from the United States was unable to get the Brazilians to alter their market access reserve policy that discriminated against American firms.

The ineffectiveness of U.S. pressure in changing Chinese and Brazilian policies contrasts sharply with the greater degree of success the United States had achieved in its trade negotiations with Japan, a country with a highly competitive trade relationship with the United States. While variations certainly existed in the degree to which the United States was successful in imposing its demands on Japan, it can be argued that, on the whole, American pressure has produced more significant market opening with Japan than with China. This study will look at the U.S.–Japan semiconductor trade conflict in the mid-1980s as well as U.S. Super 301 investigations to identify the factors that contributed to the higher level of American success with Japan. In all of these cases, American negotiators were generally successful in achieving their negotiation objectives of gaining increased access to the Japanese market, but the degree to which they were able to do so varied.[40] Focusing on these cases allows us to see why, on average, American negotiators had greater success extracting concessions from the Japanese, even though Japan yielded more in some cases than in others.

Through an exploration of these cases involving U.S. trade bargaining with Japan and China (and, to some extent, Brazil), this study hopes to shed light on the factors conditioning the effectiveness of U.S. coercive diplomacy. It will then proceed to compare trade conflicts between the United States and China, a democracy and an authoritarian state, with those between the United States and Europe, both of which are democracies. It will show that, in contrast to what the democratic peace theorists would predict, there have been many trade wars between democracies. It will be further argued that this pattern can best be accounted for by the competitive trade structure between many democratic regimes, which generates potent prosanction forces at home that constrain the "pacifying" effects of democratic institutions and processes.

As mentioned earlier, trade relations between the United States and China since the early 1980s are largely characterized by the absence of trade wars. In almost all issue areas, the United States threatened to impose economic sanctions against China, only to refrain from doing so in the end. In the negotiations over IPR that will be discussed in detail, Washington several times threatened to slap punitive tariffs on Chinese products unless China took concrete measures to police property rights infringements. In the end, however, the two sides have always managed to reach an eleventh-hour agreement, thereby avoiding a costly trade battle. In addition to looking at the intellectual property issue, this study will look at trade in textiles to further substantiate its argument. Although the record of the textile dispute conforms to the overall pattern of trade peace, the United States did impose quota restrictions on Chinese textile exports to the United States in the early 1980s, prompting Chinese retaliation in the form of a suspension of grain imports. The detailed case study will explain the general pattern of trade peace between the United States and China, as well as the anomaly involving textiles in the early 1980s.

While trade disputes between the United States and China were generally resolved peacefully, those between the United States and Europe have more often escalated into trade wars. The trade conflict between the United States and the EC over enlargement in the mid-1980s and the U.S.–Canada trade conflict over timber products will be examined closely to show why democracies have a greater tendency to engage in trade wars. Of course, not every trade conflict between democracies ended in a trade war. I did not choose to examine these low-intensity trade conflicts because it was only through an examination of cases where the dog did bark that one could possibly find out the mechanisms or stimuli that triggered the outbreak of trade wars. The factors I emphasize ought to be necessary, though not necessarily sufficient, conditions for trade wars to take place.

Contributions to the Literature

Theoretically and empirically, this work adds to the existing literature on the intersection of domestic and international politics and addresses a number of debated relationships in the study of international relations. First, by systematically relating the domestic coalitional consequences of trade structure to my two dependent variables, this study contributes to the two-level game approach. Domestic-level explanations of international politics have sometimes been criticized for their ad hoc nature and their inability to generate hypotheses that could be tested empirically. More recent works that formally model the domestic-international interaction tend to concentrate on the role of the legislature, instead of societal actors, in shaping foreign economic policy.[41] This study presents a more sophisticated treatment of domestic interests and generates more explicit, testable hypotheses of the two-level interaction. As scholars of international negotiations and of international political economy have not yet fully untangled the nexus between domestic and international politics, this research promises to enrich this research agenda.

Second, by revisiting the determinants of "aggressively unilateral"

U.S. trade actions, this book sheds light on the factors conditioning the effectiveness of unilateral market-opening pressure and, as a result, improves our understanding of the use of trade sanctions as an instrument of foreign economic policy. At a time when the United States is confronted with continued difficulties in its attempts to pry open foreign markets, this analysis provides a useful reminder that much of the limits on the effective use of pressure tactics can be found at home, among domestic interest groups. As such, it offers valuable lessons for those in the policy community interested in finding more constructive approaches for dealing with some of America's most intractable trade problems.

Third, my claim that a country in a dependent position in a relationship may be both more resistant to pressure tactics *and* less prone to conflict in trade with the partner country challenges the dependency theory. The dependency theory contends that developing countries are constrained by their dependence on export markets in the developed world in their search for economic development. In this view, the workings of the capitalist world economy tend to perpetuate and to reinforce developing countries' dependence on the markets of the core countries.[42] My argument provides a critique of such an overly pessimistic and rigid view of the bargaining power of developing countries. Since production of labor-intensive products has increasingly been phased out in the industrialized economies, import users in those countries are increasingly wary of having to cut off their supplies from their complementary trading partners. This provides trade relations between complementary trading partners with a certain degree of durability that not only serves to minimize protectionist pressures in the country issuing the threat but also enhances the leverage of the targeted country, which is usually inferior in terms of power resources, in bilateral negotiations.

In addition, although this study focuses primarily on the effect of trade structure on patterns of trade conflicts, it may be possible to extend this logic to understand patterns of military conflicts. The large body of literature on the relationship between economic interdependence and military conflict has mostly examined the effect of total trade (such as trade volumes, trade values, systemic trade levels, trade as a proportion of gross domestic product [GDP], and trade in strategic goods) on the level of military conflict.[43] But if certain kinds of trade relationships (such as a complementary trade structure) may induce some domestic actors who stand to lose from trade disruptions resulting from military actions to oppose such measures, while other kinds of relations (such as a competitive trade structure) do not exercise the same pressure, then it may indeed be necessary to develop more sophisticated models of the connection between bilateral trade structure and the possibility for conflict (or cooperation) in international military disputes.

Finally, while ostensibly a study of American foreign trade policy, this project nevertheless sheds light on the theoretical literature over the democratic peace as it applies to both security and trade issues. Importantly, the finding that the domestic pressure generated by trade structure overwhelms democratic institutions' purported conflict-constraining abilities ought to provide us with a basis to question both the audience cost theory—which posits that democratic institutions and processes ought to allow democracies to better reveal their true intentions in a bargaining situation, thereby encouraging the opponent to refrain from escalating the conflict so as to prevent a costly "war"— and theories emphasizing how institutional characteristics of democracies such as separation of powers and electoral accountability contribute to the trade-liberalizing tendencies of democratic regimes.

Furthermore, such a conclusion drawn from a study of trade conflicts may allow us to assess the validity of different strands of theories of the democratic peace in security affairs. As noted, norms-based, structure-based, and signaling arguments are the three most prominent theories developed to explain why democracies are less likely to fight with one another in the security realm. Yet scholars have not yet been able to establish the relative causal validity of these competing arguments. But if it can be shown that democratic institutions and structures do not prevent democracies from fighting each other in trade, then one can further infer that structure-based explanations may not have constituted the real causal mechanism for the democratic peace in security. The substantive findings of this project therefore have important implications for the debate over the democratic peace and may offer certain policy prescriptions for policymakers interested in finding effective solutions to ongoing international conflicts.

CHAPTER 2

Trade Structure, Threat Effectiveness, and "Democratic Trade Peace"

The previous chapter summarizes the two empirical puzzles driving this research: Why has the United States been more successful in enforcing its demands on some of its trading partners (such as Japan, Canada, and Europe) than on others (such as China, Brazil, and India), and why are democracies not necessarily less likely to be engaged in trade wars with one another? In addressing these puzzles, I draw on the two-level game approach to develop a specific model for understanding the conditions under which domestic politics supports the use of threat tactics. Before doing so, I provide a literature review describing existing approaches to international negotiations and their limitations, focusing in particular on the contribution of the two-level game approach. This brief review suggests possible avenues for developing a more systematic theory of the domestic determinants of international behavior and provides a basis for my modified two-level game model.

Alternative Explanations

Three theoretical approaches may potentially help us understand the distributional patterns of international negotiations: realism, bargaining theories, and the two-level game approach. While realist theories emphasize how disparities in the power resources of the parties involved in a dispute shape the distribution of gains in international negotiations, bargaining theories posit that power balance is not determinant and that weak states may overcome their power inferiority to strike favorable deals if they have strong motivations in gaining a positive result or if they can skillfully utilize a range of bargaining tactics to their own advantage. While some strands of the bargaining theory point out how negotiators may manipulate domestic politics by employing strategies such as "tying hands" to strengthen their credibility at the international level, bargaining theories as a whole do not have an explicit domestic focus. Instead, it is the two-level game approach that has sought to more systematically integrate domestic and international politics.

The Realist Paradigm

Existing international relations theories provide a good starting point for the analysis. As the dominant paradigm in the field of international relations, realism contends that, since anarchy is the defining character of the international system, states tend to view one another as potential threats, aim to maximize their security through the pursuit of power, and are predisposed toward conflict and competition. In international trade bargaining, realists predict, states' bargaining positions will be shaped by their interests in improving their relative power positions. International negotiating outcomes will reflect the relative power resources of the parties involved in a dispute.

Most realist analysts emphasize the primacy of military power in determining a nation's power resources, but some analysts in the realist tradition argue that economic power can be converted into bargaining resources in international negotiations as well. In particular, in situations of asymmetrical interdependence, where state A's degree of reliance on state B as an export market is much higher than B's degree of reliance on A, the less dependent one should be able to use its market power to win concessions from the more dependent one.[1] In other words, economic coercion is more likely to produce the desired effects when the power resources of the sender of threats are greater than those of the target nation.

While classical realism does not speak directly to trade dispute settlement, more recent realist theories have developed a set of critical assumptions about the international political economy. They propose that (a) states are the major actors in the world political economy; (b) states are primarily concerned about relative gains in power resources; (c) economic sanctions can serve as an important policy instrument; and (d) state policy choices are fundamentally shaped by the international economic structure and that states are predisposed to conflict rather than cooperation in international economic relations.[2]

One of the weaknesses of the realist explanation, as scholars in the liberal tradition have often pointed out, is that increasing international interdependence has made the exercise of power more difficult. Weak states are often able to stand up to the strong because of the numerous points of leverage and influence among nations created by conditions such as economic interdependence, the existence of sub-state actors, the issue-specific nature of power resources, the multiple foreign policy goals that states possess, and the utilization of different bargaining tactics.[3] Various scholars outside of the realist tradition have looked at cases of asymmetrical negotiation to explain how factors not related to aggregate raw material power can influence weak states' ability to get what they want some of the times.

William Zartman, in a study of trade negotiations between African states and the EEC, challenges the traditional conception of power in asymmetrical negotiations. He argues that power is situational and relative rather than aggregate and absolute. Powerful states may fail to impose their demands on weaker ones if they cannot effectively apply their aggregate power to the specific bilateral situation. He further suggests several conditions under which weak states may be able to overcome their power inferiority.[4]

In *Power and Tactics in International Negotiation,* William Mark Habeeb reaches similar conclusions through an analysis of several cases of asymmetrical negotiation. He illustrates that between 1958 and 1976 Iceland successfully negotiated with Britain to extend its fisheries limit from four to two hundred miles. In each stage of the negotiation, Britain backed off from its demands and eventually acceded to virtually all of Iceland's positions. Similarly, in U.S.–Panama negotiations over the status of the Panama Canal, Panama achieved considerable success not only in obtaining financial compensation from the United States but also in resuming sovereignty over the Panama Canal. In another case, involving U.S. attempts to secure additional overseas bases from Spain, Spain tried, with moderate success, to create a formula that traded bases for close military and political ties with the United States. Habeeb takes these cases as evidence that weak states are able to resist pressure from more powerful nations in a given confrontation. He examines the dynamics of the negotiation process in detail to explain why powerful states may sometimes fail to translate their aggregate power advantages into effective bargaining chips.[5] Wriggins's analysis of negotiations between Malta and Britain uncovers an identical pattern: despite the power asymmetry to its disadvantage, tiny Malta managed to substantially reduce the presence of British and North Atlantic Treaty Organization (NATO) powers on the island and to get them to pay considerable cash payments for their use of Malta's facilities by adroitly employing such ploys as making "a sufficient nuisance," dramatizing alternatives, and "protracting the negotiations interminably."[6]

John Odell presents case studies of U.S.–Korea trade negotiations as well as bilateral trade bargaining between the United States and Latin American states. He finds that both South Korea and the Latin American states were able to win some of the negotiations, attributing the weak states' victories in these cases to their superior negotiation strategies.[7] In another study of U.S.–Brazil negotiations over informatics, Odell suggests that one reason why powerful nations frequently fail to achieve their negotiation objectives despite their overall power advantage is the web of interests spawned by international interdependence. He argues that Brazil, which is inferior to the United States in terms of power resources, was able to resist American demands to change its program designed to promote a national computer industry because it knew that American firms, which had extensive investments inside Brazil, were opposed to the government's pressure tactics.[8]

These examples all point to the inability of traditional realist explanations to account for the outcomes of asymmetrical negotiations. More importantly, even though realism may explain why weak states sometimes comply with the demands of stronger ones, it has a difficult time explaining why U.S. pressure worked and did not work in degrees not predicted by raw "power." In their studies of the United States' use of retaliatory strategies under Section 301, Bayard and Elliott and Erick Duchesne have found that it is insufficient to explain bargaining power solely in terms of structural power.[9] Moreover, even negotiations between the same pair of countries have not always produced uniform results. For example, through an examination of negotiations between the United States and the EU, Sophie Meunier suggests that the strong, hegemonic United States did not always emerge as the winner and that the Europeans more frequently negotiated successfully during the Uruguay Round (1986–93) than during the Kennedy Round negotiations (1963–67) due to variations in internal voting rules and negotiating competence in the EU.[10]

Furthermore, as described in the previous section, in U.S. trade negotiations with its Asian trading partners, Asian countries differed in the extent to which they conceded to U.S. demands, even though they were similarly dependent on the U.S. market for exports. Japan, Taiwan, and South Korea, for example, were among the U.S. trading partners that were most responsive to U.S. pressure. However, China, while it already depended on the U.S. market for more than 30 percent of its exports in 1994,[11] has not offered concessions to the U.S. as readily as these other Asian states. Realist power theories clearly cannot explain why the United States was not able to influence China more. Explanations for these variations have to be found in factors other than states' relative power balances.

Critics may be quick to point out that an obvious reason why countries such as Japan, Taiwan, and South Korea are more amenable to American demands than countries such as China is the first group of countries' greater degree of security reliance on the United States. Since these smaller states are America's allies, highly dependent on U.S. security guarantees, whereas China is capable of providing for its own security, the argument goes, it is not surprising that the greater leverage the United States wields in security issues would have translated into greater bargaining power in bilateral trade disputes.

Another potential criticism, similar to the one just mentioned, emphasizes the greater expectations of future conflict, as well as the opportunity costs of coercion between adversaries rather than between allies. In a study on the use of economic coercion, Daniel Drezner contends that, because of greater concerns about relative gains and bilateral reputation, the sender of threats should be more willing to initiate economic sanctions against its adversaries. He further argues that, paradoxically, these same relative gains concerns reduce the sender's ability to obtain positive results in disputes with its adversaries, as the target will be worried about the long-run implications of caving in and hence will be reluctant to concede to the sender's demands.[12]

However, arguments along this line of reasoning are ambiguous for a number of reasons. First, it is not clear to what extent security considerations weigh in international bargaining over purely economic issues. The primary U.S. objective in most trade negotiations is to expand American exports to overseas markets or to prevent unfair foreign competition in the American market. Concerns about the political-military relationship with the target country, while not totally absent, seem marginal at best.[13]

Second, granted that U.S. allies such as Japan can be more amenable to U.S. demands because of their greater dependence on U.S. security guarantees, alliance maintenance nevertheless entails considerable costs for the United States. At various points in U.S.–Japan trade negotiations, the United States was forced to soften its demands for fear of antagonizing Japan and thereby endangering the alliance relationship. In U.S.–Japan negotiations over semiconductors in the mid-1980s, for example, considerations on the part of the State Department and the National Security Council for Japan's role as an American friend and ally complicated the decision-making process to name Japan an unfair trader, lessening the effectiveness of American pressure in the early stages of the disputes. Japan could count on those agencies within the U.S. government most concerned with security issues and refuse to negotiate seriously on semiconductors.[14] As this example suggests, the incentives provided by the security relationship are often indeterminate: the leverage the United States derives from Japan's security dependence may well be offset by its need to maintain a close alliance relationship and therefore to be more attentive to Japan's perspectives.

It could be further argued that the United States, not for purely altruistic reasons, has actively worked to extend its security umbrella to Japan to prevent Japanese rearmament and the resurgence of Japanese military power in East Asia. Cognizant of the U.S. motive, Tokyo has during most of the postwar period enjoyed the benefits of free riding in the security domain and has refused to take up its fair share of the security obligation in the Asian-Pacific region. America's self-interest in providing a security guarantee to Japan may thus have lessened the imperative for Tokyo to cave in to American pressure on either security or trade issues.

Third, even though China is not dependent on America for security, as are Japan, South Korea, and Taiwan, the argument has frequently been made that security relations between great powers similarly involve mutual dependency. During the Cold War, the United States and the Soviet Union were dependent on each other for not launching a nuclear attack; the United States also sought to play the "China card" in efforts to counter Soviet expansionism in Asia. At present the United States needs to take into consideration China's role in maintaining peace and stability in the Asian-Pacific region (especially on issues such as North Korea and Taiwan) when dealing with economic issues; and China, in turn, depends on the United States for maintaining the strategic balance in East Asia. In this sense, security considerations influence America's economic relationship with China in much the same way as they shape U.S.–Japan economic bargaining outcomes. One cannot simply attribute America's greater negotiation success with Japan on trade issues to the latter's greater degree of security reliance on the United States.

Bargaining Theories

In light of realism's inability to explain the variations in the effectiveness of U.S. coercive diplomacy, analysts in the bargaining tradition have sought to identify the conditions under which threats are more likely to work. As a modification of the realist emphasis on power asymmetries, a number of scholars suggest that the *interests* of the parties involved in a dispute play an important role in determining bargaining outcomes. It has been argued that a party can strengthen its credibility and enhance its chances of obtaining a favorable outcome if it has important stakes in the issue. For example, if the sender of threat only has peripheral interests in the issue, then the target country, knowing that the sender is unwilling to risk war (or trade war) for a relatively small gain, will most likely reject the sender's demands. Conversely, if the target country places a high priority on the issue and is dedicated to achieving its preferred outcomes, then the sender should be more likely to give up its demands.[15] By emphasizing how factors other than power resources (such as the interests of the parties involved) may lead to variations in bargaining results across issue areas, this strand of the bargaining theory provides one plausible explanation for why weak states can sometimes stand up to strong ones. However, it still does not help us understand why bargaining outcomes often vary in the same issue area where a state's interests remain more or less constant.

Another strand of the bargaining theory emphasizes the importance of bargaining tactics. Some analysts focus on negotiating tactics on the part of the sender of threats that might enhance or undermine the credibility of a threat to retaliate. Following Thomas Schelling, who emphasizes the role of commitment in making a threat credible, these analyses suggest that threats to impose sanctions will be more credible if negotiators can tie their own hands with respect to retaliating, link agreement on one issue to another issue area where one has leverage over the partner, offer side payments to foreign governments in order to obtain the acquiescence of those domestic groups opposed to change, and add parties who support one's position to the negotiations.[16] International negotiators would be able to improve the terms of the deal if they could expand the other side's perceived zone of possible agreement by using one or a number of these strategies.[17] This approach helps to illustrate both analytically and empirically how bargaining strategies can work to improve the credibility of threats. However, it says nothing about the conditions under which these strategies are most likely to work. Many of the factors that may influence whether and when threats will be most effective have simply been assumed away. For example, the target's preferences, which play an important role in determining whether tactics such as threats and persuasion could work to expand the "zone of possible agreement," have generally been left out of the analysis.[18]

How weak states can use bargaining tactics to overcome asymmetric power balances has also been examined. In his study of East Asian states' strategies for dealing with the Americans, David Yoffie emphasizes that weak bargainers can resist demands from more powerful actors if they can make a commitment to realize long-term gains. According to Yoffie, weak states can better achieve their objectives when they can negotiate for ambiguity, demand compensation for restrictions, exploit bureaucratic cleavages within the opponent, and cheat on regulations and agreements.[19] Habeeb offers a more general logic behind weak state capabilities. He argues that conclusions about state interactions drawn from a modeled structure of a static, aggregated power relationship ignore the dynamic of process. According to Habeeb, issue-specific power, which "is determined by asymmetries in alternatives, commitment, and control," is at least as important as aggregate structural power in explaining outcomes. A weak state can alter its dependence on a more powerful one if it can "gain its preferred outcomes from a relationship other than with the opposing actor," is strongly dedicated to achieving a positive outcome, or can achieve greater control in the negotiations.[20] While this emphasis on weak state bargaining tactics has considerable validity, once again it is not clear under what conditions these tactics will be more or less effective. Given the general availability of these bargaining tactics to weak states, the question remains as to why some weak states are able to resist U.S. demands more than others.

In a 1994 study directed by Thomas Bayard and Kimberly Elliott on the effectiveness of Section 301 provisions of U.S. trade law in opening overseas markets, the authors similarly attempt to identify the factors affecting the efficacy of threats in trade negotiations. They found that U.S. negotiators are more likely to obtain market-opening outcomes the "more dependent the target country is on the U.S. market, the larger the U.S. bilateral trade deficit with the target is, and the more transparent the targeted trade barrier is."[21] Another important conclusion drawn from the collaborative project is that the success of bilateral negotiations depends critically on the value that the target country places on maintaining access to the U.S. market: "Threats typically 'succeed' when the perceived economic and political costs to the target of complying with a demand are lower than the perceived costs of defiance."[22] Specifically, the United States can obtain a more favorable deal under the following conditions:

(a) the greater the harm to the targeted country from having its access to the U.S. market limited; (b) the smaller the targeted country's ability to harm the U.S. in retaliation; (c) the smaller the costs within the targeted country of complying with the U.S. demands; and (d) the greater the benefit to the United States—in the U.S. negotiators' perception—from the demanded liberalization.[23]

This project makes a valuable contribution to understanding the conditions under which the use of aggressive tactics would be more effective. But many of the factors the authors identified as having credibility-enhancing effects (such as the benefits to the sender of carrying out a threat as well as the risks of retaliation and counterretaliation by the target) have been emphasized in earlier writings on international bargaining.[24] Most of these conditions are also linked to the bilateral economic interdependence ratio.[25] Moreover, other conditions the authors hypothesized to influence threat credibility, including U.S. concerns about possible counterretaliation, public or explicit threat, and GATT procedures, turn out to be relatively insignificant in determining outcomes.

On the whole, existing bargaining theories help to advance our understanding of the dynamics of international bargaining by highlighting how certain factors not related to raw material power can impinge on negotiation outcomes. But they also suffer from important shortcomings and are not able to fully explain the puzzles described earlier. This directs our attention to a third approach in the search for answers to the research questions: the two-level game theory.

The Two-Level Game Approach

Most of the theories described previously assume that states are rational, unitary actors,[26] an assumption that is increasingly difficult to sustain considering the diversity of interests, institutions, and opinions within most democratic countries. Since trade conflicts have a substantial domestic component that cannot simply be assumed away, there has been a burgeoning literature emphasizing how politics and divisions within countries can affect international bargaining behavior. These works challenge the view that states' behavior can be explained primarily by international structural factors, explicitly arguing that failure to examine domestic conditions may result in the neglect of a crucial source of international relations.[27]

Most of this literature on how domestic politics affects international behavior has utilized the concept of the two-level game developed by Robert Putnam. The two-level game approach, in Putnam's original formulation, views national leaders as engaging in two sets of negotiations simultaneously: one with their international counterparts and the other with their respective domestic constituents. Chief negotiators not only need to "win" at the international table but also have to make sure that any deal that is cut internationally will be accepted by those who could veto or block implementation of the deal at home. An international agreement will be possible only if the two parties' "winsets"—the set of possible policies that can obtain the necessary domestic support—overlap. Putnam and other scholars working with this approach further identify three factors that affect the size of the winset: the combination of the power and preferences of possible domestic coalitions, domestic political institutions, and the strategies adopted by the negotiators.[28]

By emphasizing the interaction between domestic- and international-level variables and by integrating a number of previously disparate observations into a single theoretical framework, the two-level game approach has made a positive contribution to international relations.[29] It not only helps to remedy the neglect of domestic variables resulting from the dominance of structural realism in international relations theory but also provides a basis for organizing further empirical study.

Indeed, analyses of the domestic sources of foreign policy have mushroomed in the past decade. In the area of international security, Bueno de Mesquita and Lalman, in one of the most systematic investigations of international and domestic theories of conflict, make a strong case that domestic politics affects international conflict. But this investigation treats domestic politics as a black box, characterizing it as the vector sum of the power and interests of whatever domestic actors may be relevant in a given polity.[30]

The influence of domestic politics also has been studied in the area of trade policy. Numerous studies investigate the role of political parties on trade; the most recent writings also emphasize how divided government could affect trade policy. Lohmann and O'Halloran, for example, argue that, in the United States, different party control of Congress and the White House can lead to a more protectionist trade policy. They observe that, when the congressional majority party is confronted by a president of the opposing party, the former has an incentive to delegate to and to constrain the latter by requiring congressional approval of trade proposals, forcing the president to adopt more protectionist policies in order to bring together a congressional majority.[31] Studies such as Lohmann and O'Halloran's emphasize the importance of domestic politics but have not devoted sufficient attention to the *interaction* between domestic and international politics. Since trade politics operates at both the national and international levels, both should be included in analyses of the policy-making process.

Other studies have emphasized how domestic politics in target countries influence the distribution of gains in international negotiations. In his study of U.S. trade bargaining with Japan, for example, Leonard Schoppa develops a framework for analyzing when and how U.S. synergistic strategies can work to extract the desired concessions. U.S. pressure is most effective in influencing Japanese policy outcomes when the United States is able to employ strategies such as "synergistic linkage," "reverberation," "participation expansion," and "alternative specification" to take advantage of divisions of interests and opinions on the Japanese side.[32] Although Schoppa looks at how the effectiveness of U.S. synergistic strategies could be conditioned by domestic politics in the United States, the focus of his study is primarily on the interaction of these strategies with domestic politics in the target nation. This selective focus leaves ample room for future studies to develop explicit hypotheses about the domestic factors in the sender of threats that may have an important bearing on negotiating outcomes.

In a more recent study on the ten-year dialogue between the United States and China over IPR, Andrew Mertha extends the two-level framework to explain both the specific IPR issues being negotiated and the variations in the extent to which nationally negotiated agreements are being implemented in China. He argues that the organizational characteristics of the relevant IPR lobby critically influence the effect of transnational deterrence (i.e., implicit or explicit threat of retaliation issued by local governments in China to preempt these U.S. actors from exposing the deficiencies in China's IPR regime) and hence the kinds of issues that get onto the U.S. negotiation agenda. He further contends that the specific organizational characteristics of the various IPR enforcement bureaucracies in China determine enforcement outcomes and patterns of bureaucratic defection.[33] By looking at the organizational characteristics of both the IPR lobby and the IPR enforcement agencies in China, Mertha's work has made a valuable link between the organizational literature and international interactions.

The impact of ideas and institutions on trade policy has received attention as well. Although studies emphasizing the influence of ideas do not fall neatly into the two-level game framework, they capture an important part of the evolution of trade policy and have important implications for some of the cases examined in the following chapters. Judith Goldstein, for example, emphasizes that ideas provide decision makers with strategies or guidelines that help to maximize their interests. While material interests may explain why groups and coalitions opt for certain positions, ideas serve to legitimize or mold these societal interests. Especially when ideas become embedded in political institutions, they can exert a sustained impact on policy and may constrain the policy choice of political elites, even when the social reality that produced them in the first place may no longer be in place. Thus congressional delegation of trade policy authority to the executive in the 1930s can be explained by the rise of liberal trade ideas following the Great Depression. In the early 1980s, when the ascendance of European and Asian competition resulted in the erosion of industry support for free trade, liberal trade ideas entrenched in institutional structures permitted a broad continuity in American trade policy.[34]

Scholars have applied the two-level game approach to examine issues outside of the realm of trade policy. In her work on the domestic sources of international environmental policy, Elizabeth DeSombre systematically analyzes the conditions under which the United States will attempt to internationalize domestic environmental regulations and the degree to which the United States can successfully convince other states to adopt regulatory policies. She finds that the United States will most likely undertake efforts to internationalize its domestic environmental regulation when both environmental and industry groups in the sender country, who otherwise seem to be strange bedfellows, perceive positive results from such actions and form a variant of the Baptist-and-bootlegger coalition to push for internationalization. She further argues that the success of internationalization depends both on the market power the United States enjoys vis-à-vis the target in the commodity in question and on the continued existence and strength of the coalition initiating the threat.[35] In doing so, her study provides a valuable link between domestic coalitions and paths of internationalization.

Examining a wide array of U.S. foreign policy actions, Lisa Martin challenges the conventional view that legislative participation in the policy-making process undermines democratic regimes' ability to conclude and implement stable international agreements. She argues that institutionalized legislative-executive interactions can enhance the credibility of commitments made by democratic leaders by legitimizing and institutionalizing states' bargaining positions and international commitments, thus allowing democracies to better achieve international cooperation.[36]

By drawing our attention to the domestic sources of foreign policy, the literature just described has made a valuable contribution to our understanding of the complex interaction between domestic- and international-level games. This does not mean, though, that the existing state of the two-level game approach has not left room for theory development. Indeed, it may be argued that research inspired by the two-level game approach has two important shortcomings: first, the large body of literature on two-level games has so far generated only a few testable hypotheses about how domestic politics operates to affect international negotiating outcomes; second, where recent scholarship has tried to develop more parsimonious models of the linkage between domestic and international politics, the emphasis is primarily on how domestic conditions facilitate or impede the prospect for cooperation among nations rather than how they affect the ability of threats to extract concessions from the target country or the likelihood of trade wars. This makes efforts to develop a more systematic approach to understanding threat effectiveness and the probability of trade war a worthwhile endeavor.

In the first place, it should be noted that existing studies on two-level games have not developed systematic theories of the ways in which domestic politics can intervene in the international level of play to affect bargaining outcomes. None of these studies has taken the next step in two-level theory development: the incorporation of a model of domestic politics that accounts for the pattern of *domestic preferences* that shape international bargaining behavior. Odell's comparison of U.S.–Brazil and U.S.–EC bargaining makes a major contribution toward understanding how domestic divisions affect the distribution of gains in international bargaining. Odell finds that successful negotiating by the sender of threats hinges on the degree to which domestic actors are united on the issue in both the sender and the target. Specifically, the more united interests are within the country issuing the threat, and the more divided interests are in the target country, the more likely that the party threatening sanctions will be able to get a favorable agreement.[37] For example, U.S. negotiators were able to achieve greater success in negotiations with the EC over feed grains than with Brazil over computers primarily because domestic interest groups in the United States were unified. In the case of Brazil, the credibility of American threats was undermined because virtually no constituents supported a shift to open coercion. Even those actors who would benefit from pressure tactics were divided in their policy preferences. In the feed grains case, most directly affected groups strongly supported government policies and there was little domestic opposition to implementing the threat. Therefore, even though the United States had a far greater capacity to hurt Brazil, divisions among U.S. interest groups reduced the likelihood that this capacity would be effectively used, thus undermining compliance.

Odell's findings capture an important aspect of the negotiation dynamics by emphasizing how the degree of unity among domestic interests influences threat credibility and effectiveness. Nevertheless, he does not go one step further to develop a more general theory for understanding *when* domestic support for sanctions is more or less likely to be present, a point to which I will return later in this chapter. His analysis thus remains rather ad hoc on domestic interests, unable to tell us when trade sanctions are more likely to obtain the necessary domestic consensus.

In general, Putnam and his associates have used the two-level game concept primarily as a metaphor and have not attempted to generate hypotheses through formalization. As Andrew Moravcsik acknowledges in the introduction to the collaborative project, the case studies in the volume are intended to be "plausibility probes" regarding existing hypotheses about two-level games and an "indispensable first step" in the transition from metaphor to social scientific theory.[38] Although subsequent studies have attempted to develop more explicit hypotheses, the concept of two-level games remains underdeveloped theoretically. In particular, the structure of domestic interests and preferences that affects the international game needs to be designated more explicitly, and the mechanisms linking domestic and international politics need to be spelled out more clearly as well.

A number of recent works have attempted to develop a more rigorous and systematic treatment of the domestic game along these lines.[39] The most prominent of these studies is Helen Milner's *Interests, Institutions, and Information.* Starting from the assumption that domestic politics is polyarchic, that is, composed of at least two groups with different policy preferences that share power and decision making, Milner contends that the possibility and extent of cooperation among states are vitally affected by these factors: the structure of domestic preferences (i.e., the degree of divided government and the preferences of the executive), the nature of domestic political institutions (specifically, the institutional process of ratification), and the distribution of information internally.[40]

Milner argues that the level of divided government is an important variable affecting prospects for international cooperation. Divided government, she explains, emerges when the policy preferences of the executive and the median legislator differ. Although executives and legislators are rational actors who share a common interest in retaining office, they often hold different policy preferences due to their different constituency concerns. Typically, executives are more concerned with the general performance of the economy, whereas legislators prefer policies that would both enhance the economy and cater to their interest group supporters. In other words, executives focus more on the national constituency, while legislators have more local concerns. These differences between the policy preferences of the executive and the median legislator lead to divided government. The greater the divergence in executive-legislative preferences, the more the government is divided.[41] Divided government can be seen not only in presidential systems; it can, Milner argues, emerge in semi-presidential and parliamentary systems as well. Minority governments in parliamentary systems as well as majority coalition governments can experience divided government. Even when the same party controls both branches, divided government may occur because of the lack of party discipline or divergent policy preferences that derive from different constituency interests.

Divided government, according to Milner, makes international cooperation less likely. Since there is more than one player that can veto a deal, the need for ratification by the hawkish player within a state (i.e., the one whose preferences are further apart from those of the foreign country) places important constraints on the dovish player who is inclined to enter into cooperative arrangements with the foreign country, thus diminishing the prospect for international cooperation. The possibility for cooperation further declines and the likelihood of ratification failure increases as the policy differences between the two actors increase, because the dove is now increasingly forced to accede to terms favored by the hawk. However, if cooperation is possible at all, this should push the terms of the deal closer to the preferences of the hawkish actor, leading to more favorable deals for the country with divided government. The possibility of cooperation also declines when the more hawkish actor holds greater internal decision power. The implications of Milner's findings are pessimistic: domestic politics makes cooperation less likely and changes the terms of the agreement that could be made. Even realists may have overestimated the likelihood that states will cooperate with one another.[42]

In short, by relaxing the assumption of the state as a unitary actor and laying out clearly the logic behind the hypotheses linking domestic politics to the negotiation and ratification of international agreements, Milner's *Interests, Institutions, and Information* and other studies inspired by it have advanced the research agenda on two-level games. But these works look more at how domestic interests and institutions affect the prospects for international cooperation than at how they affect the effectiveness of threats and the probability of trade wars.[43] It is thus both necessary and possible to develop a two-level game approach to understanding threat effectiveness that includes more systematic analysis of domestic interests and institutions and their impact on international negotiations. Such an approach ought to allow us to better understand the interaction between the domestic and international games and to generate new, fruitful observations about the dynamics of international trade bargaining.

Theoretical Framework and Hypotheses

While this study draws on the concept of two-level games to address the two puzzles concerning threat effectiveness and the instances of trade wars, it also improves on the two-level game approach in two ways. First, it develops a model for understanding when threats are likely to be ratified by domestic interest groups. Second, it specifies the conditions under which domestic institutions will be united in support of trade sanctions. It will take a system-level variable—the structure of trade among nations (specifically, whether the parties involved have a complementary or competitive trade relationship)—and show how it systematically affects both the level of unity among domestic interest groups and the level of divided government in the sender of threats.

When two countries have a competitive trade relationship, both domestic interest groups and the government institutions in the sender of threats are more likely to be united in their policy preferences than when trade relations are complementary, enhancing the credibility of threats. Thus the United States will almost always find it more difficult to extract concessions from countries with which it has complementary trade relations than from those with which it has competitive ones. Paradoxically, the same set of variables, by producing stronger pressure for brinkmanship in bilateral trade games, also makes democracies more war prone in their trade relations. While democracies may indeed be more pacific in their security relations, that a fair number of democratic regimes happen to have highly competitive trade relations shapes their domestic politics in a way that pushes democracies toward less cooperative stances on trade. The contrasting pattern of democratic peace in security relations and the lack of it in trade therefore ought to have important implications for the theory of democratic peace in general.

Defining the Structure of Trade

As summarized previously, Odell's examination of two empirical cases shows that the presence or absence of support for sanctions makes a major difference to negotiation outcomes but that examination does not lead to a more general theory predicting when support for sanctions is likely to be present. The current study fills this gap by hypothesizing that the configuration of domestic interests, which bears importantly on threat effectiveness and the likelihood of trade wars, is affected to a considerable extent by a system-level variable—the structure of trade between the two parties, specifically, whether the trade relationship between the two is complementary or competitive.

Trade complementarity/competitiveness refers to the extent to which two countries engage in the production and export of a similar range of commodities. When two nations' comparative advantages differ, each has an incentive to concentrate on the production of those commodities that best utilize its comparative advantage and produce the highest profit margin and trades them for goods that it cannot produce at a reasonable cost at home. To illustrate this situation, if the United States specializes in the manufacturing of technology-intensive products and exports them to countries such as China in return for imports of labor-intensive products (such as shoes, toys, and textiles) that it no longer produces at home, then the trade structure between the two can be considered complementary. In contrast, when two countries' comparative advantages converge, both will specialize in the same set of products that will allow them to capture the greatest profits. Since their economic structures are similar, each will have home substitutes for imports from the other, and, as a result, trade is more competitive. Trade between the United States and Japan (or Europe) provides an example of a competitive trade structure, as both focus on the export of technology-intensive products.

John Conybeare uses the terms "complementary" and "competitive" in a way very similar to the way I employ the terms here. In his study of bilateral trade wars throughout history, Conybeare finds that trade complementarity/competitiveness is an important variable affecting the likelihood of bilateral trade wars. He gives the trade pattern in the ancient world as an example of a complementary trade relationship. In ancient times, the structure of trade consisted of complementary exchanges of essential commodities such as food and raw materials. Each country produced only one or a few commodities in which it had a clear comparative advantage and exchanged them for commodities that it was incapable of producing efficiently. He contrasts this pattern of trade with that in the contemporary world, where countries import commodities (such as autos, steel, and televisions) for which they have close substitutes at home. In this case, countries have higher elasticities of demands for imports and hence trade is more competitive.[44]

Conybeare's book looks primarily at the effects of the structure of trade on the likelihood of trade wars, but his insights have implications for understanding threat effectiveness as well. Conybeare considers trade relations in the contemporary world to be generally more competitive than those in the ancient world, but I would argue that there remains in the modern world a fair degree of variation in complementarity. Countries that export a similar set of products face a competitive trade structure, whereas those whose exports concentrate on a different range of commodities have a primarily complementary trade relationship.

To determine whether the United States, for example, has a complementary or competitive trade relationship with a specific country, we can compare the list of commodities that the United States exports with the list of commodities it imports from that trading partner. If there is considerable overlap between the two lists (i.e., if the leading items in U.S. exports to a country are similar to the leading commodities it imports from that trading partner), then the trade relationship is competitive. But if the items on these lists differ considerably (i.e., if the United States imports from its trading partner very different commodities than it exports to that country), then the trade relationship is complementary. An examination of the number of overlaps between the top twenty commodities the United States exports and the top twenty commodities it imports from particular countries reveals a wide range in the degrees of competitiveness in U.S. trade relations with its major trading partners (see table 2.1). Using my earlier definitions of trade competitiveness, we can see that the United States has the most competitive trade relationship with Canada, Japan, and EU member countries but has far more complementary trade relationships with countries such as China, Brazil, and India. In his study, Conybeare considers trade structure to be a determinant of the strategic game structure of bilateral trade wars. He argues that trade wars are more likely to break out between countries with competitive economies than between those with complementary ones because the costs of disrupting trade with the former are less severe: "Trade complementarity implies low elasticities of demand for each other's products, and high costs to a trade war. Countries with similar economic structures would have substitutes for each other's products and a higher elasticity."[45] Thus, trade structure is believed to influence outcomes of international

TABLE 2.1.   Number of Overlaps between Top Twenty Commodities the United States Exports to and Top Twenty Commodities It Imports from Major U.S. Trading Partners

Country	Total Volume of Trade Ranking	Number of Overlaps
United Kingdom	5	12
Canada	1	11
Germany	6	11
Mexico	3	10
Japan	2	9
Switzerland	21	9
France	10	8
Israel	24	8
Singapore	9	8
Belgium	16	7
Hong Kong	15	7
Netherlands	13	7
Taiwan	7	7
Malaysia	11	6
Philippines	19	6
Australia	22	5
Italy	12	5
South Korea	8	5
Thailand	18	4
Brazil	14	3
China	4	2
India	25	2
Indonesia	23	2
Saudi Arabia	20	2
Venezuela	17	2
Argentina	31	0

Source: U.S. Department of Commerce, U.S. Foreign Trade Highlights.

Note: Top twenty commodities in U.S. trade with individual trading partners are sorted by 1996 values and are based on three-digit SITC codes. Total volume of trade ranking is based on 1997 data.

bargaining primarily through the effects it has on the actors' evaluations of their material gains or losses from the disruption of trade. This approach is concerned primarily with factors at the system level and says nothing about domestic politics. It is possible, however, that trade structure can influence international bargaining outcomes by shaping the ways in which domestic forces respond to international structural factors.[46] In the following sections, we will see how trade structure can impinge on both threat effectiveness and the likelihood of trade wars by influencing the level of divergence of domestic interests as well as the degree of divided government in the sender of threats.

Trade Structure and Domestic Preferences

An important way in which trade structure may influence threat effectiveness is by determining the degree of *divergent preferences* among domestic interest groups. It is interesting to notice that, when trade relations are competitive (i.e., when the two nations compete in the same product lines), the nation issuing the threat will most likely have large export-seeking and import-competing sectors specializing in the production of the same commodities as the target country. In some cases, the firms seeking exports may even be the same as those that are competing with imports in the home market. U.S. efforts to pry open the Japanese construction market in 1987–88 may help to illustrate this point. In the late 1980s, convinced that U.S. construction firms, especially those involved in high-tech services, had been excluded from the Japanese public sector construction market by unfair Japanese practices, the U.S. Trade Representative (USTR) announced that a ban would be imposed on Japanese firms' participation in U.S. public works construction unless Japan modified its government procurement policy.

In this case, the U.S. construction firms pushing for trade sanctions were mainly large international firms that wanted to expand their presence in the Japanese construction market. At the same time there were also many U.S. construction firms that felt threatened by Japan's increasing success in the American construction market. These firms supported sanction threats because they would benefit from the restrictions on Japanese competition in the U.S. building market if sanctions were carried out against Japan.[47] Given this situation, American threats to impose sanctions unless Japan opened its market presented American industries with a no-lose situation. If sanction threats succeeded in extracting concessions, export-seeking interests (the larger international firms) won by obtaining greater access to Japan's market. If threats failed, and sanctions had to be imposed, import-competing interests (firms threatened by Japanese competition in the U.S. market) won. Because these firms produced the same things as the target, protectionism promised to provide them with "rents" previously unavailable under free trade. Sanction threats under these conditions consequently enjoyed much more unified support from affected organized interests and were therefore more likely to be effective.

In contrast, in the case of complementary trade relations, domestic interest groups are more likely to be divided, thus reducing the credibility and effectiveness of threats. This hypothesis derives from the observation that when trade relations are complementary the nation making the threat is likely to have both a large export-seeking industry and a virtually nonexistent import-competing sector. Trade relations between the United States and China, two countries with a high degree of trade complementarity, provide an example of this dynamic. Since the United States imports from China commodities that are no longer efficiently produced at home, there is a large import-using sector in the United States comprised of footwear, toy, and apparel manufacturers and distributors that support trade sanctions. At the same time, there are virtually no import-competing interests in the United States that want to see the threat of sanctions carried out against the Chinese. Although, in some cases, export-seeking firms (such as the intellectual property rights industry) support efforts to use trade sanctions to open up the Chinese market, oftentimes they find themselves impeded in this effort by active opposition from import-using industries. Not surprising, these domestic divisions severely reduced the credibility of American threats in the eyes of the Chinese.

Indeed, the logic developed here may help us understand the contrasting results of the two case studies described by Odell. As we have seen earlier, Odell's comparison of U.S.–EC and U.S.–Brazil negotiations illustrates how difficult it is for the United States to carry out a credible threat without strong, unified support from the affected groups. The question Odell did not ask, however, was why American interest groups were more divided in the informatics case involving Brazil than in the EC enlargement case. But if the argument developed previously has any validity, then we will see that one reason why American negotiators faced virtually no domestic opposition in the EC enlargement case was the competitive trade relationship between the United States and Europe. American feed-grain farmers, who wanted the EC to eliminate its subsidies on exports in an effort to expand

American exports, were also the ones competing with EC farm imports. Not surprising, the feed-grain sector was prepared to face the possible consequences of EC counterretaliation. Even those groups targeted by EC counterretaliation (the corn gluten feed farmers) did not press for accommodation because they faced "their own zero [duty] binding in the E.C."[48] The situation was completely different in the case of Brazil. Since trade relations between the United States and Brazil were complementary (note that Brazil is located near the bottom of the competitiveness index in table 2.1), threats to impose sanctions on Brazil enjoyed backing only from U.S. computer companies. There were no import-competing interests that supported the sanction threats. With this structure of interests, it is no wonder that the credibility of American threats was substantially reduced.

Summarized briefly, the analysis just described suggests that the structure of trade has an important impact on domestic interests in the country issuing the threat: U.S. threats to impose economic sanctions will enjoy more unified domestic support and hence will be more credible when the target has a competitive, rather than complementary, trade relationship with the United States. The domestic pressure generated by trade complementarity tends to be highly contradictory, thereby undermining the effectiveness of threat tactics.

Trade Structure, Divided Government, and
Threat Effectiveness

I further hypothesize that, in addition to influencing the pattern of interest group support for sanction threats, trade structure may also affect threat effectiveness by influencing the level of *divided government* in the sender of threats. As mentioned in the previous section, the effects of institutions on agreements to cooperate have been investigated systematically. Milner argues that divided government diminishes the prospects for international cooperation. Because the hawk exercises important veto power over the terms of the deal, the dove will be forced to modify its position and to accede to terms favored by the hawk. As the policy preferences of the two government branches diverge, the dove will have increasing difficulty getting the agreement ratified and will now have to negotiate agreements that lie closer to the hawk's preferences. As a result, divided government poses a major obstacle to international cooperation.

It should be noted at this point that in international negotiations it sometimes takes threats to get a country to move toward a cooperative deal. But for the threat to be credible, it has to be ratifiable. Typically, even though the executive and legislative branches share a common interest in retaining office, they may have different policy preferences due to their different constituency concerns. These differences in executive-legislative preferences lead to divided government. But since the ratification of threats requires the approval of both the legislative and executive branches, the more dovish actor—the one whose policy preferences are closer to those of the target—now has a veto over whether the threat can be approved. In this case, the logic that Milner describes works in reverse and the credibility of threats will again depend on the level of divided government, or the policy space between the executive and legislative branches. If the policy preferences of the executive happen to be closer to those of the legislature, the target country will perceive that the threat will have a greater possibility of being approved by the executive and of being implemented. Consequently, U.S. threats will be more credible. On the other hand, when the policy preferences of the two branches differ considerably, threats will be less credible in that it will lead the target to believe that there is only a slight chance that threats could be ratified and imposed. In short, greater unity between the two government branches increases the credibility of U.S. threats to impose trade sanctions, whereas divided government reduces threat credibility.

Which factors influence the degree of division between the two institutions? This study further hypothesizes that the structure of trade (i.e., whether trade relations are competitive or complementary) plays an important role in the level of divided government. Studies of American foreign economic policy have shown that the U.S. executive's responses to industries seeking protection will be determined by the combination of ideological considerations and institutional role pressures that a particular type of industry exerts on the executive. Ellis Krauss and Simon Reich argue that the embedded American ideology of free and fair trade implies that state intervention is legitimized only if the industry is perceived as "competitive" and is therefore likely to be able to eventually stand on its own. Noncompetitive industries, on the other hand, are more likely to be allowed to decline and disappear if they are not efficient enough.[49] Meanwhile, different types of industries tend to invoke different kinds of institutional role pressures. Specifically, since high-tech industries are perceived as crucial to the future well-being of the United States and often also to national security, they tend to invoke the role pressure of state interest on the president. On the other hand, although they may not be perceived as vital to the well-being of the country as a whole, non-high-tech industries also may induce the executive to act if they can bring to bear enough political pressure.

Using this logic, Krauss and Reich predict that, since high-tech industries such as supercomputers and satellites are both crucial to the future health of the economy and can compete in foreign markets, the American executive is likely to adopt the "fair trade" principle and attempt to open foreign markets for U.S. firms. Industries such as automobiles and machine tools are ones that traditionally have enjoyed a home market advantage and are thus generally perceived as competitive. Even though these are non-high-tech industries that have suffered a certain degree of decline, they are likely to exert sufficient pressure on the executive to act due to their political clout. In such cases, the executive is expected to come up with a moderate response by providing temporary relief for the industry and to adopt informal managed trade agreements that do not institutionalize protectionism.

U.S. industries that do not enjoy a home market advantage, on the other hand, are perceived by the executive to be undeserving of state intervention based on the executive's free trade ideology. The president will be quite reluctant to intervene in certain non-high-tech industries facing long-term structural decline, such as textiles and steel. But, in light of the pressure from organized labor to provide relief and out of practical electoral considerations, the executive would resort to "structural protectionism," adopting a series of measures to maintain the industry's employment level and to minimize the effects of terminal decline on labor. Finally, due to the executive's free trade ideology and the lack of strong political pressure, the executive branch will be least likely to undertake a major initiative on behalf of those high-tech industries (for example, high-definition television and fiber optics) that are unable to compete in foreign markets.[50]

Having posited when and how the American executive is likely to respond to domestic interests threatened with foreign competition, I now argue that, since trade conflicts between countries with competitive trade relations are most likely to occur in sectors in which U.S. firms are competitive (either high-tech sectors or mature/non-high-tech industries that have considerable political clout), the U.S. executive will be more likely to deviate from the free trade ideology to accommodate domestic pressure for protectionism or strategic trade policy when disputes involve these industries. This accommodation should bring the executive position closer to that of the legislature, which tends to be more hawkish in most trade disputes,[51] increasing the possibility that threats to impose sanctions will be ratified by the more dovish actor.

To be sure, trade conflicts between countries with competitive trade relations have taken place in noncompetitive, non-high-tech industries such as textiles and steel. But even here one would expect the American executive to respond more forcefully to domestic industries seeking relief from competition from a country with which the United States has a competitive trade relationship than to one with which it has a complementary relationship, because the level of threat posed by the former would be perceived to be higher than that by the latter.

Conversely, since trade conflicts between the United States and a country with which it has complementary trade relations are most likely to take place in noncompetitive, permanently declining industries, the U.S. executive is less likely to respond to domestic protectionist pressure, even though the industry under consideration still may hold some political power. Moreover, the interests of the import-using sectors in the continuation of normal trade relations should give the executive an additional incentive to resist the tougher approach. The policy space between the two government institutions will be wider, and there will be a higher possibility that threats may not be approved by the dove. The wider gap between executive and legislative preferences should make U.S. threats of sanctions less credible to the target.

This analysis leads to one of the key hypotheses of this study: the United States will be able to make more effective use of threats to extract concessions from nations with which it has competitive trade relations (such as Japan or Europe) than it will from nations with which it has complementary trade relations (such as China). In the case of competitive trade, not only are domestic interests more likely to be united in favor of trade sanctions, but the degree of division between the two government institutions will also be considerably lower, making the use of threats more effective. In the case of complementary trade, on the other hand, divisions in domestic interests and a more divided government all serve to undermine the credibility of U.S. threats.

Explaining Patterns of Trade War

Having developed a modified two-level game approach to explain the variations in the effectiveness of U.S. coercive diplomacy, we are still left with the question of why there have been many trade wars between democracies. This study proposes that the same factors that account for the variable degrees of threat credibility can also help us understand the lack of democratic peace in trade. The structure of trade—by influencing the structure of societal preferences, the preferences of the executive, and the degree of divided government—alters the incentives created by the nature of the regime (whether a state is democratic or not) that prevent democracies from going to war with one another in the security realm. Since a good number of democracies happen to be advanced industrial countries whose trade with one another tends to be competitive, strong domestic pressure for sanctions, coupled with an executive more inclined to go along with the tougher approach, will likely push these democracies toward fairly conflictual stances in trade disputes, resulting in high instances of trade wars among democracies.

In the case of competitive trade, domestic interest groups are generally unanimous in support of aggressive trade negotiation strategies, since both exporting and import-competing interests gain from aggressive tactics that promise benefits whether the threat succeeds or fails (and results in sanctions). This should produce strong pressure for brinkmanship in bilateral trade disputes. Meanwhile, for the reasons already enumerated, the executive is also more likely to approve of the need to impose sanctions if he or she perceives that domestic pressure for compensation is strong enough or that an industry vital to the future economic well-being of the nation is genuinely threatened by foreign competition.

When it comes to trade disputes between two countries with complementary trade relations, the structure of domestic interests differs. Divisions between exporting and import-using interests mean that an internal consensus will be harder to obtain. When one group of actors clamors for policies that will restrict the target's access to the home market, chances are that this will be offset by the pressure from another group that has an interest in the continuation of normal trade relations. This should reduce the incentives for defection in bilateral trade. Moreover, the more hawkish legislative branch will find it more difficult to get the executive, whose policy stance will differ even more sharply with that of the legislature, to ratify the decision. Given the difficulty of securing domestic ratification of threats, it is hardly surprising that the United States has rarely imposed sanctions to initiate a trade war with a trading partner with which it has a complementary trade relationship.

As we can see from the analysis in this chapter, the degree to which domestic actors are united over sanction threats plays an important role in determining the likelihood of trade wars. Having domestic groups opposed to sanction threats not only reduces threat effectiveness but also makes trade wars less likely. Similar to Conybeare's analysis of bilateral trade wars, this study emphasizes the importance of trade structure in affecting the outcomes of international commercial conflicts. But the argument advanced here also differs from that of Conybeare in important ways. For Conybeare, the structure of bilateral trade games is the primary factor determining the outcomes of commercial rivalries. Trade structure is important insofar as it affects the structure of payoffs in bilateral trade wars. Even though he considers the impact of domestic politics in some of his cases, he essentially adopts a game-theoretic approach that treats states as rational, unitary actors. In his framework, the influence of domestic politics is peripheral. The approach adopted here, in contrast, seeks to disaggregate the effects of trade structure at the domestic level by showing how it can affect states' propensity to engage in trade wars by influencing the level of polarization among domestic interest groups and the level of divided government. In doing so, it provides a plausible theoretical mechanism linking domestic and international variables.

In short, even though the theory of democratic peace would have led us to expect fewer democratic trade wars, that most democratic countries happen to have highly competitive trade relations generates societal and institutional forces that make democracies no less war prone with one another in trade than with nondemocracies.[52] While the theory of democratic peace may have considerable validity when applied to security issues, it does not fully capture the dynamics of international trade conflicts: democracies may be no less inclined to fight trade wars due to forces that can be traced to trade structure. The one strand of the democratic peace theory that is most applicable to trade issues—the theory of "democratic signaling" emphasized by Fearon—obviously has trouble explaining the pattern of trade wars we have observed. In the concluding chapter, I further discuss the implications of this finding for both trade policy-making and for the "democratic peace" literature.

Conclusion

This chapter develops a framework showing how the structure of trade among nations, by influencing the structure of domestic interests and the level of divided government in the sender of threats, affects international trade negotiation outcomes. It advances explicit hypotheses about the influence of domestic politics on international behavior. This framework will be used to organize the following analysis of America's negotiation record with its major trading partners. We will find that the factors emphasized in this chapter do have the hypothesized effects on threat effectiveness and the probability of trade war. Because of the way in which its domestic topography is shaped by varying trade structure, the United States not only has considerable difficulty imposing its demands on its weaker trading partners but has also been involved in a fairly large number of trade wars with its democratic trading partners, a pattern that clearly is not explicable in terms of the democratic peace theory.

CHAPTER 3

The Empirical Record

The analysis in the previous chapter provides a plausible explanation for the two empirical puzzles laid out in the opening pages of the book by looking at the interaction between domestic and international politics. If the theoretical mechanism suggested here is what really drives the negotiation dynamics, then the reason that U.S. pressure is more effective with countries such as Japan than with countries such as China resides in the different structure of these dyadic trade relationships and in the ways in which trade structure divides or unites domestic actors. Before delving into detailed case studies to see how these factors play out in the negotiation processes, I will first provide an overview of the record of trade negotiations between the United States and its major trading partners to establish the empirical validity of the research questions and to show that, rather than deliberately setting up an analytical straw man, the book explains two puzzling patterns that do exist in the real world.

Drawing primarily on the database on Section 301 cases provided by Bayard and Elliott, I show that substantial differences exist in the effectiveness of American pressure across countries and that these differences cannot be readily explained by the degree to which the target countries are dependent on the U.S. markets for exports. Rather, trade competitiveness/complementarity better predicts the variations in threat effectiveness. This chapter also looks at the record of trade conflicts initiated by the United States and shows that trade wars have taken place more frequently between the United States and its competitive trading partners and that regime type is irrelevant to understanding patterns of trade war.[1] Although the theory of democratic peace may offer accurate predictions of the pattern of interstate military wars, it does a less good job describing the pattern of trade wars among nations. Once again, my quantitative analysis reveals the importance of trade competitiveness/complementarity in explaining patterns of trade wars.

A Profile of Recent U.S. Trade Actions

Before proceeding to the empirical test, I first provide an overview of
the policy instruments frequently invoked by the United States at the
unilateral, bilateral, and multilateral levels designed to address
allegedly unfair foreign trade practices and the recent trade actions
undertaken by the United States pursuant to these relevant provisions
in order to lay out the general context of American trade policy.
Although this study will focus primarily on unilateral market-opening
measures under Section 301, it may be argued that the political dynamics characterizing unilateral trade sanctions is equally applicable to
U.S. bilateral and multilateral trade actions since the initiation and resolution of these other trade actions similarly depend on the degree to
which domestic actors support such measures designed to address the
alleged unfair trade practices of foreign actors. Due to space limitations, this study will not undertake detailed analyses of the connection
between trade structure and the outcome of each set of U.S. trade
actions and will instead leave this task to future investigation.

Administration of U.S. Trade Laws and Regulations

A wide range of legal statutes in the United States provides trade-remedy measures to deal with allegedly harmful effects of unfair foreign
trade practices. The most frequently utilized trade-remedy measures
include Section 301 of U.S. trade law, antidumping (AD) and countervailing duties (CVD), safeguard actions, and special arrangements for
agricultural products and for textiles and clothing.

Section 301 and Related Actions

The United States has frequently invoked what has been dubbed
"aggressively unilateral" trade strategy in an attempt to open foreign
markets. Section 301 of the U.S. trade law, which came into existence
in 1974 in response to industry concerns about unfair foreign competition, provides the USTR with enhanced authority either to self-initiate
a case or to launch a Section 301 investigation into an alleged unfair
trade barrier at the request of private parties. Under the Section 301
statute, the USTR is required to undertake consultations with the relevant foreign government in order to reach a settlement. In the event
that a settlement cannot be reached, the USTR would either invoke
dispute settlement procedures of the GATT/WTO if a trade agreement

is involved or decide on the measures to be pursued to compensate for the losses of American business interests.

There are two variations of the Section 301 procedure: the Super 301 provisions incorporated in the Omnibus Trade and Competitiveness Act of 1988 and Special 301 provisions. Reflecting Congress's desire for the USTR to set priorities and to pursue them vigorously, the Super 301 provision of the 1988 trade act authorized the USTR both to identify foreign practices, "the elimination of which are likely to have the most significant potential to increase U.S. exports (either directly or through establishing a beneficial precedent)" and to identify "priority foreign countries" on the basis of the "number and pervasiveness" of the únfair trade practices and "the level of United States exports of goods and services that would be reasonably expected from full implementation of existing trade agreements."[2]

Special 301, in turn, provides for investigation against "priority foreign countries" that may infringe on U.S. IPR. In its annual *National Trade Estimate Report,* the USTR typically singles out countries to be named in the following lists: priority foreign country, priority watch list, and special mention. Table 3.4 provides a breakdown by country of Section 301 (including both Super and Special 301) actions the United States initiated between 1975 and 1995. Between January 1995 and August 1999, the USTR initiated another twenty-five Section 301 cases targeted at a greater number of countries. Notably, the institution of new dispute settlement procedures of the WTO did not lead to a decline in the frequency of Section 301 investigations. Indeed, the USTR has continued to supplement multilateral and bilateral trade negotiations with the aggressive pursuit of unilateral market-opening strategies in order to address unfair trade practices of non-WTO member countries or those in areas not yet covered by the WTO. It is reasonable to expect that aggressive unilateralism will continue to be an important component of U.S. trade policy.

Antidumping and Countervailing Duties

The rise in international competition in recent decades has led many U.S. firms to resort increasingly to U.S. "unfair" trade laws, including the AD and CVD laws to seek relief from foreign imports. The AD law allows U.S. firms or industries to seek protection from "unfair" pricing practices of foreign firms, whereas the CVD law is designed to protect domestic firms and industries from subsidies provided by foreign government. Typically, requests for AD and CVD actions are made by firms and industries directly to the International Trade Administration (ITA) of the Commerce Department and the U.S. International Trade Commission (USITC), two agencies with congressionally mandated authority to determine whether unfair practice has occurred or whether such practice has injured the U.S. industry. In cases where both the ITA and the USITC make an affirmative decision, an AD or CVD duty is usually imposed to counter the effects of the alleged unfair practice.

Table 3.1 lists the AD investigations the United States initiated, ordered, and revoked between 1980 and 1999. As we can see, industry resort to AD laws has risen steadily since the late 1980s. It reached its peak in 1992 and then declined in the late 1990s, dropping to only fifteen cases in 1997. In terms of the geographical distribution of AD actions, Japan has been singled out most frequently, accounting for 16 percent of all the AD duties in effect in 1999. As to the product distribution of AD actions, iron and steel products take up the lion's share, accounting for 41 percent of all affected products in 1999.[3]

The pattern of CVD actions (see table 3.2) parallels that of AD actions, as CVD actions also peaked in 1992, with twenty-two cases, and then fell to six in 1997 and eleven in 1998. Iron and steel products again take up a disproportionately large share of CVD actions, accounting for 58.8 percent of all CVD duties in effect in 1999.[4]

Safeguard Actions

Under Section 201 of the U.S. Trade Act of 1974, an industry can apply for safeguard relief with the USITC. An affirmative decision by the USITC that an industry has been injured by increased imports will result in the application of safeguard measures for up to four years, or even eight years at the maximum. As of March 2000, safeguard measures were being provided for the following products: wheat gluten, lamb meat, certain wire (wire rod), and circular-welded, carbon-quality line pipe.

U.S. Bilateral Trade Policy Initiatives

In addition to addressing unfair foreign trade practices through existing U.S. trade laws, Washington has conducted extensive bilateral discussions with many of its trading partners to achieve expanded market access for U.S. firms. The following discussion of U.S. bilateral trade initiatives focuses mainly on U.S. trade negotiations with its major trading partners, such as China, Japan, and the EU.

TABLE 3.1. U.S. Antidumping (AD) Investigations, 1980–99

	1980–85	1986	1987	1988	1989	1990	1991	1992	1993	1994	1995	1996	1997	1998	1999	1980–99
Initiations	218	83	16	42	24	35	66	84	37	51	14	21	15	36	46	788
Preliminary Determinations	156	52	45	35	23	25	43	54	67	46	23	16	16	28	34	663
Final Determinations	117	43	58	17	40	18	28	28	80	31	38	12	15	17	37	579
Duty Orders	59	26	53	12	24	14	19	16	42	16	24	9	7	9	19	349
Revocations	37	8	9	0	5	10	7	1	3	28	12	6	4	25	48	203

Source: International Trade Administration, <http://ia.ita.doc.gov/stats/ad8099.htm>.

TABLE 3.2. U.S. Countervailing Duty Investigations, 1980–99

	1980–85	1986	1987	1988	1989	1990	1991	1992	1993	1994	1995	1996	1997	1998	1999	1980–99
Initiations	173	28	8	17	7	7	11	22	5	7	2	1	6	11	10	315
Preliminary Determinations	144	28	10	18	6	4	9	26	1	7	3	0	3	7	9	275
Final Determinations	104	22	20	14	12	4	5	7	20	2	6	2	0	2	15	235
Duty Orders	65	13	14	7	6	2	2	4	16	1	2	2	0	1	6	141
Revocations	68	4	2	1	5	4	6	0	1	5	35	1	1	4	19	156

Source: International Trade Administration, <http://ia.ita.doc.gov/stats/cvd-1980-2002.html>.

According to the Trade and Related Agreements Database (TARA) compiled by the Trade Compliance Center (TCC), which covers active, binding agreements between the United States and its trading partners in manufactured products and services, the United States has reached fifteen major bilateral trade agreements with the People's Republic of China since 1992. The agreements cover such issues as IPR, market access, textile products, and commercial launch services.[5]

In terms of U.S. bilateral trade initiatives vis-à-vis Japan, the U.S. government has managed to reach over forty market-opening agreements with that country since 1989. Many of these agreements were accompanied by extensive monitoring and enforcement mechanisms and incorporated "objective" criteria as the basis for the evaluation of progress. Some of the most prominent issues covered by the agreements include auto and auto parts, government procurement (especially in the areas of telecommunications, computers, supercomputers, public works, and medical technology), deregulation of financial services, insurance, and the telecommunication sectors. Finally, fifteen bilateral trade agreements between the United States and the EU are currently in effect, covering such areas as civil aircraft, government procurement, and enlargement.[6]

U.S. Dispute Settlement Actions in the Multilateral Context

In addition to addressing alleged unfair foreign practices either bilaterally or within the framework of U.S. unfair trade laws and regulations, the United States has frequently resorted to the multilateral forum provided by the GATT and its successor, the WTO, to settle disputes with its trading partners. The launching of the WTO in January 1995, with the redesign and strengthening of the Dispute Settlement Mechanism (DSM), has introduced some important changes in dispute resolution procedures. Compared to the dispute settlement procedures in the GATT, several features of the new DSM may have affected the degree to which the United States can effectively utilize the multilateral forum to pursue its trade policy objectives. For example, under the new DSM rules, it is no longer possible for a nation that does not want another country to take the dispute to the WTO to indefinitely delay the establishment of a dispute panel. A nation that is not happy with the WTO panel ruling gains the ability to block the finding on appeal. The new dispute settlement procedures also increase opportunities for arbitration, specify standard terms of reference, and enhance surveillance of the implementation of the panel reports.[7]

Due to the broader coverage of the WTO, the number of consultation requests has risen since 1995. While a total of 278 cases were initiated in the first four decades of the GATT between 1948 and 1987, a total of 317 cases were initiated between 1988 and 1998.[8] As the breakdown of the consultation requests made under the WTO suggests (see table 3.3), the United States has most frequently resorted to the DSM, initiating 65 out of the total of 202 consultation requests filed between January 1995 and June 2000, including 25 against the EU and individual EU member countries, 5 against Japan, 6 against other industrialized countries, and 29 against developing/emerging economies.

As mentioned earlier, this study will not undertake detailed analysis of the relevance of trade structure to each of the sets of trade actions discussed previously. Instead, it will focus primarily on the relationship between trade structure and the United States' aggressively unilateral trade actions under Section 301 in testing its argument. If trade structure exerts a significant impact on the effectiveness of America's unilateral trade actions, then this should provide a basis for extending my analysis to other facets of U.S. trade policy.

Trade Structure and the Effectiveness of America's "Aggressively Unilateral" Trade Policy

Using U.S. trade action under Section 301 as an example, this section tests the relationship between trade structure and threat effectiveness.

TABLE 3.3.   WTO Disputes: Consultation Requests, 1995–2000

	Respondents					
Complainants	United States	Japan	EU (including individual EC members)	Other Industrialized Countries	Developing/ Emerging Economies	Total
United States	—	5	25	6	29	65
Japan	4	—	—	1	2	7
EU	18	6	—	3	24	51
Other Industrialized Countries	5	1	7	3	11	27
Developing/ Emerging Economies	21	—	18	2	27	68
Total	48	12	50	15	93	218

Source: World Trade Organization, "Overview of the State-of-Play of WTO Disputes," see WTO website.

Chapter 1 briefly outlines the cross-national variations in American threat effectiveness under Section 301. Based on a few examples, I argue that U.S. pressure was more effective with countries such as Japan, Taiwan, and South Korea than with countries such as China, Brazil, and India. This contrast is given more empirical weight, however, if I can illustrate, through a more general survey of the record of negotiations between the United States and its major trading partners, that American economic coercion has produced more tangible results with competitive trading partners than with complementary ones. Toward this end, I examine the overall record of Section 301 negotiations conducted by the United States between 1975 and 1995.

An Overview of U.S. Section 301 Actions

To substantiate the claim that there exists substantial cross-national variations in the effectiveness of America's "aggressively unilateral" trade policy, I first calculate the average concession rates of major U.S. trading partners in Section 301 investigations, relying primarily on Bayard and Elliott's evaluation of the success of U.S. economic coercion in Section 301 cases and on Elliott and Richardson's updated and expanded data set. In both Bayard and Elliott's and Elliott and Richardson's classification schemes, the United States is "largely successful" if there is substantial compliance with U.S. demands in all issue areas; "partially successful" if the target capitulates to American demands on some, but not all, of the issues under dispute; "nominally successful" if the issue reoccurs or if the target fails to implement the agreement; and "not at all successful" if the United States fails to reach any agreement with the target.[9] Following these criteria, I rate "not at all successful" cases as "0" up through "largely successful" cases as "3" and average the results of American pressure by country. The results, reported in table 3.4, indicate that the effectiveness of American pressure varies widely with each bilateral relationship. For example, while Japan, Taiwan, South Korea, and Canada are among the U.S. trading partners most responsive to American pressure, China, India, and Argentina end up on the lower end of the responsiveness scale. The Japanese, who are most responsive to American pressure, achieve an average score of 2.07, compared with only 1 for China and 0.5 for India.

A Comparison of Section 301 Cases Involving China and Japan

If we look closely at the effectiveness of American coercive diplomacy in cases involving China and Japan, the contrast in negotiation outcomes

TABLE 3.4. Effectiveness of U.S. Pressure under Section 301

Cases Involving Japan	Degree to Which U.S. Objectives Achieved	Quantitative Score
Thrown silk (1977–78)	Largely successful	3
Leather (1977–85)	Partially successful	2
Cigars (1979–81)	Nominally successful	1
Pipe tobacco (1979–81)	Nominally successful	1
Footwear (1982–85)	Partially successful	2
Semiconductors (1985–91)	Nominally successful	1
Cigarettes (1985–86)	Largely successful	3
Citrus (1988)	Largely successful	3
Construction (1988–91)	Partially successful	2
Satellites (1989–90)	Largely successful	3
Supercomputers (1989–90)	Partially successful	2
Wood products (1989–90)	Partially successful	2
Auto parts (1994–95)	Nominally successful	1
Agricultural products (1997)*	Largely successful	3
Average result	Partially successful	2.07

Cases Involving China		
Market access (1991–92)	Nominally successful	1
IP protection (1991–92)	Nominally successful	1
IP protection (1994–96)*	Nominally successful	1
Average result	Nominally successful	1

Cases Involving EU		
Egg albumin (1975–80)	Partially successful	2
Canned fruit and vegetables (1975–79)	Nominally successful	1
Malt (1975–80)	Not at all successful	0
Wheat flour (1975–83)	Not at all successful	0
Canned fruit (1976–80)	Nominally successful	1
Soybeans and soymeal (1976–79)	Nominally successful	1
Citrus (1976–86)	Partially successful	2
Wheat (1978–80)	Nominally successful	1
Sugar (1981–82)	Not at all successful	0
Poultry (1981–84)	Nominally successful	1
Pasta (1981–87)	Partially successful	2
Canned fruit and raisins (1981–85)	Nominally successful	1
Corn, sorghum, oilseeds (1986–87)	Largely successful	3
Meatpacking (1987–89)	Not at all successful	0
Beef (1987–89)	Not at all successful	0
Soybeans (1987–90)	Nominally successful	1
Fabricated copper (1988–90)	Largely successful	3
Canned fruit (1989)	Partially successful	2
Corn, sorghum, oilseeds (1990)	Partially successful	2
Meatpacking (1990–93)	Nominally successful	1
Bananas (1995–98)*	Partially successful	2
Enlargement (1995–96)*	Nominally successful	1
Modified starch (1997)*	Partially successful	2
Average result	Nominally successful	1.3

TABLE 3.4.—*Continued*

Cases Involving Canada	Degree to Which U.S. Objectives Achieved	Quantitative Score
Eggs (1975–76)	Largely successful	3
Broadcasting (1978–84)	Not at all successful	0
Fish (1986–90)	Partially successful	2
Beer (1990–93)	Nominally successful	1
Service (1994–95)	Partially successful	2
Periodicals (1996–97)*	Partially successful	2
Average result	Nominally successful	1.67

Cases Involving Brazil		
Footwear (1982–85)	Partially successful	2
Soybean oil and meal (1983–85)	Partially successful	2
Informatics (1985–89)	Partially successful	2
Pharmaceuticals (1987–90)	Nominally successful	1
Import licensing (1989–90)	Largely successful	3
Intellectual property (1993–94)	Nominally successful	1
Automobiles (1996–98)*	Partially successful	2
Average result	Nominally successful	1.86

Cases Involving Argentina		
Marine insurance (1979–80)	Nominally successful	1
Leather (1981–82)	Not at all successful	0
Air couriers (1983–89)	Partially successful	2
Soybean oil and meal (1986–88)	Nominally successful	2
Textiles (1988–89)*	Nominally successful	1
Average result	Nominally successful	1.2

Cases Involving Korea		
Insurance (1979–80)	Nominally successful	1
Footwear (1982–85)	Partially successful	2
Insurance (1985–86)	Partially successful	2
Intellectual property (1985–86)	Nominally successful	1
Cigarettes (1988)	Partially successful	2
Beef (1988–90)	Partially successful	2
Wine (1988–89)	Partially successful	2
Agricultural market access restrictions (1994–95)*	Partially successful	2
Automobiles (1997)*	Partially successful	2
Average result	Nominally successful	1.78

Cases Involving Taiwan		
Home appliances (1976–77)	Largely successful	3
Rice (1983–84)	Partially successful	2
Motion picture films (1983–84)	Partially successful	2
Customs evaluation (1986)	Partially successful	2
Beer, wine, tobacco (1986)	Partially successful	2
Intellectual property (1992)	Partially successful	1
Average result	Partially successful	2

(continued)

TABLE 3.4.—*Continued*

Cases Involving India	Degree to Which U.S. Objectives Achieved	Quantitative Score
Almonds (1987–88)	Partially successful	2
Investment (1989–90)	Not at all successful	0
Insurance (1989–90)	Not at all successful	0
Intellectual property (1991–92)	Not at all successful	0
Pharmaceuticals (1996–98)*	Nominally successful	1
Average result	Not at all successful	0.6

Note: Unless indicated by an asterisk, the degree to which U.S. negotiating objectives were achieved is based on Bayard and Elliott, *Reciprocity and Retaliation,* and Elliott and Richardson, "Determinants and Effectiveness." Since Bayard and Elliott's data only cover cases resolved as of 1992 and Elliott and Richardson only dealt with cases resolved as of 1995, evaluations of cases completed after 1995 are made using similar criteria.

is obvious. The application of pressure tactics against China resulted in only nominal success in both of the Section 301 cases involving that country.[10] Indeed, China is the second least responsive American trading partner behind India. Before the conclusion of the U.S.–China agreement on terms for China's entry into the WTO in November 1999, the United States threatened trade sanctions in an attempt to obtain unilateral concessions from the Chinese. American negotiators repeatedly found themselves defeated in efforts to force the Chinese to reduce tariffs and other trade barriers, to improve the transparency of their trade regime, to police intellectual property protection, and to strictly adhere to quota restrictions on textile trade. As the detailed case studies in chapters 4 and 6 suggest, the United States was able to extract very few meaningful concessions from China in these sets of negotiations and had to several times reinvoke threats of trade retaliation to get the Chinese to move closer to American demands. The reemergence of these issues in bilateral trade negotiations itself suggests the ineffectiveness of American pressure.

In comparison with the China cases, U.S. pressure against Japan seems to be remarkably successful. The utilization of unilateral market-opening measures against Japan turned out to be largely successful five out of fourteen times, resulted in partial success in another five cases, and was only nominally successful in the remaining four cases, thus making Japan the country most responsive to American pressure. The claim that Tokyo has most frequently caved in to American pressure is perhaps hard to believe, given the enduring complaints about Japanese trade barriers emanating from industry officials and their representatives on Capitol Hill. In particular, critics are apt to question the extent to which Japanese concessions have produced genuine market-opening outcomes.[11] But as Bayard and Elliott's study points out, the United States has derived significant economic gains from the concessions Japan made during Section 301 negotiations. For example, under threats of Section 301 retaliation, the United States was able to increase its exports of cigarettes to Japan from less than $95 million in 1985 to more than $1 billion by 1990. U.S. exports of beef to Japan increased by $750 million, from $350 million in 1987 to $1.1 billion in 1990. Similarly, the semiconductor agreement allowed U.S. producers to increase their exports to Japan by $1 billion a year. The beef, tobacco, and semiconductor cases together accounted for more than three-fourths of the total gains the United States accrued through the use of Section 301.[12] While market barriers remained in Japan, it seems fair to say that the level of Japanese trade barriers would have been a lot higher in the absence of American pressure.

The high-profile semiconductor trade conflict between the United States and Japan provides an example of the effectiveness of American pressure in opening the Japanese market. In this case, described in more detail in chapter 5, sustained American pressure, backed by the threat and actual implementation of trade retaliation, played a crucial role in helping American manufacturers gain enhanced market access in Japan and in preventing Japanese firms from dumping in the U.S. market. As a result of Japanese concessions, American producers were able to increase their shares of the Japanese market, capturing $1 billion in additional sales between 1987 and 1990.[13] While U.S. firms might have hoped to achieve even more through trade negotiations, U.S. coercive diplomacy clearly helped to resuscitate a critical industry on the edge of extinction.

American pressure also turned out to be highly successful in the Super 301 cases over supercomputers, satellites, and forest products that will be examined in more detail in chapter 5. In these cases, U.S. threats of retaliation led to the conclusion of bilateral agreements that helped to address industry complaint about Japanese "targeting" of high-technology industries and other nontariffs barriers that impeded American manufacturers' access to the Japanese market.

To be sure, that the United States was more successful in negotiations with Japan than in negotiations with China does not mean that U.S. pressure has been uniformly successful in extracting concessions from the Japanese. In fact, a fair amount of variations exist in the degree to which Japan has yielded to U.S. demands. While the United States largely achieved its negotiation objectives in a number of Section 301 cases involving such products as thrown silk, cigarettes, citrus, and satellites, it has met more Japanese resistance in other areas.

For example, in U.S.–Japan negotiations over satellites in 1989–90, the United States largely achieved its negotiating objectives. Under strong U.S. pressure to open up Japan's public procurement of satellites, the Japanese government eventually acceded to virtually all American demands, committing itself and entities under its control to "procure non-R&D satellites on an open, transparent and nondiscriminatory basis, and in accordance with the GATT Procurement Code."[14] Not only did Japanese observers consider the agreement "a complete acceptance of American demands" in all respects, but U.S. trade officials also regarded it as a significant setback for Japanese commercial satellite development.[15]

But if the United States has largely achieved its negotiating objective of opening Japanese government procurement to foreign bidders in the satellite case, it has had considerably less success in other negotiations with Japan. American efforts to open up Japan's public sector construction market in 1988–91, for example, only partly succeeded in improving access for U.S. firms. U.S. retaliatory threats to bar Japanese firms from bidding for U.S. public contracts led the Japanese government to commit itself to a more open and competitive bidding system and to establish more objective and transparent standards for bidding and contracting procedures. But although the list of projects open to U.S. bidding was increased, it was not implemented as the United States would have wanted. Actual U.S. export gains also appeared to be rather limited. Furthermore, U.S. firms seemed to have difficulty bidding on projects not on the list. Even though the subsequent agreement addressed additional U.S. concerns, there was much more the United States hoped to achieve through the negotiations. The outcome in this case therefore appears to represent only partial fulfillment of U.S. objectives.[16]

Moreover, there were also areas in which the United States failed to induce Japanese commitments to specific American objectives. For instance, in the years between 1993 and 1995, the Clinton administration stepped up the pressure on the Japanese government to increase the use of U.S.–made auto parts in Japanese cars and to enhance access to dealership networks by foreign carmakers. Under U.S. threats to impose prohibitive tariffs on $5.9 billion of imports of Japanese luxury cars, Japan eventually entered into an agreement with the United States in 1995. But the 1995 auto accord contained only very vague language on the expected direction and scope of change. The "results" specified in the accord were mostly based on "voluntary plans" announced by the Japanese automakers. Without any explicit criteria, the United States had found it very difficult to monitor Japan's enforcement of the deal in any meaningful way.[17] In this case the Clinton administration was unable to achieve its core objectives through coercive diplomacy.

This brief survey of the record of U.S. trade negotiations with Japan is intended to show that, even though U.S. pressure on Japan is highly effective overall, there are also cases in which U.S. pressure only marginally succeeded in affecting Japanese behavior. What is most important for the purposes of the present study, however, is that when compared with America's other trading partners Japan still shows up as the country most responsive to American demands.

Realism and Variations in Threat Effectiveness

In view of the wide variations in U.S. threat effectiveness previously described, one may want to ask to what extent these variations could have been explained by the differences in the contexts of U.S.–Japan and U.S.–China trade negotiations. For example, it may be argued that the United States was able to achieve greater success in negotiations with the Japanese because the U.S. trade relationship with Japan is both more developed and sector specific than are U.S. trade relations with China. It may also be argued that the variations in threat effectiveness previously described may be better understood in terms of states' power balances, a variable emphasized by the realist theory.

However, not entirely in line with realists' predictions, many nations' level of responsiveness to American pressure differs from what one would predict based on their level of asymmetrical export dependence on the United States. Here I measure asymmetrical trade dependence by comparing the percentage of a target country's exports to the United States in the target's GDP to the percentage of U.S. exports to the target country in U.S. GDP.[18] Using this procedure, I calculate the level of asymmetrical trade dependence for major U.S. trading partners in each of the years between 1975 and 1995 and arrive at an average for each country. I then construct a responsiveness index based on the average concession rates reported in table 3.4. The results, plotted in figure 3.1, reveal that countries that are least responsive to American pressure (such as China and India) have a higher level of asymmetrical export dependence on the United States than several of America's other trading partners. Japan, the trading partner most responsive to

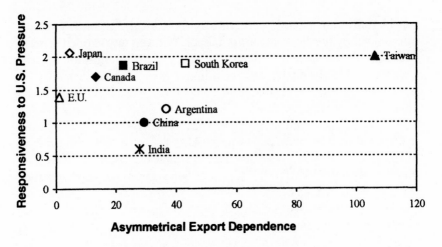

FIGURE 3.1. Asymmetrical export dependence and responsiveness to U.S. pressure

American pressure, actually has one of the lowest asymmetrical export dependence levels on the American export market. The EU, whose responsiveness index is comparable to those of Canada and Argentina, does not rely on the U.S. export market as much as these two trading partners. Therefore, it seems that states' power balances do not fully explain these patterns. It is necessary for us to look at factors other than raw material power and to unpack the black box of domestic politics to account for these paradoxical outcomes.

Trade Structure and Threat Effectiveness: Statistical Analysis

If countries' underlying power balances do not adequately account for the pattern of U.S. threat effectiveness, how well does the alternative variable emphasized by this study, the structure of trade, explain this pattern? Figure 3.2 presents the relationship between trade structure and the degree of responsiveness of several major U.S. trading partners. As we can see, there is a generally positive relationship between trade structure and threat effectiveness: countries having more competitive trade relations with the United States (such as Japan, Canada, South Korea, and Taiwan) also are the ones that have yielded more frequently to American pressure. In contrast, countries having a primarily complementary trade structure with the United States (such as China and India) are significantly less responsive to America's sanction threats.

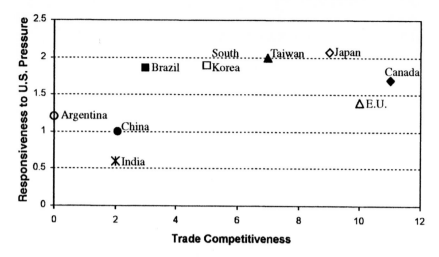

FIGURE 3.2.   Structure of trade and responsiveness to U.S. pressure. (*Note:* See table 3.2 for the responsiveness index. The trade competitiveness index is constructed using data in table 2.1, with larger numbers indicating a higher level of trade competitiveness.)

To better assess the relationship between trade structure and threat effectiveness, I estimate a model of the level of success the United States achieved in using Section 301 to open overseas markets. The estimation sample is based primarily on Bayard and Elliott's comprehensive evaluation of seventy-two Section 301 cases concluded by 1994.[19] But it also takes into account six cases from Elliott and Richardson's updated and expanded sample of Section 301 cases settled by 1995. The addition of these six cases produces a sample of seventy-eight cases involving fifteen countries.[20] To test the influence of trade competitiveness on Section 301 success, I essentially replicate Bayard and Elliott's and Elliott and Richardson's earlier works by including all of the variables in their analyses and adopting the same statistical methods they employed. I then run the same model, adding my trade competitiveness/complementarity variable.

The dependent variable SUCCESS, based on the degree to which the United States was able to achieve its negotiation objectives in each individual case, is a dichotomous variable. It equals 0 if American negotiators were "not at all successful" or "nominally successful" in pursuing their negotiation objectives in a given case and 1 if the United States partially or largely fulfilled its negotiating objectives. Both Bayard and Elliott and Elliott and Richardson used the same coding scheme, although the latter also assessed the influence of various explanatory variables on an ordinal-scale measure of the target's responsiveness to U.S. pressure, in addition to the dichotomous measure of success. My statistical tests using the ordinal measure success variable yielded similar, indeed even stronger, results than those described later and are not reported here.

To examine the relationship between trade structure and the odds of Section 301 success, I first estimate a model (Model 1) that incorporates all of the variables, measured in exactly the same ways, as those used by Bayard and Elliott in their 1994 study. Explanatory variables for Model 1 include the following:

TBAL. Bilateral trade balance has often been considered as a crude measure of reciprocity in international trade negotiations. It is expected that larger U.S. trade deficits will produce greater protectionist pressure toward the target, increasing the chances of a successful outcome.[21]

TXDEP. To test the realist argument that power resources in a country's favor would enhance its bargaining leverage and chances for successful outcomes, I include the degree of the target's export dependence on the American market (TXDEP) in the analysis. A positive relationship is expected between TXDEP and SUCCESS.[22] TXDEP is measured by the percentage of the target's exports to the United States in the target's GDP during the year(s) of the dispute.

RULING. The variable RULING makes a distinction between those cases in which a GATT panel issued a ruling against the target country (in which case RULING is set to equal 1) and those in which the GATT did not issue such a ruling during the dispute settlement process (in which case RULING equals 0). It is expected that a negative GATT panel ruling can increase the chance for a successful outcome by raising the costs to the target government of defying international rules.[23]

BORDER. Bayard and Elliott and Elliott and Richardson have found that, compared to such trade barriers as subsidies, "domestic" regulatory access barriers, services trade, or intellectual property protection, unfair border barriers to U.S. exports (such as import and export quotas and tariffs) have a better chance of success because of their transparency, ease of definition and measurement, and greater likelihood of being GATT-illegal.[24] Following their lead, a dummy variable BORDER is included to control for the effect of different types of trade barriers on the success of U.S. negotiation strategy. This variable is coded as 1 if the case involves traditional border barriers that impede merchandise access and 0 if otherwise.

COUNTER. Bayard and Elliott have found some evidence that American negotiators' perceptions of U.S. vulnerability to counterretaliation, shaped in part by whether the target has responded to America's aggressive negotiation tactics in the past with similar moves, play an important role in determining outcomes. The variable COUNTER, intended to capture the effect of U.S. concerns about possible counter-retaliation, is set to equal 1 if the target has retaliated against the United States in a past trade dispute (whether under Section 301 or not); otherwise it is 0.[25] A negative relationship is expected between COUNTER and SUCCESS.

TPAP. Following the lead of Bayard and Elliott, I include a time-related dummy variable, TPAP, in Model 1 to see if the adoption of more aggressive negotiation tactics by the USTR since the mid-1980s, especially after the announcement of President Reagan's Trade Policy Action Plan (TPAP) in 1985, played any role in increasing the effectiveness of U.S. negotiation strategy. TPAP equals 1 if a case was settled before September 1985 and 0 otherwise.

SUPER301. The passage of the 1988 Omnibus Trade and Competitiveness Act, including Super 301 provisions, presumably enhances threat credibility by providing trade negotiators with greater discretion and by signaling the United States' strengthened resolve for a positive outcome. Thus, like Bayard and Elliott, I incorporate a dummy variable SUPER301, coded as 1 if the case was initiated after the signing of the congressional trade bill in 1988 and 0 otherwise, to account for the possible strengthening of U.S. credibility under Super 301.

All of these variables are adopted by Bayard and Elliott in their model estimates. To see how trade structure, my key explanatory variable, would affect model estimates, I run a second model (Model 2), adding the degree of trade competitiveness (COMPET) between the United States and its trading partners to Model 1. By adding COMPET to Bayard and Elliott's and Elliott and Richardson's analyses, I am testing the influence of trade structure on threat credibility. The causal logic developed in the previous chapter would lead us to expect a positive relationship between COMPET and SUCCESS. The trade competitiveness index for each case is calculated using the procedure described in the previous section.[26] Because it is possible for a country having a highly competitive trade relationship with the United States in a given year to nevertheless have a relatively small absolute number of overlaps, the raw data for each dyad year is adjusted in relation to that of the country with the most overlaps in that particular year.[27] In other words, even though the raw numbers reflect the countries' relative degree of trade competitiveness in a given year, they may bias comparisons of trade structure across time, as a given raw score may not reflect the same level of trade competitiveness from year to year. The adjustment described earlier should therefore provide a more objective basis for comparing trade competitiveness indices across dyad years.

Based on these results, I estimate a third model (Model 3), which takes into consideration a couple of other control variables that Elliott and Richardson examined in their study that could potentially affect the probability of Section 301 success, in addition to the variables previously given. These control variables include the following:

INITIATE. The ability of U.S. negotiators to make a threat public may help to open foreign markets by sending a signal to the target country that the issue was high on the U.S. negotiation agenda and that "the administration meant business."[28] To test the hypothesis that USTR initiation of a case will have a positive effect on threat credibility and the successful pursuit of U.S. negotiation objectives, I add a dummy variable INITIATE that takes on a value of 1 if the USTR self-initiates a case and 0 otherwise.

BULLY. This variable measures the number of cases initiated against a particular target country as a percentage of all Section 301 cases started over a three-year period. A negative association is expected between this variable and the likelihood of success due to the phenomenon of diminishing returns.

Tables 3.5 and 3.6 provide a concise description of the dependent and explanatory variables and their frequency distributions.

Test Results

To understand the pattern of Section 301 success, I use the same statistical method adopted by Bayard and Elliott and Elliott and Richardson, the probit approach, to assess the influence of the aforementioned variables on Section 301 negotiation outcome (SUCCESS). The probit method is appropriate for estimating a dichotomous variable such as success/failure.[29] The estimates for the models just described, reported in table 3.7, lend strong support to the hypothesis about the relationship between trade competitiveness and the degree of Section 301 success. In both Model 2 and Model 3, the variable measuring the degree of trade competitiveness, COMPET, holds up quite well. Regardless of the mix of variables included in the analysis, the relationship between COMPET and SUCCESS is consistently positive and significant, reaching a significance level of 95 percent in Model 2 and 90 percent in Model 3. This result seems to be quite robust considering the relatively large number of control variables included in the analysis.

The type of trade barriers under consideration (BORDER) and the time-related variable (TPAP) also perform quite well in these tests. Consistent with the findings of both Bayard and Elliott and Elliott and Richardson, traditional, transparent border barriers enhance the ability of U.S. negotiators to liberalize foreign markets through Section 301 negotiations. The coefficient for this variable is significant at the 99 percent level. Also corroborating previous study results is the finding

TABLE 3.5. Variable Descriptions

	Name	Description
Dependent Variable	SUCCESS	Dichotomous measure of the degree to which the United States successfully achieved its negotiation objectives: 1 = "largely successful" or "partially successful"; 0 = "nominally successful" or "not at all successful."
Explanatory Variables	COMPET	Ordinal measure of the degree of trade competitiveness between the United States and the target country in a particular dyad year. Ranges between 0 and 10.
	TBAL	Trade balance between the United States and a given trading partner.
	TXDEP	The percentage of the target's exports to the United States in the target's GDP. Averaged over the years in which the dispute was active.
	COUNTER	1 if the target has retaliated against the United States in past trade disputes; 0 otherwise.
	RULING	1 if a GATT panel issued a ruling against the target; 0 otherwise.
	BORDER	1 if the dispute involved a border barrier to merchandise trade (such as import and export quotas and tariffs); 0 otherwise.
	TPAP	1 if a case is settled before September 1985; 0 otherwise.
	SUPER301	1 if a case is initiated after 1988; 0 otherwise.
	INITIATE	1 if the case is initiated by the USTR; 0 otherwise.
	BULLY	Number of cases initiated against a given target country as a percentage of all investigations started during the current year and two preceding years. The number of cases in 1973 and 1974 is set to equal 0.

that legislative and executive changes in the mid-1980s (TPAP) have contributed to the significantly higher success rates of Section 301 investigations in the late 1980s and early 1990s. The Trade Policy Action Plan, by signaling U.S. negotiators' increasingly tough posture toward trade issues, has increased the odds of obtaining a successful outcome.

The results also provide some support for the variable representing the degree of the target's vulnerability to U.S. retaliation (TXDEP). The United States did wring more concessions from its relatively weak trading partners. Somewhat surprisingly, the variable emphasized by liberal institutionalism, the presence of a negative GATT ruling against the target, while statistically significant in each of the three models, is in the direction opposite from that expected. A GATT panel finding of impairment and nullification actually decreases, rather than increases, the probability of obtaining a successful negotiation outcome. It is possible that, analogous to what the literature on alliances and extended deterrence posits, GATT "commitment" on behalf of the United States could have enhanced the possibilities of conflict. According to the extended deterrence literature, state A's public statement of willingness to intervene on state B's behalf in an international crisis may lead state B to be more intransigent and to refuse to make concessions in a dispute involving state B and a third party, state C, thereby creating the problem of entrapment.[30] Extending this logic to trade disputes, it can be argued that a GATT panel ruling in favor of the United States may produce a similar effect by encouraging a more confrontational and aggressive approach to the dispute, which in turn results in greater conflict.

TABLE 3.6.   Descriptive Statistics of the Estimation Sample

Variable	Observations	Mean	Standard Deviation	Min	Max
SUCCESS	78	1.449	.907	0	3
COMPET	78	6.195	2.920	0	10
TBAL	78	8643.84	16188.75	−65942.5	10822
TXDEP	78	.066	.084	.003	.359
COUNTER	78	.256	.439	0	1
RULING	78	.167	.375	0	1
BORDER	78	.308	.465	0	1
TPAP	78	.346	.479	0	1
SUPER301	78	.308	.465	0	1
INITIATE	78	.295	.459	0	1
BULLY	78	.230	.175	.048	.7

TABLE 3.7. Probit Estimates for the Success of Section 301 Investigations (Models 1–3)

Explanatory Variable	Model 1			Model 2			Model 3		
	Coefficient	Standard Error	t-statistic	Coefficient	Standard Error	t-statistic	Coefficient	Standard Error	t-statistic
TBAL	-8.53e-06	.00001	-.771	.00001	.00002	.810	.00002	.00002	.932
TXDEP	7.661	2.938	2.608***	8.831	3.084	.864***	8.595	3.292	2.611***
COUNTER	.229	.427	.054	-.493	.522	-.943	-.483	.522	0.924
RULING	-.494	.518	-.955	-.828	.567	1.459	-.703	.599	1.175
BORDER	1.895	.515	3.682***	2.189	.593	3.691***	2.161	.595	3.631***
TPAP	-1.611	.543	-2.969***	-2.332	.721	-3.232***	-2.195	.755	-2.907***
SUPER301	-.302	.426	-.708	-.215	.449	-.479	-.307	.471	-.625
COMPET				.192	.097	1.975**	.202	.106	.906*
INITIATE							.371	.518	.716
BULLY							-.284	.499	-.190
Log likelihood	-35.54			-33.35			-33.09		

Note: * indicates significance at the 90 percent level; ** indicates significance at the 95 percent level; ***indicates significance at the 99 percent level.

Statistical tests fail to establish the importance of a number of variables that are presumably important to understanding the pattern of Section 301 outcomes. U.S. concerns about possible counterretaliation (COUNTER) prove to have no effect on the effectiveness of U.S. threats in Section 301 cases in any way. The relationship between COUNTER and SUCCESS is not statistically significant in any of the models. In addition, the trade balance between the United States and the target (TBAL), a rough measure of reciprocity in trade relations, does not reach statistical significance in either of the models.[31] Counterintuitively, the bigger stick American negotiators carried under Super 301 provisions did not improve the chances for opening foreign markets. The coefficient for SUPER301, while in the expected direction, is not statistically significant.

The addition of the trade competitiveness variable in Model 2 and the two control variables in Model 3 does not affect the sign and significance of the variables in Model 1. These additional tests lend strong support to the hypothesis about the relationship between trade competitiveness and the degree of Section 301 success. In both models, the variable measuring the degree of trade competitiveness, COMPET, exhibits a positive and statistically significant relationship with SUCCESS. The two control variables, INITIATE and BULLY, do not appear to add any leverage. Public announcement of U.S. negotiation resolve, represented by the USTR initiation of Section 301 investigations, does not have the expected credibility-enhancing effect. Nor did the variable representing the intensity of U.S. investigation activities against a specific target country (BULLY) play any role in explaining Section 301 success. Although, similar to Elliott and Richardson's findings, a period of concentrated activities against a particular country results in decreased, rather than improved, credibility for American negotiators, this variable does not reach statistical significance in Model 3.

In addition to these tests, I experimented with a few alternative specifications, including testing a model that adds to Model 2 three other control variables measuring the regime type of the target (REGIME), the target's level of economic development (GDP-CAPITA), and the nature of the security relationship between the United States and the target (ALIGNMENT), respectively. In this test, the REGIME variable is added to control for the possibility that democratic pairs may be more likely to pursue free trade policies or that they resolve trade disputes more effectively.[32] I also control for the possibility that developed countries may be better able to resist demands to liberalize trade through a variable measuring the target's average per capita GDP during the years in which the dispute was active (GDPCAPITA). Finally, to account for the possibility that American demands will encounter far less resistance from its strategic partners because of the latter's reluctance to jeopardize their security relationship with the United States or because of the greater concerns about relative gains between adversaries than between allies,[33] I add a trichotomous variable (ALIGNMENT) measuring the target's security relationship with the United States based on the degree to which the target has either an antagonistic, neutral, or cordial relationship with the United States.[34] Test results show that the addition of these control variables does not alter my central finding about the significance of trade structure and that the degree of trade competitiveness is a significant determinant of the success of Section 301 actions.[35]

I further experimented with the ordered probit approach to assess the probability of success using the ordinal-scale measure of success. These tests yield very similar results to those described already. Regardless of the variables added or dropped, the degree of trade competitiveness, the nature of the trade barrier, the degree of the target's trade dependence on the United States, and the adoption of the trade policy action plan have generally retained their sign and significance.

Based on Model 2, I calculate the predicted probabilities of threat effectiveness for countries with low, average, and high levels of export dependence on the United States while holding all other variables at their means. As figure 3.3 suggests, when all other variables are held at their means, the United States would be 8.49 times more likely to obtain a successful outcome from a country with low export dependence on the United States, 4.39 times more likely to be successful with a country with average export dependence on the United States, and 1.05 times more likely to achieve a successful outcome with a country with high levels of export dependence on the United States should the trade competitiveness index increase from 1 to 10. Although the effect of trade structure on threat credibility is not particularly pronounced when the target country is highly dependent on the United States, figure 3.3 nevertheless reveals the influence that varying degrees of trade competitiveness could exert on threat effectiveness.

In conclusion, after taking into account other potentially confounding factors, trade competitiveness still has a statistically significant effect on the degree of threat effectiveness. The evidence from my statistical analysis provides overwhelming support to my argument.

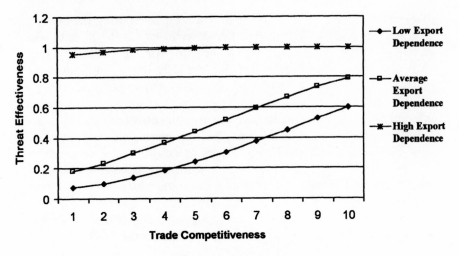

FIGURE 3.3.   Predicted probability of threat effectiveness

Understanding Patterns of Trade War

The second empirical puzzle that is of particular interest to this study is why trade wars seem to have broken out so frequently between democracies. The growing literature on democratic peace provides substantial evidence that democracies are indeed less war prone in their security relations.[36] The connection between regime type and the likelihood of trade wars, however, has been understudied. To see whether democracies are indeed more war prone in their trade relations and the extent to which the key variable emphasized by this study, the structure of trade, can help us predict the outcome of international trade conflicts, I examine the record of bilateral trade disputes between the United States and its top twenty-five trading partners between 1980 and 1995. The subsequent study will first present a brief summary of those trade disputes initiated by the United States (mostly GATT/WTO and Section 301 cases) that have escalated into tit-for-tat trade wars. It will then provide a regression analysis of the effects of trade structure, regime type, and a number of other factors on the probability of trade war by the United States. Both the summary of recent trade conflicts and the regression analysis confirm that there is no "democratic peace" when it comes to trade and that trade wars are indeed more likely among nations with competitive trade relations. The United States has more frequently been engaged in trade wars against countries with whom it has competitive trade relations, even after controlling for variables that could potentially influence the chances for trade retaliation. This result lends further support to my argument that competitive trade relations can increase the risks of aggressive escalation in trade disputes.

Trade Wars: The Cases

In chapter 1, I define "trade war" as a sustained, high-intensity trade conflict involving at least one round of mutual retaliation. If we apply these criteria to examine the record of trade conflicts involving the United States (mostly those waged under the framework of GATT/WTO and Section 301 of U.S. trade law), we will see that the frequent use of aggressive tactics in international trade disputes did not spark a large number of trade wars. Trade wars that have occurred, however, have been fought almost exclusively between the United States and its democratic trading partners (see table 3.8). Unfortunately, due to the lack of data on the composition of U.S. imports and exports from each trading partner for years prior to 1980, I had to limit the scope of this research to cases that took place after 1980. I also had to restrict my data set to pairs involving the United States because of the difficulty of compiling an exhaustive list of trade wars that covers all available country dyads. Despite these limitations, the evidence presented ought to provide a useful first cut at the relationship between trade structure and the probability of trade war.

The history of trade wars between the United States and the EC can be traced back to the Chicken War in the 1960s and the Turkey War in the 1970s, both of which occurred as a response to the EC's scheme for protecting its agricultural sector, the Common Agricultural Policy (CAP). In the 1980s, the increasingly heavy protection that CAP afforded European farmers again engendered several heated agricultural trade confrontations between the two sides of the Atlantic, including the dispute over EC agricultural export subsidies in third markets, EC tariff preferences in favor of Mediterranean citrus fruits, and EC enlargement that imposed new restrictions against third-country agricultural imports. All of these disputes resulted in the mutual imposition of trade sanctions and are discussed in greater detail in chapter 7.

In addition to agricultural trade wars, trade battles also took place in the steel industry between the United States and the EC. The Amer-

TABLE 3.8. Trade Wars Involving the United States, 1980–95

Target Country	Duration	Issue	Amount of Trade Retaliation
EC (301-6)	1982–85	*Agricultural subsidies in third markets:* In 1983 the Reagan administration announced a $250 million subsidy to farm exports (mostly to Egypt) in response to EC subsidies on agricultural products. The EC replied by announcing a subsidized wheat sale to China in 1983. In 1985 the United States announced another subsidized wheat sale to Algeria and allocated $2 billion through the Export Enhancement Program (EEP) to subsidize agricultural exports.	The subsidy war cost the United States over $2 billion in additional outlays.
China	1983	*Textiles:* In 1983 the United States failed to negotiate a new bilateral textile agreement with more stringent quota restrictions on Chinese textile exports and, as a result, imposed a new unilateral agreement with a substantial increase in the number of product categories subject to quantitative restrictions. China retaliated by suspending agricultural imports from the United States.	Chinese retaliation resulted in $600 million in loss for United States farmers.
EC	1983–84	*Specialty steel:* To prevent European producers from dumping in the United States market, the United States in 1983 imposed quotas and higher tariffs on the import of specialty steel. The EC demanded compensation and, when no agreement could be reached on the appropriate level of compensation, retaliated against United States exports of chemicals, plastics, and selected other products.	EC's total share of the United States steel market decreased from 6.31 percent to 4.64 percent as a result of the United States quota restrictions. EC retaliation against United States quotas was worth $160 million annually.
EC (301-11)	1985–86	*Tariff preferences on citrus, export subsidies for pasta:* In 1985, in retaliation for EC tariff preferences in favor of Mediterranean citrus fruits, the United States imposed penalty duties of 25 to 40 percent on EC pasta, prompting EC counterretaliation against United States lemons and walnuts. Both sides withdrew their penalty tariffs in 1986.	The United States retaliation led to a 28 percent decrease in EC pasta exports, worth about $36 million. United States exports of nuts in shells and lemons to the EC, which averaged about $33 million a year, plunged by 85 percent in the first five months of EC retaliation.

EC (301-54)	1986–91	*Accession of Spain and Portugal*: The EC placed new restrictions against third-country agricultural imports (particularly feed grains) when Spain and Portugal acceded to the EC in 1986. The United States imposed retaliatory QRs on EC agricultural exports in retaliation for the Portuguese quotas on United States soybeans and soybean oil. The United States also imposed a 200 percent ad valorem tariff on EC agricultural products in response to import levies on Spanish imports. The EC promptly retaliated against the United States sanctions with similar tariffs and QRs.	The quotas the United States imposed in May 1986 on EC imports in response to the EC's quantitative restrictions on oilseeds and grains in Portugal amounted to $500 million a year.
Canada	1986	*Timber products*: In 1986 the Reagan administration ruled that Canada was subsidizing its lumber producers and imposed tariffs on imported Canadian softwoods. Canada retaliated by imposing a 70 percent CVD on corn imported from the United States.	The 15 percent export tax Canada eventually agreed to levy on softwood lumber exports to the United States translated into $450 million in lost sales a year.
EC (301-62)	1989	*Beef hormone*: In 1989 the EC announced a ban on imports of meat treated with growth hormones. The United States retaliated against the ban by blocking $100 million EC exports to the United States. The EC counterretaliated against $100 million of United States exports.	United States retaliation and EC counterretaliation each affected $100 million of imports from the other side.
Canada	1991–92	*Softwood lumber exports*: In 1991 Canada suspended the Canada-United States softwood lumber agreement. The United States imposed a bonding requirement on Canadian lumber exports to the United States.	The ITA imposed a 11.54 percent CVD on softwood lumber imports from Canada.
Canada	1992	*Provincial restrictions on beer sales*: In response to Canadian restrictions on beer imports from the United States, the United States imposed a 50 percent duty on beer imported from Ontario in 1992. Canada retaliated by imposing a 50 percent duty on United States beer exported to Ontario.	The United States retaliation affected $80 million in Canadian imports.
Canada	1993	*Steel*: In 1993 the United States imposed duties on a variety of Canadian steel products. Canada fired back by placing provisional duties on some steel exports from the United States.	United States duties on Canadian steel products were as high as 68.7 percent, whereas Canadian duties on United States steel exports ranged between 4.5 and 124.2 percent.

Source: Hudec, *Enforcing International Trade Law*; Section 301 case summaries, in Bayard and Elliott, *Reciprocity and Retaliation*; and various newspaper articles.

ican steel industry, which had been in serious decline, started to focus on the competitive threats that Japan and the EC posed in the domestic U.S. market in the late 1970s. In December 1981, American steel producers filed dumping charges against specialty steel imports from France, West Germany, Italy, Britain, Brazil, Austria, Sweden, and Spain. In June 1983 the United States announced that it would place quotas and higher tariffs on the import of specialty steel. The EEC initially refused to bargain for the market share quota and later filed a claim with GATT for compensation. When negotiations between the two sides broke down, the EEC retaliated in 1984 and imposed quotas and tariffs against U.S. exports of chemicals, plastics, and sporting goods.

A more recent trade war took place between the United States and Canada over Canadian provincial restrictions on U.S. beer exports. In 1990, U.S. beer manufacturers filed a Section 301 petition alleging that Canadian provincial restrictions on distribution of beer discriminated against imports and violated both the GATT and the Canada–United States Free Trade Agreement (FTA). The two sides managed to reach an agreement in April 1992. At the end of April, however, Ontario decided to double its tax on nonrefillable cans of beer, wine, and spirits. In June, it announced additional new rules for beer imports that directly affected the United States. In July 1992 the United States imposed a 50 percent duty on beer imported from Ontario. Canada retaliated by imposing a 50 percent duty on U.S. beer exported to Ontario.

It is fairly obvious that all of the trade wars described here have been fought between democratic countries. Trade wars did occur between dyads that consist of a democracy and an autocracy, but this happened far more sporadically. For example, as explained earlier, the United States and China did engage in a trade war over textiles in the early 1980s. In 1983, unable to curb the flow of Chinese textile exports to the United States, Washington unilaterally imposed quantitative restrictions on Chinese textile imports. China retaliated by suspending their imports from the United States of chemical fibers, cotton, soybeans, and wheat, products for which China was an important international market.[37]

However, other than this case, trade conflicts between democracies and authoritarian regimes have rarely escalated into full-blown trade wars. Trade relations between the United States and China since the early 1980s, for instance, have been characterized by the complete absence of trade wars. In almost all contentious issue areas, the United

States had threatened to impose economic sanctions on China, only to refrain from doing so in the end. The overall pattern of trade peace was clearly reflected in the two Section 301 cases involving IPR and market access, where the United States always managed to reach an eleventh-hour agreement with the Chinese despite its various sanction threats.

In the area of market access, the United States initiated a Section 301 investigation into China's general practices restricting the entry of U.S. goods into the Chinese markets. The alleged unfair practices, which were not sector specific, included quantitative restrictions (QRs), import licensing requirements, technical barriers to trade, and lack of transparency of laws and regulations pertaining to restrictions on imports. The Chinese argued that some of these measures were necessary as infant industry protection and, therefore, were unwilling to set specific timetables for phasing out their QRs and other trade restrictions. In August 1992 the USTR threatened to impose retaliatory tariffs worth $3.9 billion of Chinese exports, including goods that topped the Chinese export list (such as footwear, silk apparel, leather goods, minerals, industrial hardware, and electronics products). China responded with its own list of U.S. exports worth $4 billion (including aircraft, computers, chemicals, wood products, and cotton) that could suffer retaliation should Washington carry through with its threatened sanctions.

But right before the deadline, the two sides reached an agreement in which China pledged to publish all "laws, regulations, policies and guidance" regarding trade; to eliminate most quantitative restrictions within two years and on products such as telecommunications equipment by the end of 1992; to reduce some tariffs; and to resolve problems involving phytosanitary and other technical standards.[38] A trade war was thus averted at the last minute.

Even textile trade, an area where the two sides failed to conclude a negotiated settlement in the early 1980s, has become more cooperative in outcome. In the 1990s, in response to industry complaints of Chinese textile and apparel quota noncompliance in the forms of counterfeit export visas and country-of-origin evasions, the U.S. government on several occasions threatened to substantially reduce Chinese quotas. But although China protested and threatened to impose retaliatory tariffs on various U.S. products, the two countries eventually signed new bilateral textile agreements and managed to head off potential wars at the threatened deadline.

This survey of the record of bilateral trade wars involving the United States suggests that the democratic peace argument may not provide accurate predictions of the pattern of trade war: only very rarely have trade disputes between the United States and authoritarian regimes resulted in trade wars. Trade disputes between the United States and its democratic trading partners, in contrast, have shown a greater propensity to escalate into trade wars. Since the signaling strand of the democratic peace literature predicts that democracies' greater capacity to signal their true preferences in a crisis situation should help to prevent disputes between democracies from escalating into war, the lack of democratic peace in trade, as far as cases involving the United States are concerned, thus presents a major challenge to the theory.

The review also points to the structure of trade as a possible alternative explanation for the pattern of trade war. As we can see, most of the countries that have been involved in tit-for-tat trade retaliation against the United States also are the ones that have highly competitive trade relations with the United States. For instance, Canada and the EC, two trading partners that are the frequent targets of U.S. retaliatory action, have trade competitiveness scores of as high as 11 with the United States. In contrast, very few of the trade war cases listed earlier involve a partner country with a complementary trade relationship with the United States. Indeed, only one trade war was directed against such a partner country (i.e., China, with a trade competitiveness score of only 2). My preliminary review of the trade war cases thus suggests that trade structure may potentially play an important role in explaining the pattern of trade war.

Statistical Analysis of the Determinants of Trade War

While the United States seems to have fought a greater number of trade wars with its competitive trading partners, it is plausible that factors other than the structure of trade could have contributed to the higher probability of trade war between these countries. For example, one might expect the probability of trade war to be higher if the two parties trade more with each other or if the target country enjoys a larger trade surplus with the United States. Thus, in this section, I report the results of my statistical analyses of the relationship between trade structure and the probability of trade war. These results suggest that, even after controlling for other potentially confounding variables, the level of trade competitiveness still shows up as a significant factor in explaining patterns of trade retaliation.

To test the relationship between trade structure and the probability of trade war, I estimate a model that takes into consideration the following explanatory variables: the degree of trade competitiveness, the regime type of the U.S. trading partner, the volume of trade, the size of the bilateral trade balance, the size of the target economy, the target country's dependence on the American export market, and the political relations between the two parties to the disputes.

This model is evaluated on the basis of dyad years. Given the limited availability of data on the composition of bilateral trade for the years prior to 1980, as well as the difficulties of capturing all bilateral trade wars in which the United States is not a party, the analysis focuses on trade disputes between the United States and its top twenty-five trading partners between 1980 and 1995.[39] The resulting data set encompasses sixteen years for a total of four hundred dyad observations.

My dependent variable is simply the probability of trade war, which refers to the odds that a trade war breaks out in a given dyad year. It is coded as 1 if a trade war occurs and 0 otherwise. Trade wars that last several years are coded as 1 in each year they were in place. Explanatory variables for this analysis include the following:

COMPET. The degree of trade competitiveness (COMPET) is the key explanatory variable in this test. It is expected that highly competitive trade relationships are likely to result in higher incidences of trade wars, as discussed in the previous chapter.

REGIME. To see if states' regime type is related to the probability of trade war in any way, I include the trading partner's regime type into this analysis. If the democratic peace theory, particularly the audience cost version of that theory, is valid, then we should expect a statistically negative relationship between democracies and the likelihood of trade war.

The definition of "democracy" I adopt here is consistent with the commonly used definition of democracy seen in the democratic peace literature, which emphasizes the competitiveness and openness of the process through which a country's government is brought to power, the degree to which a country's chief executive's decision-making authority is bounded by institutionalized rules and arrangements, and the degree of political participation within a country. In addition, this definition provides that a state should have established these democratic institutions and processes for a reasonable amount of time so that both its citizens and its adversaries regard it as one governed by democratic principles.[40] According to this criteria, the EU and Canada, two trading partners that have frequently fought trade wars with the United States, are clearly democracies, while

China, which has been involved in only one trade war with the United States, is not.

The widely used Polity III data developed by Jaggers and Gurr are used to measure the regime type of each of the major U.S. trading partners (REGIME).[41] The Polity III data (and earlier versions of them) broadly follow the definition of democracy just described and have been used by various studies of the relationship between regime type and international security conflict.[42] Jaggers and Gurr develop a measure of a state's democratic characteristics (DEMOC) on a 1–11 scale and another measure of its autocratic characteristics (AUTOC) on a 1–11 scale. The measure of a state's regime type is derived by subtracting its autocratic index from its democratic index, that is, REGIME = DEMOC – AUTOC. This summary measure is a continuous variable with values ranging from 10 for a highly autocratic state to +10 for a highly democratic one.[43]

VOLUME. I include the volume of trade between the United States and its trading partner (VOLUME) to account for the possibility that, since countries that trade more with one another tend to have more trade disputes, the chances for such trade disputes to escalate into trade war will be higher. Volume of trade statistics is derived primarily from U.S. Foreign Trade Highlights.[44]

TBAL. In addition, trade balance between the United States and the target country (TBAL) is taken into account because it is expected that the size of the trade deficit could either increase or decrease the likelihood of trade wars. A more negative trade balance could make trade wars more likely because one would assume that there would be stronger domestic pressure for trade sanctions against countries enjoying large trade surpluses with the United States. But it is also plausible that having a larger trade deficit with the target country could reduce the chances of trade wars because the United States would have a greater demand for goods produced in the target country. The costs of having to restrict trade with the target would consequently be higher.

GDPRATIO. To control for the possible influence of country size on the probability of trade war, I take into consideration the partner country's GDP as a percentage of U.S. GDP in each of the dyad years. It is expected that the United States ought to be involved in fewer trade wars with its relatively small trading partners, who are less likely to be able to resist U.S. pressure.

TRDEP. I include a measure of a country's dependence on trade with the United States (TRDEP), measured by the percentage of the total volume of trade between the target and the United States in the target's GDP, to account for the vulnerability (besides their small size) of certain countries to U.S. retaliation. A negative relationship is expected between each of the previous two variables and TRWAR.

ALIGNMENT. Previous studies have shown that allies tend to trade more with one another.[45] To control for the possibility that countries with cordial political relationships ought to be less likely to fight trade wars when their trade volumes are taken into account, I include a variable (ALIGNMENT) representing the nature of the political relationship between the United States and the target country into the analysis. Alignment is measured using the same procedure described in the previous section. A negative relationship is expected between ALIGNMENT and the probability of trade war.

YEAR. To check to see if there is any secular trend in the probability of having a trade war, I include a time-related variable (YEAR), set consecutively for each dyad, into the analysis.[46]

The parameters in the equation are estimated using the logit model. The logit model has widely been used to estimate the effects of a set of regressors on a binary dependent variable (such as the probability of war or deterrence). Regression analysis using the logit model yields the results shown in table 3.9.

As expected, the relationship between the volume of trade and the probability of trade war is positive and is statistically significant at the $p < 0.1$ level. This suggests that trade wars did break out more frequently between countries that trade more with one another. The variable representing the disparities between the size of the target economy and that of the U.S. market (GDPRATIO) also performed well in this case. Larger economies seem to be more likely to take on a trade war due to their greater ability to withstand the effects of trade restrictions. The variable representing the degree of the target's dependence on the

TABLE 3.9. Logit Estimates for the Probability of Trade War (full model)

TRWAR	Coefficient	Standard Error	Z	$p > z$
VOLUME	.0000308	.0000166	1.85	.064
REGIME	−.038	.111	−.35	.729
TBAL	−.0000207	.0000306	−.68	.500
COMPET	.633	.295	2.15	.032
GDPRATIO	7.906	4.602	1.72	.086
TRDEP	6.582	8.971	.73	.463
ALIGNMENT	−2.161	1.551	−1.39	.164
YEAR	−.584	.252	−2.32	.020
CONSTANT	−1.525	3.231	−.47	.637

log likelihood = −29.004; chi-square = 69.92

American export market performed less well and did not reach statistical significance. The size of the U.S. trade surplus (BALANCE) and the nature of the political relationship between the two parties (ALIGNMENT), although in the expected direction, did not reach statistical significance in the model.

Consistent with theoretical expectations, after controlling for the confounding influence of other explanatory variables, trade competitiveness has a robust and independent effect on the probability of trade war. The relationship between trade competitiveness and the probability of trade war is positive and is statistically significant at the $p < .05$ level. Although the trade competitiveness variable did not achieve statistical significance at the $p < .01$ level, this may have to do with specific attributes of the statistical analysis (such as the magnitude of the raw data) and in no way indicates that trade competitiveness is less significant than trade volume or the size of the trade deficit in predicting the trade war outcome.

Also of great interest is the finding that the regime measure has failed to achieve statistical significance. When the influence of other relevant variables is taken into consideration, regime type clearly plays no major role in predicting the trade war outcome.

Since the regime measure is clearly insignificant, I re-ran the model without it (see table 3.10). The likelihood ratio test yields a p value that is greater than 0.05, indicating that removal of the regime variable had no significant effect on the model. In addition, the log likelihood of the constrained model (−29.06) was nearly identical to that of the full model (−29.004). These results suggest that the constrained model is superior than the full model in predicting the trade war outcome, as the reduction in the number of independent variables makes the specification somewhat more parsimonious. Note that in the con-

TABLE 3.10.   Logit Estimates for the Probability of Trade War (constrained model)

TRWAR	Coefficient	Standard Error	Z	$p > z$
VOLUME	.00003	.000016	1.81	.070
TBAL	−.000018	.000029	−.61	.540
COMPET	.603	.279	2.16	.031
GDPRATIO	7.841	4.611	1.70	.089
TRDEP	6.691	8.979	.75	.456
ALIGNMENT	−2.239	1.622	−1.38	.168
YEAR	−.558	.235	−2.37	.018
CONSTANT	−1.408	3.427	−.41	.681

log likelihood = −29.06; chi-square = 69.81

strained model trade competitiveness remains statistically significant at the $p < .05$ level.

To illustrate the impact of trade competitiveness on the probability of trade war, I report the changes in the probability of trade war with the United States for several of America's leading trading partners for a model consisting of four variables (i.e., VOLUME, GDPRATIO, COMPET, and YEAR), holding all other variables constant and varying only the trade competitiveness variable. In figure 3.4, I show how each of America's five leading trading partners—given their trade volume, GDP ratio, and year (the mean for each over the sample period used)—would be affected were their competitiveness index to change. The chart suggests that varying the trade competitiveness index will result in substantial changes in the probability of trade war. For example, the EC, whose average trade competitiveness index was approximately 9 on a 10-point scale between 1980 and 1995, would be 75 percent less likely to be involved in a trade war with the United States (the probability drops from 0.72 to 0.18) were its competitiveness ratio to fall to 2. Similarly, Canada would be almost 90 percent less likely to fight a trade war with the United States (the probability falls from 0.2 to 0.012) if its trade competitiveness index dropped from an average of 8 over the sample period to 2. Conversely, the probability that China will have a trade war with the United States will be thirty-two times higher (the probability increases from 0.0006 to 0.02) if its competitiveness index rises from 2 to that of the EC's level (9 on a 10-point scale). In reality, most countries' competitiveness index had remained more or less constant over the years; nevertheless, figure 3.4 reveals the effect that increasing competitiveness ratios would have had on the probability of trade war when the other two variables are held at a given level.

Conclusion

The empirical analysis in this chapter confirms the two puzzling patterns that motivate this study. U.S. sanction threats proved to be more effective in opening markets in some countries (e.g., Japan, Canada, and the EC) than in others (e.g., China, Brazil, and India). Interestingly, the bilateral trade structure does play an important role in explaining these variations. It has also been shown that the likelihood of trade war was not necessarily higher between dyads that include at least one party that is nondemocratic than between democracies. If

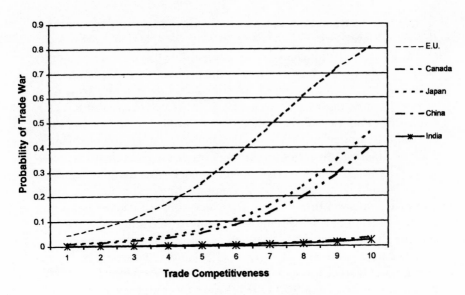

FIGURE 3.4. Predicted probabilities of trade war

these puzzling patterns do exist in the real world, and if neither realism nor the democratic peace thesis can adequately explain these patterns, then how can we best go about tackling these puzzles? To what extent does the structure of trade affect the pattern of trade war and threat effectiveness? Does domestic politics exert such an important influence on negotiation outcomes? Through detailed case studies of trade negotiations between the United States and some of its major trading partners, the following chapters will piece together the answers to these questions and will show how trade structure, by shaping the domestic political landscape, drives the negotiation dynamics and helps to produce the puzzling patterns observed in this study.

American Threats and U.S.–China Negotiations over Most-Favored-Nation Status and Market Access

This chapter assesses the influence of complementary trade structure on negotiation outcomes by examining trade disputes between the United States and China over MFN status and market access issues. While the primary focus of this chapter is on U.S.–China negotiations, I also supplement the China cases with a brief discussion of U.S.–Brazil negotiations over informatics in the mid-1980s to show that the pattern of interest group coalition generated by complementary trade structure is not restricted to a country such as China, which not only has a large internal market but is also undergoing a transition from a closed economy to a market system, which tends to produce greater uncertainty dampening American businesses' opposition to the sanctions strategy. All of these cases lend support to my argument that complementary trade can give rise to a powerful import lobby opposed to trade sanctions, thus reducing the credibility and effectiveness of American pressure.

Since the late 1980s, the question of whether to renew China's MFN status has occupied center stage in U.S.–China economic relations. Given the tremendous pressure exerted by Congress and various domestic constituents to get China to adjust both its economic and human rights policies seen as detrimental to American interests, and in view of the power asymmetries between the two countries, one would expect that the United States should have had considerable success securing Chinese compromises. But has it? Has Beijing made substantial modifications in its trade practices in response to American pressure?

If we examine the period when the United States threatened to revoke China's MFN status to obtain *unilateral* concessions in such issue areas as human rights, trade, and weapons proliferation, the compromises won by the United States over many years, measured against the original American demands, have been paltry. In each of these issue areas mentioned, the United States has by and large failed to obtain the desired concessions. While the Chinese were perhaps most unyielding on the human rights issue, their responses to the other *economic* demands that Washington made under threats of MFN revocation (including providing better protection for IPR and removing trade barriers) were equally disappointing. Although, with the conclusion of the U.S.–China bilateral agreement on terms for China's accession to the WTO in November 1999 the United States does seem to have won a significant market opening in exchange for Chinese firms' greater access to the American market,[1] it seems fair to say that America's unilateral sanction threats against China have yielded only suboptimal results. As one China scholar summarizes the MFN debate:

> The process has produced virtually no discernible change in Beijing's policies and has weakened the elite and popular base of those in China most inclined toward genuine reform; it has locked successive administrations and Congress in unproductive debate annually for eight years; it has encouraged presidents to make commitments they cannot keep; and all this has made U.S. administrations look impotent to Beijing and dangerously unpredictable to allies and friends in the region and throughout the world. In short, the MFN debate has been the poorest imaginable way to make coherent policy or to be credible to Beijing.[2]

America's attempt to tackle pervasive market access barriers in the Chinese market in the early 1990s through threats of retaliation under Section 301 of U.S. trade law has similarly encountered a fair amount of Chinese resistance. In 1991, to exert more focused pressure on the Chinese on market access issues, the United States initiated a Section 301 negotiation, separate from the MFN process, and threatened sanctions against Chinese exports unless Beijing agreed to relax various quantitative restrictions, dismantle technical barriers to trade, and improve the transparency of its trade regulation. Although Beijing agreed to make its trade regulations more transparent and to cut tariffs on a wide range of U.S. goods in a bilateral market access accord in 1992, the agreement signified the beginning, rather than the completion, of the process of moving China's foreign trade regime closer to international norms and practices. Later China threatened to halt the implementation of the 1992 agreement for alleged U.S. failure to keep its commitments, instead charging the Americans with impeding the development of bilateral trade relations by keeping in place the post-1989 sanctions and by failing to keep its commitment to support China's bid for WTO membership.[3] In the end, Washington had to once again threaten sanctions to get Beijing to honor its promises and was unable to achieve concrete results in the market access talks. Partly because of the continued existence of trade barriers, American trade deficits with China continued to soar in the 1990s.

In view of the inability of American trade pressure to effect change in China, it is intriguing to ask why the United States, as the world's largest economy and as the country that provides most of China's hard currency, has encountered so much resistance from Beijing? The following empirical study finds answers to this question in the realm of domestic politics: trade complementarity between the two nations structured political forces in the United States in a way that prevented the emergence of a unified and coherent *American* position credible to Beijing. Whenever human rights advocates, groups concerned about China's protectionist trade policies, or the intellectual property industry tried to strike out against China, they met uniform resistance from other business groups that favored continued normal relations with China. The existence of a large import-using constituency consisting of American importers and retailers of such Chinese products as footwear, toys, and apparel provided a powerful counterbalance to forces supporting MFN revocation. Moreover, the executive branch, due to its institutional prerogatives and priorities, tended to emphasize the importance of a viable commercial relationship with China and thus opposed the tough approach advocated by Congress. These divisions in American politics sent highly mixed and confusing messages to the Chinese, sharply reducing the credibility of American threats.

The U.S.–Brazil informatics dispute similarly demonstrates how complementary trade structure between the two nations created a strong import lobby that eroded U.S. credibility. In this case, resistance by importers of such Brazilian products as footwear, orange juice concentrates, and auto parts aggravated the divisions that exporters with different market positions held with respect to the Brazilian market, contributing to the difficulties of getting Brasília to modify its restrictive informatics program. In the case studies that follow, I will employ the process-tracing method to illuminate these competing interests and pressures in American politics. By weighing my argument against other competing explanations, I will try to show that there exists a causal relationship, not simply a statistical correlation, between trade structure and threat credibility.

American Threats and China's MFN Status

Tiananmen and the Initiation of the MFN Debate

Up until the advent of the Tiananmen incident in 1989, China had been able to secure the annual renewal of its MFN status on the basis of a presidential waiver of the freedom of emigration requirements and of subsequent congressional consent, as required of all communist countries, under the Jackson-Vanik amendment of the Trade Act of 1974.[4] It was only in 1989, when the Tiananmen incident shattered a decade of consensus on China policy in the United States, allowing a wider array of domestic interests access to the decision-making process, that the U.S. Congress turned to the annual renewal of China's MFN status as the key to influencing the general direction of U.S.–China policy.[5] Each year between 1990 and 1994, the U.S. Congress attempted dozens of pieces of legislation that would have made the continuation of China's MFN status contingent upon presidential certification in the areas of human rights, trade, and arms proliferation.[6]

However, none of these threats has been materialized. Nor did China's performance in the targeted areas of trade, human rights, and weapons proliferation live up to American expectations. Although President George H. W. Bush repeatedly vetoed legislation seeking to revoke or to attach conditions to China's MFN renewal, by the end of his administration Chinese performance in the targeted issue areas remained far from satisfactory.[7] Even the coming to power of Bill Clinton, who had accused President Bush of "coddling the dictators" in Beijing during his presidential campaign, did nothing to reverse this situation. Clinton soon backed off from his campaign promises and, on May 28, 1993, signed an executive order linking trade preferences granted by the United States to China's human rights behavior. While the executive order was intended to be sufficiently tough on Beijing without breaking the back of U.S.–China relations, it again proved ineffectual. In the face of continued Chinese resistance, Clinton had to acknowledge the futility of attempts to force changes in China through the leverage provided by MFN status, signing an executive order in 1994 "delinking" China's

MFN status with its domestic practices. In the executive order, Clinton acknowledged that

> The Chinese did not achieve overall significant progress in all the areas outlined in the executive order relating to human rights, even though clearly there was some progress made in important areas. . . . I believe . . . that we have reached the end of the usefulness of that policy, and it is time to take a new path toward the achievement of our constant objectives. We need to place our relationship into a larger and more productive framework.[8]

That the MFN sanction threats against China were so ineffective was not surprising if we take into consideration the divisions in American politics on the MFN issue. First, since the United States was no longer a major producer of such goods as apparel, toys, shoes, and consumer electronics, there was a large constituency in America heavily dependent on imports of these materials. These import-using interests strongly opposed MFN conditionality or withdrawal, arguing that such a measure would impose significant costs on American consumers and retailers. Second, there existed considerable differences between the policy preferences of the executive and legislative branches. President Bush, for example, had consistently opposed efforts to attach any conditions to China's MFN renewal. His repeated assertion that he would veto any legislation denying or placing further conditions on China's MFN eligibility made any potential legislative action on conditionality appear more symbolic than substantive. Moreover, even though President Clinton had initially taken a tough stance on MFN, he was soon forced by the reality of U.S.–China relations to reverse course and to pursue a more realistic policy with China. That China did not pose a competitive challenge to American industries prompted the executive branch to accord higher priority to America's overall economic and strategic relationship with the Chinese.

The net effect of these competing forces in American politics—the trade lobby's campaign for normal trade relations and the different policy orientations of the executive and legislative branches—was to substantially reduce the effectiveness of U.S. threats against China. They contributed to Beijing's perception that it was highly unlikely that the United States would carry out its threats and that therefore China did not need to kowtow to American pressure. In the end, Washington was forced to acknowledge that China had made only minimal concessions.

The China Trade Lobby

An important factor weakening the credibility of American threats was the business community's active support for continued MFN tariff treatment for China. As the debate over MFN status unfolded, affected interest groups rushed to Capitol Hill to make their cases. While human rights advocates, trade unions, and groups concerned with China's unfair trade practices lashed out at China, a large pro-MFN coalition had been formed to push for unconditional renewal of China's trade status. The pro-MFN forces, composed of toy makers, apparel manufacturers, farmers, and aircraft manufacturers, as well as businesses in Hong Kong, launched a massive campaign defending U.S. trade with China, swamping Capitol Hill with letters and position papers detailing the damage that denial of MFN status or its equivalent—conditional MFN—might inflict on the U.S. economy.

What was most distinctive about this pro-MFN coalition was that it united both American exporters and importers behind a major trade expansion. Because the United States exported to China very different commodities from what it imported from that country (see figure 4.1, which depicts the lack of overlap between the top five commodities the United States exports to and imports from China),[9] American importers of toys, apparel, footwear, electronics, and other consumer goods coalesced into a major political force actively opposing the imposition of sanctions that could adversely affect their sales in the United States. At the same time, American investors and some exporters with no direct stakes in using MFN to open the Chinese market opposed the MFN linkage, a linkage that, they worried, could hurt both their exports to and their investment in China by creating more uncertainty in the business environment. As a result, importers and many businesses with an interest in the China market mobilized early in defense of China's trade status.

In 1991, large companies and leading trade groups—including the Emergency Committee for American Trade (ECAT); the U.S. Chamber of Commerce; the five-hundred-member National Foreign Trade Council; and the U.S.–China Business Council, a Washington-based group representing the interests of companies doing business with China—formed an umbrella organization, the Business Coalition for U.S.–China Trade, in support of President Bush's position for unconditional extension of MFN status. By 1996, the coalition had expanded to include over eight hundred member companies and trade associations heavily involved in trade with China. The composition of the

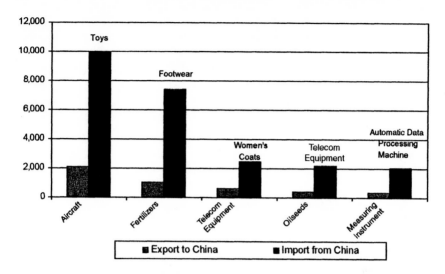

FIGURE 4.1.   Top five commodities in U.S. trade with China (SITC-3), 1997–2001 (in millions of dollars). Data from U.S. Department of Commerce, International Trade Administration, *U.S. Foreign Trade Highlights.*

association ranged from firms importing labor-intensive manufactured goods made in China to exporters of high-tech, agricultural, aviation, telecommunications, and transportation goods.[10] Also outspoken on the MFN issue were business groups representing both American exporters and importers doing business with China, such as the American Association of Exporters and Importers, the National Association of Wheat Growers, the North American Export Grain Association, and the Toy Manufacturers of America.[11]

In dollar terms, U.S. companies importing from China had a higher stake in the battle over MFN status than did firms exporting to China. For the three years before 1991, American exports to China held at roughly $5 billion a year, while Chinese exports to the United States increased rapidly during the same period, reaching a record high of $15 billion in 1990.[12] For American importers, MFN status could be a crucial competitive advantage. If MFN status were revoked, U.S. tariffs on Chinese-made toys, footwear, apparel, and other goods would soar to prohibitive levels. For example, in the absence of MFN status, the tariff on imported toys would soar from 6.8 percent to 70 percent.[13] Terminating MFN status would therefore require a vast number of U.S. importers and retailers to find new sources for goods upon which

many low-income consumers had come to rely. For many smaller manufacturers that simply could not find sources elsewhere, the effects of
MFN revocation would simply be devastating. Even large manufacturers and retailers that could shift some of their manufacturing to
other countries would have to bear added costs of production as new
factories would have to be reconfigured for new lines and increased
output.

Toy makers and apparel manufacturers argued along these lines.
For example, at an economic conference held in Little Rock in December 1992, soon before Clinton's swearing-in, Jill Barad, the president
and chief executive officer of the American toy company Mattel,
explicitly warned Clinton of the repercussions of MFN withdrawal on
American toy makers. She argued that the sanctions would cost companies such as Mattel significant market shares as they would raise tariffs on toys imported from China to a prohibitive 70 percent level. It
was further asserted that the damage of MFN withdrawal would not
be limited to toy manufacturers but would also extend to American
shoe companies, which acquired 60 percent of their products from
China, and textile importers, which imported nearly $4 billion of tex-
tile and apparel from China each year.[14] In addition, retailers such as
Toys "R" Us and J.C. Penney contended that trade restrictions would
hurt American consumers by driving up the cost of Chinese goods and
that low-income consumers in particular would bear a disproportion-
ate burden in such an event.[15]

Footwear distributors echoed these concerns, pointing out that
China was the biggest supplier of imported footwear to the United
States, accounting for 38 percent of all shoes sold in the United States
in 1990 and 63 percent of all low-priced shoe imports.[16] China's share
of the American footwear market increased further in the early 1990s
so that by 1994 China accounted for one of every two pairs of shoes
sold in the United States.[17] Footwear Distributors and Retailers of
America argued that, since it was difficult to find competitive alternatives for footwear outside of China, American consumers, particularly
low- and middle-income families who depended on China-produced
shoes, would be the real losers should China lose its MFN status.[18]
Athletic footwear companies such as Nike shared this view, as the
company sourced about one-third of its shoes in China.

While importers emphasized the costs of MFN denial to American
consumers, exporters, especially those that faced no market impediments in China, focused on the consequences of a closed Chinese market to the United States. While some exporters such as the IPR indus-

try made a successful case for applying the leverage of MFN to secure Chinese agreement to provide more adequate protection for American IPR, many other exporters with no direct stakes involved instead focused on the consequences of a closed Chinese market to American interests. They emphasized that, since China had become one of the fastest growing American markets, rescinding MFN status and the subsequent Chinese retaliation would result not only in lost sales over the short term but also in lost markets to European and Japanese competitors, forcing a cut in U.S. production and employment.[19] Importantly, if the United States made good on its promises to impose sanctions, likely Chinese retaliation would only limit American firms' access to the Chinese market.

U.S. aircraft manufacturers, which held 76 percent of the huge Chinese market, would face severe losses if China's trade status were revoked. Since the late 1980s, companies such as Boeing and McDonnell Douglas had been courting Chinese authorities, bidding to supply China's domestic route airplanes well into the next century. By 1993, China was already Boeing's biggest overseas market next to Japan, with one of every six aircrafts produced by Boeing going to China.[20] Both companies were worried that withdrawal of MFN status and subsequent Chinese retaliation would undercut their competitive advantage, forcing them to cede market shares and suffer an estimated loss of $41 billion in deliveries to European aerospace companies at a time when transatlantic competition in the aerospace industry was heating up. In light of these potential costs, the aerospace industry began early to urge Congress to renew China's MFN status, arguing that denying MFN status to China would not only close off the opportunity to cut lucrative deals with the Chinese but also cost jobs at home.

Telecommunications and consumer electronics companies such as AT&T, General Electric (GE), IBM, General Motors (GM), and Motorola all made China their top international goal. Companies such as GE were on the outlook for increased sales in a wide range of products, including aircraft engines, power-generation equipment, locomotives, medical equipment, plastics, and electric lighting.[21] GM's joint venture in northern China expected to be assembling fifty thousand trucks by 1998. For Motorola, China already was its biggest market outside the United States by 1993 and was expected to deliver a 20 to 30 percent annual growth rate in phone sales for the next decade.[22]

Similarly, AT&T, which had been locked out of the Chinese market for years, was able to conclude a landmark deal in 1993 to help upgrade China's overburdened telecommunications system. The deal represented an important breakthrough in the company's plan to tap into a Chinese market projected to expand tenfold by the year 2000. Furthermore, the increase in Chinese purchasing power following the implementation of reform led to drastically expanded opportunities for U.S. consumer-product companies, substantially raising their expectations about the China market.[23]

In short, U.S.–China trade relations had expanded so rapidly that by the early 1990s a broad spectrum of American business had developed a huge stake in the China trade. This pro-MFN coalition maintained that ending MFN status would inaugurate a trade war with China that would increase the price of Chinese imports to American consumers, reduce American exports, yield market shares to foreign competitors, and threaten the viability of American investment in China. As outlined in a position paper prepared by the U.S.–China Business Council, revoking or conditioning MFN status would likely increase consumer prices and the U.S. trade deficit, lead to the loss of a major export market and over one hundred thousand American jobs, dampen the nearly $5 billion investment in China, and seriously harm Hong Kong and the semi-private sector in South China.[24] In light of the cost of revoking China's MFN status, business groups strongly urged the government to adopt alternative measures to influence Chinese behavior and focused in particular on influencing votes in the Senate to help sustain Bush's veto on conditioning MFN status.[25]

While business groups were relatively restrained in their campaign for unconditional MFN status under Bush by strongly negative media coverage of developments in China and by unfavorable popular opinion in the United States, they became increasingly assertive and vocal in pressing their demands during the Clinton administration. In 1992, following Deng Xiaoping's visit to southern China, Beijing abandoned the austerity measures adopted in the aftermath of Tiananmen in favor of a more open, liberal economic policy. This reorientation of economic policy brought the Chinese economy out of the recession toward a period of more sustained economic growth. China's phenomenal annual growth rates of 12 to 13 percent between 1993 and 1994 produced a spurt in U.S. business activity in China. This development reinforced U.S. business's perception of the importance of the Chinese market,[26] causing business lobby to intensify during the Clinton administration.

Business strategy between 1993 and 1994 focused on exposing the electoral consequences of the MFN issue to elected officials. In 1993, with the election for the entire House of Representatives (and one-third of the Senate) approaching, more than four hundred California companies in the Business Coalition for U.S.–China Trade wrote to President Clinton reminding him that MFN revocation would put at risk California's $1.7 billion in exports to China and the thirty-five thousand jobs generated by the China trade.[27] In April 1994, nearly eight hundred representatives of large and small businesses, trade associations, and consumer groups wrote to Clinton reminding him that a failure to renew MFN status to China would "jeopardize over 180,000 high-wage jobs."[28]

The National Association of Manufacturers (NAM), an organization representing 1,250 American manufacturers that account for roughly 90 percent of U.S. industrial output, maintained that Clinton's decision would have a "profound impact" on U.S. firms, workers, and industrial competitiveness. The organization released a statement calling MFN "the minimum requirement of meaningful economic exchanges between the two countries." Since MFN was the "*sine qua non* of the U.S.–China commercial relationship," NAM argued, "it cannot be the basis for the exercise of U.S. leverage within that relationship."[29] NAM's active opposition to sanction threats against China contrasted sharply with its attitude toward U.S. trade disputes with Japan. As we will see in the next chapter, when the United States threatened trade sanctions against the Japanese for their protectionist practices concerning supercomputers and satellites under Super 301 provision of the U.S. trade law, NAM turned out to be one of the foremost advocates of threats to impose sanctions against the Japanese. Since many of its member companies representing a broad range of industrial sectors were confronted with stiff Japanese competition, NAM supported the threatened sanctions, which, if carried out, would help to bring down the level of competition that NAM members faced in both the Japanese and U.S. domestic markets.

Similarly, U.S.–China Business Council president Donald Anderson, whose association represents about 200 American businesses in China, testified before a panel of the House Foreign Affairs Committee that withdrawing or conditioning MFN status "would be a recipe for disaster for U.S. workers, consumers and employers."[30] In May 1993, the business community sent Clinton a letter signed by 298 companies and 37 trade associations opposing any conditioning or compromising of MFN status. Prominent were firms such as Boeing, GM, AT&T, Coca-Cola, Caterpillar, and IBM, which feared loss of current and future export markets. Also active were wheat growers and footwear retailers. The latter, which "flooded the White House with letters from thousands of shoe store managers," argued that they simply did not "have any leverage" with China, since few companies had the luxury of pulling out of China or of having trade with China cut off.[31]

Business interests were careful to supplement their lobbying campaign with efforts to influence public opinion. For example, when Chinese president Jiang Zeming attended the Asia-Pacific Economic Cooperation (APEC) leaders' meeting in Seattle in November 1993, his visits to the Boeing aircraft production facility and to a working family's home received extra media coverage. Following Jiang's visit, Representative Jim McDermott, whose district is home to thousands of Boeing employees, submitted a letter to President Clinton signed by 106 congressional colleagues in May 1994.[32]

At this time, forces that favored revoking or placing conditions on China's MFN status were mainly to be found in a small number of U.S. industries hurt by the China trade (e.g., the textile and IPR industries), human rights and religious groups, conservative-leaning organizations, and some Chinese dissidents. While these groups held considerable sway in the early stages of the debate, their influence soon vanished because of the lack of financial strength and organizational cohesion. Importantly, even though these groups shared a common concern with China's offensive domestic policies, they often had different policy preferences due to their different ideologies and worldviews, which severely undermined the coalition's effectiveness and strength.[33]

On the whole, the China trade lobby achieved a considerable amount of success in pushing for its policy agenda. The coalition had been trying to reiterate to the White House the importance of maintaining a strong U.S. commercial relationship with China, to convince members of Congress to support an executive branch–led China policy that would not pivot on the MFN issue, and to urge the Chinese government to continue talks with the United States on the three key issue areas. Their active lobby not only helped to influence a number of congressional members' position on the MFN issue but also contributed to Beijing's perception that it had active supporters within the United States. Knowing that there was a large constituency in the United States that had vested interests in preserving China's MFN status, Beijing could afford to resist American demands. The Chinese government capitalized on its leverage on several occasions, explicitly warning that U.S. businesses would suffer in the event of MFN withdrawal. Beijing's threats turned out to be entirely credible to the American business community. Given the business groups' divergent views on the MFN issue, there is little wonder that America's high-profile threats to revoke China's MFN status did so little to induce Chinese concessions.

Institutional Divisions under the Bush Administration

Differences between the executive and legislative branches over China policy goals and priorities further complicated the task of using aggressive negotiation tactics to elicit change in Chinese policies. While Congress repeatedly pushed for measures to punish China, the Bush administration consistently demonstrated a strong willingness to preserve China's normal trade status. The differences between executive and legislative preferences began to surface soon after Tiananmen. In the wake of Tiananmen, President Bush and his aides played a leading role in designing U.S. policy response toward the crisis. Essentially, Bush pursued a two-pronged strategy for dealing with the Chinese government: at the same time as he sought to avoid imposing what he saw as overly stringent measures on China demanded by Congress, interest groups, and the media, he privately pressed the Chinese authorities to take actions to improve the strained U.S.–China relationship.[34] Throughout the year, the administration adopted a considerably "lenient" China policy, as reflected by his decision to send two secret delegations to Beijing in the immediate aftermath of Tiananmen, to lift a number of sanctions soon after they were imposed on Beijing, to veto the Emergency Chinese Immigration Relief Act, and to adopt a low public profile on the issue.

In late 1990, when Congress refocused its attention on China's trade status following the conclusion of the Gulf War, the Bush administration became more attuned to the need to take tougher actions to address the three key issues in order to mollify congressional frustration and to avoid legislative restrictions on Chinese exports. But this modus vivendi did not in any way diminish the importance of continuation of China's MFN status and the policy of engagement as the centerpiece of Bush's China policy.[35] At the same time as Bush made public announcements enunciating both the economic and political reasons for preserving China's preferential trade status,[36] the Bush administration adopted a series of carefully orchestrated actions designed to demonstrate its resolve to deal with China's offensive policies in an attempt to send a clear signal to Congress and the public that the three targeted issue areas were at the top of the administration's agenda and that the executive was pursuing a vigorous dialogue with

Beijing on these questions.[37] Furthermore, to defeat congressional legislative attempt at conditional MFN status, the Bush team both mobilized societal groups interested in preserving U.S.–China trade to press congressional members for unconditional MFN status and went out of its way to persuade Republican senators to vote in line with the president's position. Due in large part to its active defense of China's unconditional MFN status, the White House in the end managed to garner enough support in the Senate to sustain a presidential veto.

The tug of war between the president and Congress intensified in 1992. As Congress became increasingly impatient with the Chinese government and approved two bills that would have attached conditions to China's MFN status renewal in 1993, the Bush administration tapped all available resources to muster enough support to sustain presidential vetoes of the bills. The Bush administration's opposition to congressionally mandated conditions was above all rooted in its perception of the significance of a viable U.S.–China commercial relationship to long-term U.S. interests. From the Bush team's point of view, revoking or conditioning MFN status would have reduced the volume of bilateral trade, cost the United States a major overseas market, and damaged the reputation of the United States as a reliable trading partner. If MFN status were withdrawn, Chinese goods would be subject to tariffs five to ten times as high as when the status was retained, significantly reducing Chinese exports to the United States and imposing substantial costs on American importers, retailers, and consumers, particularly those who relied on China's low-end products. The Chinese retaliation provoked by the U.S. sanctions would in turn significantly reduce American exports to China, costing the United States a good number of jobs and large export contracts to its European and Japanese competitors. This reduction in bilateral trade and the resulting downward spiral in bilateral economic relations would likely exacerbate America's overall trade deficit, reduce further the flow of U.S. foreign direct investment into China, and negatively affect the most economically dynamic areas in southern China.[38]

In addition to voicing these economic considerations, administration officials repeatedly affirmed that a comprehensive and institutionalized economic relationship with China would contribute to the stabilization of Asian affairs as well as a balanced global strategic posture. Bush judged that, even though the end of the Cold War might have reduced China's importance as a lever against the Soviet Union, China remained important to the U.S. leadership role in the emerging world order because of its size, location, and potential impact on world developments.[39] In other words, the Bush team believed that the deterioration in bilateral economic and political relationships that would result from conditioning China's MFN status would significantly affect the ability of the United States to develop strategic cooperation with Beijing at both the regional and the global level. Since administration officials did not view China's trade practices as directly threatening the viability and survival of American industries, considerations for the overall economic and political costs of disrupting trade with China prevailed in the Bush administration's decision to extend MFN status to China without any conditions.

Hence, throughout 1990–92, the Bush administration and Congress had displayed widely divergent policy preferences with respect to China's MFN status. Indeed, Congress and the Bush administration were perhaps more at loggerheads on China than on any other foreign policy issue. The White House's repeated assertion that it did not want to see MFN status for China withdrawn, its firm stance, and its willingness to use the last resort of presidential veto strengthened Beijing's belief that the threat to cut off its MFN status was mere bluff. The White House's willingness to come to the defense of China's preferential trade status, which was rooted in the executive's consideration for broad, long-term American economic and political interests, effectively served as a check on Congress's more hawkish position. Such institutional divisions characteristic of many democratic polities constrained the proclivity of an aggressive legislature to take the dispute to the next level by imposing punitive tariff barriers. Reinforced by the sharply divergent interests held by interest groups, these divisions sent highly mixed signals to the Chinese and substantially reduced the effectiveness of America threats. Thus although the pressure on China to change various domestic politics was greater than any other time since the normalization of U.S.–China relations, in the end Beijing made no fundamental changes in its policies and only offered a few symbolic concessions to appease critics of the executive branch's "soft" approach.[40] As a result, Congress and China critics remained deeply dissatisfied with Beijing's performance in the areas of human rights, trade, and weapons proliferation. They elevated their hope that the coming to power of a new president who had promised during his presidential campaign to get tough with Beijing could help to orchestrate a more unified policy that could exert sufficient pressure on Beijing. The extent to which the United States was able to influence the direction of Beijing's policies under the new Clinton team will be the focus of the next section.

The Clinton Administration and MFN Status: 1993–94

Between his election in 1992 and 1994, President Clinton's approach toward China had undergone a series of modifications such that, by 1994, the Bill Clinton who had accused President Bush of "coddling the dictators" in Beijing during his presidential campaign had gone so far as to abandon the MFN linkage. From hindsight, it appears that Clinton's linkage approach was undermined by internal disagreements. Not only did the China trade advocates campaign aggressively to oppose the linkage policy, but many of those in the administration who had publicly indicated approval of the president's executive order worked diligently to overturn the policy once it came into existence.[41] Domestic opposition not only forced Clinton to reorient his China policy but also contributed to Beijing's belief that the president was not serious about his threat to terminate MFN status for China. The Chinese were able to infer, from what they learned from the American media, that Clinton simply could not get his threats ratified by domestic business groups and his own economic team and that, even in the highly unlikely event that Clinton implemented the threat, the divisions within American society would soon reverse his policy. For example, a week after Secretary of State Warren Christopher's visit to Beijing in March 1994, Chinese foreign minister Qian Qichen reportedly recalled Christopher's meeting with representatives of major U.S. corporations in Beijing, where all the American business representatives "voiced their strong opposition to the revoking of China's trade status."[42] Beijing's calculations turned out to be right. Therefore, despite a temporary toughening of policy, Clinton was soon forced to reorient his China policy. The following section will examine in detail Clinton's China policy and the process leading to his policy reversal to show how highly conflicting forces in the U.S. government undermined the credibility of the MFN threat.

Clinton's views concerning MFN tariff treatment for China underwent a fundamental metamorphosis between June 1992 and May 1993. While Clinton had vehemently attacked Bush's China policy for its brazen "indifference to democracy"[43] and indicated his support for the *legislative imposition* of a broad range of conditions on the extension of MFN status for China during his presidential campaign, the conflicting pressure on his China policy became more intense once he was sworn into office. On the one hand, some congressional members implied that, should the administration's policy fail to satisfy them, they would insist on availing of the opportunity provided by the annual renewal of China's MFN status to moderate Chinese behavior. On the other hand, the business community and many members of the Clinton team emphasized China's economic and strategic significance and positively called for unconditional MFN status. Clinton then began to tread a middle course between these two polar opinions.

By the spring of 1993, President Clinton had come to believe that administratively imposed conditions on future MFN renewal was a suitable compromise between the rhetoric of the campaign and the realities of growing U.S. economic interests in China. On May 28, 1993, Clinton officially informed Congress that he planned to renew China's MFN status. In response to congressional insistence on some form of MFN conditions, however, he signed an executive order making the next renewal of China's performance contingent on evidence of "overall, significant progress" made by China in seven areas related to human rights.[44] In opting for administratively imposed conditions, Clinton adopted an approach that was a notch higher than that of the Bush administration, which repeatedly resisted all efforts by a Democratic Congress to attach any conditions to the annual renewal of China's trade benefits. But by avoiding legislatively imposed sanctions and by relaxing the criteria set for Beijing in the executive order, such an approach also represented a significant moderation of the one advocated by Congress over the past three years.

Events during the following year transpired to undermine the very intent of the executive order. In the first place, much of the business community organized to articulate their interests more effectively to congressional members and to the administration. While corporate America refrained from arguing vigorously and publicly for unconditional MFN status for China in light of highly critical media reports about Chinese policies in the past, the announcement of the executive order left them with no choice but to take a proactive stance on MFN policy and to launch a better orchestrated campaign in order to influence the government's China policy.

Equally important was that President Clinton and many in the administration soon began to realize that the executive order had given insufficient weight to economic interests. In the summer of 1993, in view of the downward slide in U.S.–China relations, Winston Lord, assistant secretary of state for East Asian and Pacific Affairs, began to advocate "comprehensive engagement" with China, a policy that would form the basis for a series of high-level exchanges during the next year. Even President Clinton himself began to have doubts about the executive order soon after its release. For example, through his participation in the APEC meeting and his talks with President Jiang Zemin in Seattle in November 1993, the president came to realize that China was "too big to punish and too important to isolate."[45] The president's doubts deepened with Secretary Christopher's March 1994 visit to Beijing, when Christopher received a reception "as frigid as the winter wind blowing down from Mongolia" while trying to educate the Chinese on the need to improve their record on human rights.[46]

A changing mood within the executive branch further compelled Clinton to modify his position. Following the release of the executive order, a growing number of administration officials, in particular many members of Clinton's economic team, felt that the executive order overemphasized human rights at the expense of economic opportunity and subsequently articulated these economic interests more forcefully when China's preferential trade status came up for renewal in 1994. At the Treasury Department, Secretary Lloyd Bentsen, who came back from a January 1994 trip to China with a favorable assessment of America's stake in China's economic growth, cautioned strongly against unilateral economic sanctions.[47] At the Commerce Department, Undersecretary for International Trade Jeffery Garten called on the administration to more fully incorporate economic analysis into decision making in a classified economic report titled "U.S. Commercial Interest in China to the Year 2000."[48] With China being placed on the top of the Commerce Department's "Big Emerging Markets" list,[49] Commerce Secretary Ron Brown made a strong case that the pursuit of better human rights performance in China should not come at the expense of economic growth in America.[50]

The newly established National Economic Council (NEC), led by Robert E. Rubin, also played a positive role in the campaign for the unconditional renewal of China's trade status. Feeling that the president's executive order had attached excessive weight to the views of agencies such as the National Security Council (NSC), Rubin and his deputy, Bowman Cutter, urged the Clinton administration to ultimately sever the MFN linkage. The NEC turned out to be the strongest advocate of renewal in the MFN debate in both 1993 and 1994.[51] The increasingly prevalent view at agencies such as the Treasury Department, Commerce Department, and the USTR was that Winston Lord still was placing excessive conditions on human rights and security issues at the expense of trade and economics. After these agencies relayed their concerns to the NEC and the NSC, further adjustments in the policy process were made to better reflect the preferences of the economic officials.

As a result, the president's views on China had changed 180 degrees so that by May 1994 he renewed China's favorable trade status without any conditions and announced that he would abandon his effort to use trade as a lever to force Beijing to make progress on human rights, even though plainly acknowledging that China had fallen short. In making the announcement, Clinton offered perhaps the most eloquent defense of the Bush administration's China policy ever uttered at the White House: "To those who argue that in view of China's human rights abuses we should revoke MFN status, let me ask you the same question that I have asked myself: Will we do more to advance the cause of human rights if China is isolated, or if our nations are engaged in a growing web of political cooperation and contacts?"[52] In adopting such an approach, Clinton was acknowledging the growing importance of economic concerns in foreign affairs. It seems justified to say that it was the economic officials and the China trade lobby that had prevailed in the decision to delink.

Chinese Perceptions and Strategy

The intense conflict between various domestic actors in the United States over the appropriate China policy substantially reduced the credibility of American threats to terminate China's MFN status. In particular, as various bureaucracies and individuals expressed their views about China's trade status both in private and in public forums in the process leading up to Clinton's decision to delink, they diminished the credibility of the administration's position in the eyes of the Chinese government.[53] A series of visits by high-ranking Chinese officials to the United States further confirmed Beijing's belief that the United States wanted good relations with Beijing, that there were serious divisions within the Clinton administration with respect to U.S. policy toward China and, importantly, that there was latent support in corporate America, both in the importing and in the exporting and investing community, for good economic relations with China.[54]

For instance, before President Clinton was to make a decision on the renewal of China's MFN status in 1994, Chinese officials warned that cancellation of China's MFN status would cripple access for American importers as well as for U.S. businesses investing in China.[55] During a visit to San Francisco in April 1993, Hu Ding Yi, secretary-general of the All China Federation of Industry and Commerce hinted that MFN was a mutually beneficial financial arrangement and that U.S. businesses would forgo considerable economic benefits in the event that the United States withdrew MFN status from China.[56] Also, during another trip to Washington, Zheng Hongye, chairman of the China Council for the Promotion of International Trade, cautioned that withdrawal of MFN status for China would negatively impinge on the interests of American firms that either imported from or exported to China, in addition to inflicting considerable costs on Hong Kong businesses because so much two-way trade went through Hong Kong.[57] With the firm belief that loss of MFN status would hurt the United States more than it would hurt China, China's minister in charge of foreign trade, Wu Yi, who had gained the reputation as China's "iron lady" due to her uncompromising and aggressive negotiation style, stated that China was not "afraid of losing it [MFN status]," as the United States "would also have to suffer" if MFN status for China were rescinded.[58]

Well aware that both American importers and exporters were actively lobbying for China's MFN status and confident that "it is the view of U.S. business to solve this issue once and for all," Beijing simply could not believe that Washington would revoke MFN status and was thus able to avoid making any major adjustments in its domestic policies.[59] By early 1994 Beijing seemed to have come to believe that it could simply defy American pressure and that the administration would back down even in the absence of significant concessions.

Indeed, Beijing had adopted its own policy for dealing with American pressure. The "four nots" policy (not to desire confrontation, not to provoke confrontation, not to dodge confrontation, and not to be afraid of sanctions and to resist them) was based on the premises that the United States still needed China's cooperation and that Clinton's domestic and foreign policies reflected considerations for conflicts at the domestic level.[60]

In short, Beijing's leaders appeared to be convinced that American politics was fundamentally driven by economic interests and that it would be difficult for President Clinton, who had placed so much emphasis on stimulating economic growth and improving competitiveness, to change his mind and cut off America's ties with one of its most important trading partners.[61] As a result, Beijing felt it could mobilize the economically oriented segment of the American polity in the battle over MFN status. The active cooperation that Beijing was able to forge with the American business community led some Clinton administration officials, including Winston Lord, to complain that business executives "were not only not supporting us, but they were undercutting us with the Chinese."[62] An important strategy adopted by Beijing toward that end was to carry out a series of high-level trips to the United States, sometimes shopping trips carefully timed to coincide with major decisions on MFN status, to showcase China's importance to America. For example, in April 1994, Chinese trade minister Wu Yi led "the largest Chinese trade initiative ever to the U.S."[63] Another part of Beijing's strategy was to show Washington that it was alone in threatening to impose sanctions on China and that market shares would go to its competitors if MFN status were withdrawn. Beijing on several occasions awarded business deals to the Europeans and to the Japanese ostensibly in retaliation for the United States' tough stance on the MFN issue.[64]

The result, therefore, was that Beijing ended up giving President Clinton just enough face by making a number of symbolic concessions so that he could reverse his earlier decision. As Secretary Christopher candidly conceded in his recommendations to President Clinton, the Chinese concessions "cannot be said to meet the expectations set forth in the EO [executive order]."[65] The Chinese were right to see the realism in Clinton's China policy: "The U.S. is rather pragmatic when it sees its policies aren't working, so the Clinton administration will become more pragmatic."[66]

United States–China: Market Access Negotiations

As the U.S. trade deficit with China began to climb steadily in the early 1990s, from $6 billion in 1989 to $13 billion in 1991, the United States resorted to pressure tactics to address high tariff and nontariff barriers limiting the expansion of American sales in the Chinese market. Failing to secure greater market access for American businesses by applying the leverage of MFN status, the Bush administration on October 10, 1991, initiated a regular Section 301 case to address a wide range of import impediments in China that have effectively kept American products out of the Chinese market, including QRs, import licensing requirements, internal (*neibu*) trade barriers, and other nontariff barriers.[67] Instead of targeting any specific industry, the investigation sought to tackle the web of import barriers embedded in China's existing trade regime. American negotiators stressed that the trade barriers being singled out not only seriously impeded American exports to China but also would most likely violate the multilateral trading principles enshrined in the GATT were China to become a member of that regime.

While the USTR sought to narrow the differences with the Chinese on a variety of tariff- and nontariff-related issues, a year of negotiations failed to get the Chinese to commit to a specific timetable for phasing out their quantitative restrictions, as the Chinese negotiators insisted that many infant industries in China would face extinctions absent QRs and other trade restrictions.[68] In light of this stalemate, the USTR on August 21, 1992, threatened to impose retaliatory tariffs on $3.9 billion of Chinese products to the United States if no satisfactory settlement could be reached on the market access issue by the October 10 deadline. Beijing reacted swiftly by threatening to counterretaliate against $4 billion of U.S. exports should Washington implement the threatened sanctions.[69]

The Section 301 threat and China's counterthreat immediately brought American businesses into the fray. Although the dispute was not initiated over any specific industry complaint, a range of American exporters that were expecting to benefit from China's import liberalization rallied behind the sanction threat. Producers of aircraft, computers, industrial machinery, fertilizer, and chemicals stood to gain the most from a market-opening agreement with China. Through their representative associations such as the U.S.–China Business Council, these producers expressed their support for an aggressive negotiation approach that promised to knock down the myriad of nontariff barriers that existed in China.[70] Textile manufacturers, under the lead of the powerful American Textile Manufacturers Institute (ATMI), called on the government to impose retaliatory tariffs on Chinese products to compensate for the losses that China's trade barriers inflicted on American producers. The organization even urged the U.S. government to target those products considered as high-priority export items by Beijing to get the Chinese leadership to back down in the confrontation.[71]

But even though exporters were eager to open the Chinese market, they again found themselves caught in a tug of war with the American importing and retailing community. The American threat negatively impinged upon the interests of importers, whose stake in the China market had grown substantially in the past decade. These importers protested against the threat under Section 301, which, if implemented, would have disrupted the supply of low-cost imports from that country. In early 1991, when the USTR called for public comment to determine which Chinese products to target for retaliation should Beijing refuse to comply with American demands to remove trade barriers, most of the trade groups and companies that responded emphasized that it was important for the government to defuse the trade row by reaching a fair trade agreement with Beijing instead of resorting to punitive action. In the worst case scenario that retaliation had to be carried out against China, these groups scrambled to urge the USTR to exclude their own products from the list of Chinese goods to be included in the hit list.

The Toy Manufacturers of America, for example, pointed out that the toy industry was being placed in a very vulnerable dependent position, as imports from China accounted for more than 40 percent of all the toys sold in the United States. The organization further explained that, even though toy manufacturers had undertaken efforts to spread sourcing to other parts of the world, including some Asian and Latin American countries, the toy industry's commitment to China was already too substantial and specific to permit any drastic changes. In the words of one of the representatives of the association, it would be extremely difficult to "turn your back on an infrastructure that has taken 10 years to build."[72]

Footwear importers, fearing a full-blown U.S.–China trade war, undertook a two-pronged strategy designed to minimize the damage of potential retaliatory measures. While undertaking a serious effort to impress upon government officials the cost of disrupting trade with China, they began to more consciously reduce their dependence on Chinese imports. But while the latter strategy was feasible for large companies with worldwide operations, it was more difficult for the greater number of importers who were constrained by world quotas and by China's attractive low production costs to look for alternative sources of supply. Even large athletic shoe manufacturers, such as Nike, felt the effect. Nike, which sourced between 12 and 15 million pairs of shoes from China each year, or roughly 15 percent of the company's total production, complained that if punitive tariffs were imposed the company would have no other option but to sharply raise prices or to shut down its entire operation in China. The latter course of action would have seriously hurt the company's regional headquarter in Hong Kong as well. Together with Adidas, another major industry player, Nike sought to drive home the point that trade retaliation would seriously undermine the position of the footwear and athletic equipment industry, including their affiliates in Hong Kong.[73]

Leather luggage importers faced the same dilemma. Since China supplied the U.S. market with nearly 90 percent of all attaché cases priced under two hundred dollars, many leather goods importers found that locating new sources of supply would not only be time-consuming but also would likely increase costs substantially. Leather goods importers such as Kingport International therefore joined other importers in urging moderation.[74]

Importers found an unusual ally in the market access negotiations in Hong Kong. Since nearly two-thirds of the Chinese products on the U.S. hit list valued at $2.4 billion were reexports via the territory, Hong Kong businesses, which were becoming increasingly agitated about the prospect of a trade war, appeared before hearings held in Washington strongly against trade retaliation. The Hong Kong Electronics Association, the Hong Kong General Chamber of Commerce, and the Chinese Manufacturers' Association argued that, since nearly two-thirds of the commodities targeted for trade sanctions (such as footwear, electrical appliances, telecommunications gear, and parts and plastic items) were reexports via Hong Kong and over half of Hong Kong's manufacturing was undertaken in China, sanctions could greatly hurt Hong Kong's economy.[75] Furthermore, as 95 percent of China's toy exports to the United States were produced by Hong Kong firms on the mainland, the Hong Kong Toys Council warned the USTR that retaliation against China would "critically threaten" Hong Kong's toy manufacturers. The Hong Kong Watch Manufacturers Association also pleaded against retaliation, warning that such action could result in hundreds of thousands of job losses. Many of the associations mentioned here, together with the Federation of Hong Kong Industries, urged U.S. officials to exclude from the hit list "those items which in your opinion might damage HK industry" in the event that retaliation had to be carried out.[76]

Importers' plea for moderation reduced the level of domestic cohesion that the Bush administration would have wanted to project over the market access issue. It should be noted that administration officials initiated the market access talks at the urging of congressional members, in the absence of substantial industry input. An important motivation for the Bush administration's decision to initiate separate, more targeted talks over market access was to relieve congressional pressure on the annual debate over China's MFN status. Thus it was in response to a letter from Senator Max Baucus and several other senators encouraging administrative action that President Bush promised to launch Section 301 investigations in the summer of 1991. In justifying the administration's position, President Bush stated that China's protectionist policies "undoubtedly contributed to a 17 percent decline in U.S. sales to China in 1990."[77] Thus, the Bush administration did adopt a position closer to that of Congress on the market access issue than on the MFN issue both to address congressional concerns about China's pervasive market access barriers, which were by then starting to pose an increasingly formidable challenge for American businesses in the late 1980s, and to alleviate their worries about the bilateral trade deficit, which doubled again from $13 billion in 1991 to $23 billion in 1993, a figure that placed China as the country with the second largest trade surplus with the United States.

Yet even with this greater executive resolve for a positive outcome, the negotiations fell short of U.S. expectations. While Beijing promised to undertake a series of liberalization measures under U.S. retaliatory threats in a Memorandum of Understanding (MOU) signed on October 10, 1992, Beijing's willingness to compromise proved to be a tactical temporization as subsequent Chinese practices failed to fulfill the expectations of the United States, prompting Deputy USTR Charlene Barshefsky on October 25, 1993, to again set a deadline for China to comply with the MOU. To relieve American pressure, China dismantled quotas and import licenses on 283 products and reduced tariffs on 234 products on January 1, 1994. These positive developments notwithstanding, China simultaneously tightened import controls on a wide range of other products, some of which already enjoyed protection through unpublished quotas. Furthermore, Beijing imposed international bidding procedures on a list of 171 products to ensure that Chinese products could successfully compete with imports. On the whole, although the agreement on paper suggests quite substantial liberalization by China, implementation problems suggest that the U.S. market access initiative against China in the early 1990s produced rather limited results.

One reason that the market access talks were so unsuccessful in changing Chinese behavior had to do with the fact that the tariff regime constituted an important component of China's plan for industrial development and, as a result, was supported by various industrial ministries and the enterprises under their control. Thus, the Chinese leadership might agree to modifications in its tariff regime as a quid pro quo to avoid the imposition of sanctions, yet eventually proved unwilling to introduce any fundamental changes that would threaten the relationship between the state and the industries under its control. Once tensions receded and it became clear that Washington was backtracking on its pledge to support China's bid for the GATT, Beijing quickly reverted back to the old methods of protecting domestic industries behind high tariff walls.

But an equally plausible explanation for Beijing's unyielding posture was that the Chinese leadership was confident that, even if Beijing failed to abide by its commitments, countervailing pressure from import-using industries in the United States would minimize the chances that the United States really would carry out the threatened sanctions against China. In response to Washington's threat tactics during the market access negotiations, Tong Zhiguang, China's vice minister of foreign economic relations and trade (MOFERT) several times stated that "China is not afraid of a trade war, especially if the opposite side is using trade retaliation as a threat."[78] A MOFERT official explained the rationale behind the announcement: "China has a large domestic market and our exports are needed in many other countries. The United States will need to do business with China. In the worst case scenario of a trade war, we can always find other alternatives."[79] In other words, there did exist sentiments in Beijing that the United States faced internal constraints. Once the Americans left and once it became clear that Washington was backtracking on its pledge to support China's GATT bid, the incentive for Beijing to honor the agreement was substantially reduced.

United States–Brazil: Informatics

In September 1985 the United States initiated a Section 301 investigation into Brazil's informatics program, which, from the point of view of American computer manufacturers, promoted the development of a national computer industry at the expense of American and other multinational firms. Brazil was chosen as a Section 301 target in part to avoid the exclusive geographic focus of Section 301 actions on Asian countries such as Japan and South Korea. Negotiations over this issue lasted for over three years but failed to produce a lasting agreement leading to market liberalization in favor of U.S. commercial interests. As Odell's account of the informatics dispute suggests, the contrasting views of American computer companies with different market positions in Brazil was a main reason why American pressure did so little to alter the status quo.[80] But equally important to explaining dispute outcome was resistance by importers of Brazilian-made low-end and intermediary products to a retaliatory strategy that threatened to disrupt their supplies. Importers' and retailers' opposition to the sanctions strategy reinforced the ambivalence of computer manufacturers and eroded the credibility of American negotiators vis-à-vis Brasília.

In the first place, American computer manufacturers could not reach a consensus among themselves with respect to the Reagan administration's decision to cite Brazil's informatics program under the Section 301 threat. Companies favoring a more aggressive bargaining strategy were mainly ones like Tektronix that were interested in Brazil but had nevertheless been hindered by the market reserve program's restrictions from gaining a greater foothold in the Brazilian market. Associations such as the American Electronics Association (AEA), which represented electronics manufacturers, were also in favor of a firm negotiation approach so as to showcase the U.S. resolve for a fair trade outcome both in Brazil and in the global market. In August 1985, even before the initiation of the informatics dispute, the AEA had served as a lead actor in urging the Reagan administration to remove the zero-duty treatment that Brazil, along with several other developing countries, enjoyed under the Generalized System of Preferences (GSP) unless they promised enhanced protection for IPR. The AEA's support for the Section 301 designation of Brazil likewise stemmed from a desire to negotiate market opening globally.

Other than these firms and associations just cited, however, many other U.S. computer manufacturers were at best lukewarm about the decision to designate Brazil as an unfair trader. A fair number of AEA members were indifferent to the case, as they had neither exposure nor investment in that country. More importantly, some companies that had managed to develop a market niche in Brazil were themselves benefactors of the market reserve program that was the focus of the Reagan administration's attack. Not only were these firms less than enthusiastic about the designation, but they sought to constrain the Reagan administration in its trade offensive. IBM was a case in point. As a company highly dependent on global production and having developed a substantial presence in the office machines market in Brazil, IBM did not seem to see any reason for change. In particular, as the market reserve program had assisted the company in fending off competition from its commercial rivals such as Digital Equipment, Japanese mainframe manufacturers, and other minicomputer makers, IBM actually viewed the informatics law as codifying long-standing practices rather than as signifying any fundamental change.

A few other large multinational companies shared the same attitude as IBM. For instance, both Hewlett-Packard and Burroughs had investment exposure in Brazil; and, just like IBM, Burroughs was heavily dependent on world markets. With the capital and wherewithal to weather the storm and reap long-term gains, these companies actually opposed imposing sanctions on Brazil. At a hearing held in Washington in October 1985, the organization representing the interests of these large firms, the Computer and Business Equipment Manufacturers Association (CBEMA), testified against attempts to modify the informatics law, instead advocating a negotiation approach aimed at preventing the expansion of the restrictive scope of the market reserve program, improving enforcement and implementation of the law, and ensuring the eventual abolition of the program. In other words, the priority of the CBEMA was to cushion the impact of Reagan's blow for long-term commercial benefits. In the absence of active industry lobbying, reaction to the initiation of the informatics case had been mixed. For example, when the Reagan administration notified industry representatives of the decision to slap Brazil's informatics policy a day before the announcement was made, industry representatives were reportedly shocked. One industry representative even stated that "There was *never* any enthusiasm for the case from those who knew Brazil."[81] In a private symposium held in Washington a few days after Reagan made his announcement, IBM and Burroughs officials, even in the presence of Brazilian officials, directly challenged Reagan's actions as inopportune.

In addition to the different positions U.S. computer manufacturers held regarding the informatics dispute, U.S. importers and retailers had been lobbying against imposing restrictions on Brazilian exports on which they depended. Although by the mid-1980s Brazil had acquired the ability to produce and export intermediary industrial products such as automobile and aircraft parts and components, a sizable portion of Brazil's exports to the United States still consisted of labor-intensive products such as footwear and orange juice concentrates.[82] Thus when USTR officials sought to draw up a retaliation list against Brazil in the summer of 1986 and then again in 1987, American businesses likely to be negatively impacted by the retaliation spoke out against the move, in the process complicating the task of forging a credible negotiation stance toward the Brazilians. Indeed, the decision to restrict Brazilian products had triggered a storm of protest from a fair number of American firms that did not want to see an increase in the price of Brazilian products. For example, as Brazilian citrus growers supplied about 40 percent of the U.S. orange juice market, companies such as Coca-Cola, Procter and Gamble, and Beatrice Foods, which were highly dependent on orange juice concentrate imported from Brazil, lobbied against placing that item on the retaliation list.[83] The American Heritage Trading Corporation and its affiliates, which specialized in food and beverage containers and ingredients, went even further to argue that they would be forced out of business if sanctions had to be imposed on Brazilian products upon which they relied heavily. Automobile manufacturers, particularly those based in Detroit, likewise were averse to the idea of placing restrictions on imports of auto components from Brazil, a move that would threaten to disrupt their integrated global production system. The U.S. footwear industry was divided over the possibility of placing restrictions against imports of footwear from Brazil as well. While footwear producers supported the inclusion of footwear on the retaliation list, shoe retailers spoke out against the proposal. Moreover, since American negotiators had very recently vetoed the idea of placing quotas on footwear, they did not want to see the U.S. industry launch a second comeback and try to use the leverage provided by Section 301 to combat unfair foreign competition.

Resistance to the sanctions strategy could also be found among aircraft manufacturers. In particular, as Brazil had acquired the ability to produce and export airplanes, a number of smaller airlines in the United States that purchased Brazil's planes resisted any move to impose restrictions against imports from Brazil. As an unlikely opponent to trade sanctions, a Midwestern convention center argued that imposing higher duties on Brazil's Embauer 120 aircraft could hold back regional airline companies' plans to expand commuter services, thus reducing the number of conventions that could be held in an area that already lagged behind economically.[84] Even cosmetics companies such as Avon lodged a complaint against the proposed tariffs on ceramic mugs, for which Brazil was a major supplier.

In short, as a trade war with Brazil was looming, a good number of American companies rushed to lobby the administration to exempt the products on which they were dependent. Some firms cautioned that they faced extinction should Washington proceed with plans to levy punitive tariffs on Brazilian products. Other firms couched their pitches with a view to the administration's desire to reduce U.S. trade deficits with Asian nations, emphasizing that they could find no cost-effective alternative to imports from Brazil other than Asian countries such as Taiwan, South Korea, and Hong Kong. The barrage of complaints from American importers left USTR officials with little leeway in selecting the products they could hit, prompting a USTR staff member to lament that "we were down to porcelain toilet bowl covers."[85]

These divisions in American politics by no means lost the Brazilians. Importantly, judging from the reaction of U.S. computer manufacturers in discussion involving Brazilian representatives, Brazilian negotiators were able to come to the conclusion that American computer man-ufacturers themselves were divided. According to one Brazilian nego-tiator, "The U.S. companies were divided. IBM was neutral. They passed the word that they had not asked for the 301; it was really gov-ernment inspired. The companies knew better than the U.S. govern-ment how difficult it would be in Brazil."[86]

Equally important was that many business interests in Brazil were well aware of the importance of Brazil to the United States as an export market. For example, the organization representing Brazilian exporting interests, the Brazilian Association of Commercial Exporters, reportedly responded to the U.S. sanction threat by claim-ing that "coordinated action by Brazilian importers of U.S. goods could force the U.S. to withdraw its reprisals without forcing a general revision of the new software bill."[87] Brazilian business interests were also prepared to undertake counterretaliatory moves against U.S. products (such as canceling orders for Boeing aircrafts) in the worst case scenario that the United States followed through with its threats.[88] Other Brazilian exporters focused on the reliance of the United States on Brazilian consumer products. One of Brazil's largest footwear exporters noted that U.S. sanctions against footwear would result in increased prices for American consumers and the substitution of plas-tic for leather in lower-priced lines.[89] Given these perceptions, it was only natural that Brazil would have offered only token concessions to American demands.

Conclusion

The analyses presented here should make it clear why heavy-handed American pressure has failed to extract significant concessions from Beijing and Brasília. In the MFN and market access negotiations with China, the messages the United States sent to Beijing were so mixed and confusing that China simply did not find it necessary to make any concessions. As we have seen, due to the complementary trade rela-tionship between the United States and China, a great number of busi-ness groups voiced their opposition to threats to put restrictions on Chinese exports. In particular, American importers and retailers of toys, apparel, footwear, and consumer electronics, goods that the United States no longer produced itself, staunchly opposed trade sanc-tions, arguing that they could not always acquire these goods from other countries at competitive prices. Furthermore, in the MFN case,

American manufacturers of aircraft, autos, and telecommunications equipment also actively lobbied against the imposition of sanctions, a measure that would cut off their access to the world's fastest growing economy and largest market. Thus, whenever the United States tried to strike out at China for its offensive domestic policies, it almost always was hamstrung by strong opposition from the business community for doing so. While supporters of a sanctions strategy in the MFN case— the human rights lobby and other conservative groups—had aggressively pushed for MFN revocation at the outset, they simply could not match the China trade lobby in terms of organizational cohesion and financial strength. Since they did not have a policy alternative other than one that would result in Chinese retaliation and international isolation, these groups eventually lost ground to the MFN advocates.

The short discussion of the U.S.–Brazil informatics dispute illustrates a similar dynamic. Importantly, importers of Brazilian products such as footwear, orange juice concentrates, and auto components had lodged complaints against the decision to retaliate against Brazilian products. Their opposition reinforced the different opinions held by software manufacturers with different market positions in Brazil, thus undercutting the credibility of USTR officials. Table 4.1 summarizes the position and impact of each of the groups involved in the negotiations.

These divergent domestic interests were exacerbated by the divisions within the U.S. government. The cases involving China most vividly demonstrate this dynamic. In the debate over MFN status, the legislative branch, more sensitive to issues with strong domestic implications, was determined to punish China's perceived intransigence through existing trade laws. In contrast, the executive branch, considering conflicting domestic pressures and long-term American economic and strategic interests in China, was more inclined to maintain the status quo. As we have seen, the Bush administration consistently opted to oppose efforts to attach legislative conditions to MFN status for China. It was committed to its own perspectives on U.S.–China relations and devoted considerable resources to deflecting congressional pressure. The president even used the last resort of a presidential veto to preserve China's normal trade status. Later, President Clinton, even though he had initially confronted China on human rights issues, was compelled by the realities of U.S.–China relations to temper his rhetoric and to repudiate pressure tactics that have proved to be both futile and counterproductive. Clinton's about-face in part reflected intense pressure from the trade lobby, but it also stemmed from his

TABLE 4.1. Profiles of Main Actors Involved in U.S.–China and U.S.–Brazil Negotiations

	Companies and Associations	Position	Impact
U.S.–China: MFN Directly Affected Exporters	—	—	—
Exporters Not Directly Affected	Emergency Committee for American Trade; U.S. Chamber of Commerce; National Foreign Trade Council; U.S.–China Business Council; Business Coalition for U.S.–China Trade; American Association of Exporters & Importers; National Association of Wheat Growers; North American Export Grain Association; Aircraft manufacturers: Boeing; AT&T; GE; IBM; GM; Motorola; NAM	Sanctions would reduce American exports, yield market shares to foreign competitors, threaten the viability of American investment in China, jeopardize U.S. jobs, and lead to the loss of a major export market	Very influential in opposing sanction threats.
Import-Competing Interests	Textile industry	Argued that Chinese textile imports hurt the American industry. Joined human rights and religious groups, conservative-leaning organizations, and other critics of China in pushing for trade sanctions.	Relatively visible in the early stage of the debate; eventually lost ground to the pro-MFN interests.
Import-Using Interests	Importers of toy, apparel, footwear, and consumer electronics; Toys "R" Us; J.C. Penney; Footwear Distributors & Retailers of America; Nike	Trade restrictions would hurt American consumers, particularly low- and middle-income families. It would be difficult to find alternative sources for many low-cost products outside of China.	Very influential; launched intensive campaign against sanction threats.

U.S.–China Market Access Negotiations			
Directly Affected Exporters	U.S.-China Business Council, representing producers of aircraft, computers, industrial machinery, fertilizer, and chemicals; American Textile Manufacturers Institute	Supported the administration's efforts to liberalize the Chinese market.	Provided some support for the administration's negotiation strategy.
Exporters Not Directly Affected	—	—	—
Import-Competing Interests	—	—	—
Import-Using Interests	Toy Manufacturers of America; footwear importers; importers of leather luggage; and businesses in Hong Kong	Argued that trade sanctions would force importers to bear substantially increased prices and significant adjustment costs.	Their strong resistance to the sanctions strategy reduced the homogeneity of the U.S. negotiation position.
U.S.–Brazil Informatics Dispute			
Directly Affected Exporters	IBM; Hewlett-Packard; Burroughs; Tektronix; American Electronics Association; Computer and Business Equipment Manufacturers Association	While companies that were hindered by the market access provisions of the informatics program supported the designation, businesses that were dependent on global production and had benefited from the restrictions of the informatics program opposed the retaliatory move.	Divisions among American computer manufacturers reduced the credibility of American threat to the Brazilians.

TABLE 4.1.—Continued

	Companies and Associations	Position	Impact
Exporters Not Directly Affected	—	—	—
Import-Competing Interests	—	—	—
Import-Using Interests	Coca-Cola; Procter & Gamble; Beatrice Foods; footwear retailers; American Heritage Trading Corporation; automobile manufacturers	Argued that, by increasing the price of Brazilian goods on which they depended, sanctions would either cause some American firms to go out of business or exacerbate U.S. trade deficits with Asian countries, which offered the only cost-effective alternative source of supply.	Import users' opposition exacerbated the division among exporters, further reducing the cohesion of the U.S. negotiation position.

economic team's determination to move toward positive bilateral economic cooperation. Since it knew MFN revocation or conditionality would adversely affect a broad sector of the American economy as well as the overall competitiveness of American industry, it was difficult for the executive to forge a long-lasting consensus with Congress on the need to terminate China's MFN tariff treatment. Moreover, even in the negotiations over market access, where the executive branch seems to have adopted a position closer to that preferred by Congress both to deflect congressional pressure on the MFN issue and to address the growing U.S. trade deficit with China, the coherence of the U.S. negotiation stance had nevertheless been undermined by dissenting voices in the U.S. business community.

Given these divisions in American politics, it is hardly surprising that American threats have failed to extract any meaningful concessions from China. Although the United States was seriously interested in finding solutions to its trade problems, it was constrained by the structure of U.S.–China trade relations from obtaining a favorable outcome. Once the Chinese figured out that they had nothing to lose, threat tactics lost much of their utility. With intense conflict among U.S. domestic constituencies and with MFN status for China down on the executive's foreign policy priority list, it was extremely difficult for the United States to carry out a credible threat. In the end, it was Beijing who was able to adopt a coherent strategy because it was a critical foreign policy issue and there was virtually no domestic constituency opposed to its policy. Ironically, as an authoritarian regime, Beijing turned out to be in a better position to play with American politics than vice versa. Because the United States is a democracy, the Chinese could see exactly what was going on in the United States by reading the editorial pages and listening to the debates. And because Beijing is an authoritarian regime, it could implement coherent policies, such as awarding contracts to the Japanese and European firms, to exacerbate the divisions in American society. There is little wonder, then, why American threats against China to modify its domestic practices have been so futile.

Before closing this chapter, a caveat is in order. The two cases in this chapter involve China and Brazil, two countries that, by dint of their large internal markets, were able to dangle the carrot of substantial export opportunities for American businesses and hence better co-opt American exporting interests. For instance, in the MFN debate, many non–directly involved export-oriented industries opposed sanctions due to both their current reliance on the Chinese market and their expectations of even greater profits in the future. In the informatics dispute with Brazil, American software companies wishing to maintain or expand their investments in the Brazilian market similarly objected to the Reagan administration's plans to impose sanctions against Brazilian products. While my argument about the conditions under which trade pressure will be most effective in opening foreign markets centers primarily on the role of import users in counterbalancing the sanctions strategy, exporters worried about counterretaliatory moves that would likely shut them out of the target market nevertheless frequently join import users against the imposition of sanctions. Participation by these non–directly involved exporters in the anti-sanctions coalition may make U.S. threats particularly ineffective vis-à-vis those complementary trading partners with large internal markets. Future studies could more specifically examine cases involving the United States and its complementary trading partners with smaller domestic markets to tease out the role of non–directly involved exporters in negotiations between these trading partners.

CHAPTER 5

U.S.–Japan Trade Conflicts:
Semiconductors and Super 301

The U.S.–Japan trade conflicts over semiconductors as well as the Super 301 negotiations over supercomputers, satellites, and forest products highlight the importance of broad consensus in the United States in favor of sanctions for bargaining outcomes. The negotiation over semiconductors was one of the most drawn out and acrimonious between the two countries. It started in the early 1980s, when the United States began efforts to deal with the undercutting of the American semiconductor industry by increasingly competitive Japanese firms. Since then, sustained American pressure, backed by the threat of further action, helped to produce a major bilateral agreement in 1986 and another one in 1990, providing American chip producers with some relief from Japanese dumping in the U.S. market and with greater access to the Japanese market. Although the negotiations were often protracted and difficult, tough talk by both the Reagan and Bush administrations forced Japan to halt its predatory pricing behavior and to open up its protected domestic market to American semiconductor products. American pressure thus played a crucial role in preventing the further slide of the U.S. semiconductor industry.

The Super 301 investigations between 1989 and 1990 in turn stemmed from U.S. concerns about Japan's protectionist policies in the satellite, supercomputer, and forest products industries. In the first two issue areas, the United States complained that Japan, through policies of industrial targeting designed to promote the development of autonomous supercomputer and satellite industries, had effectively excluded American producers, who were very competitive elsewhere in the world, from its public-sector market. In the area of forest products, the United States directly challenged a wide array of tariff and nontariff barriers in the Japanese forest products market that not only were GATT-illegal but also impeded American producers' access to the

Japanese market. The negotiation in each of the cases presented here allowed the United States to achieve its most immediate objective of opening Japanese government procurement to foreign bidders or of forcing the much-desired Japanese tariff cuts. Although, in the super-computer and satellite cases, the United States may not have achieved its long-term objective of deterring Japanese government targeting of these industries, by prying open Japan's protected home market, it at least succeeded in thwarting the rapid ascent of Japanese industries in the global market.

In each of the cases cited here, domestic interest groups' unified support for threat tactics enhanced the chances for American negotiators to obtain a favorable outcome. Unlike in U.S. trade negotiations with China, where efforts by export-seeking industries to impose sanctions on the target were often undercut by import-using interests who were unwilling to see their access to their potential suppliers cut off, export-oriented American producers involved in each of these cases did not encounter any major opposition from other segments of the business community. Indeed, since the United States and Japan competed in so many product categories, there was a large constituency in the United States that faced Japanese competition. Under these circumstances, sanction threats won support not only from the semiconductor, super-computer, satellite, and wood producers, who were interested in expanding U.S. market access in Japan, but also from other import-competing interests (such as electronics and auto manufacturers in the semiconductor case) who would benefit from the restrictions placed on Japanese exports to the United States. In the Super 301 cases, organizations such as the U.S. Chamber of Commerce and NAM that were opposed to sanctions in the China cases all came out in favor of sanction threats against Japan. The pervasive feeling within the U.S. business community that Japanese nurturing of its domestic industries seriously injured American producers in various sectors further fed this protectionist sentiment. Since the sanction threats promised benefits to either the export-seeking interests (if sanctions succeeded in extracting concessions) or the import-competing interests (if they had to be imposed), they enjoyed wide support from the U.S. business community. This unprecedented unity signaled to Japan that it could hardly escape some form of sanctions should it fail to make meaningful concessions, prompting the Japanese to take U.S. demands more seriously.

Reinforcing unified industry support was the executive branch's greater willingness to adopt a proactive trade policy in order to lessen congressional pressure to level the playing field for American industries. Especially when the issue involved high-technology industries with significant military and economic implications, the executive branch had demonstrated considerable assertiveness, frequently shifting from a policy of benign neglect in favor of "managed trade" to reshape comparative advantage in such leading industrial sectors and to maintain the overall competitiveness of the American economy. Even in the wood products case, where such "strategic trade" considerations were less prominent, the consensus that the field on which the trade game was being played was unfairly tilted against the United States produced strong incentives for executive action.

Lack of strong domestic opposition, combined with the executive's greater willingness to intervene, demonstrated to the Japanese the U.S. resolve in seeking a fair trade outcome, indicating that sanction threats had the full support of the major domestic actors. Domestic unity enhanced American threat credibility, leading to the conclusion of several agreements that increased the U.S. share of the Japanese market. A highly competitive trade structure between the United States and Japan thus facilitated the effective use of aggressive bargaining tactics toward that country.

The U.S.–Japan Semiconductor Trade Conflict

Industry Initiatives

The semiconductor dispute was initiated over industry complaints that the Japanese government, through its classical strategy of promotion and protection, had created a highly competitive domestic industry that, by the mid-1980s, had outperformed American firms in terms of both the quantity and quality of semiconductor production.[1] As Japanese companies had displaced American firms as the leading merchant semiconductor producers and as the phenomenal rise in Japan's share of the global semiconductor market had put American firms at a distinctive comparative disadvantage, U.S. chip manufacturers began to direct their attention to two particularly irritating forms of Japanese practices: Japanese dumping in both the United States and the world market and the lack of access to the Japanese domestic market.

It was at the urging of American chip producers that Washington initiated market access negotiations with the Japanese government. Early industry pressure forced the Japanese to enter into negotiations with the United States under the auspices of the U.S.–Japan Working

Group on High Technology in April 1982. This early set of talks produced an agreement in which the Japanese government committed itself to using its authority to prevent dumping, providing U.S. firms with greater access to Japanese patents, refraining from copying U.S. propriety circuits, and encouraging Japanese firms to increase purchases of U.S. semiconductor products through administrative guidance.[2] Throughout 1983, the semiconductor industry released numerous reports and studies with detailed accounts of the unfair trade practices pursued by Japanese chip makers and the Japanese government. In April 1983, as the second round of bilateral negotiations over market barriers got under way, industry representatives explicitly called on the government to demand a 30 percent share of the Japanese market, a share that they maintained was what they would have deserved if the Japanese market were open.[3] The industry went even further to draft a Section 301 petition in the summer of 1983.

Between 1983 and 1985, the situation of the semiconductor industry further deteriorated. By 1985, the aggressive pricing strategies of Japanese producers, the exit of almost all merchant American companies from the production of DRAM chips, and the sustained cyclical slump in industry demand combined to produce a sense of crisis among U.S. semiconductor manufacturers. Such dismal industry performance induced a pervasive sentiment among industry representatives that, should the U.S. government fail to come to the rescue of the semiconductor industry, the United States would have let the larger, better-financed Japanese competitors continue to strengthen their dominance of the world market in the late 1980s and 1990s. The aggravation of industry plight also convinced U.S. semiconductor makers that ad hoc bilateral agreements such as the one brokered by the U.S.–Japan Working Group on High Technology were inadequate and that it might take sanctions to get Japan to alter its behavior. Thus, in a crisis atmosphere, U.S. semiconductor producers began to call on the government to redress the trade balance. These actions dovetailed with mounting congressional and administrative concerns about the growing U.S. trade deficit with Japan. Through extensive and continuous lobbying activities, the semiconductor manufacturers exercised considerable political clout and successfully brought to the attention of the government and the public the connection between the industry's troubles and unfair Japanese competitive tactics.

The Semiconductor Industry Association (SIA) played an indispensable leadership role during the industry's extended campaign for government intervention. Formed in 1977 in explicit response to the increasing competitive challenge from Japan, the SIA played a pivotal role in the industry's successful effort to realize a number of its trade policy objectives between 1979 and 1986.[4] By the mid-1980s, the SIA had developed into a major industry association representing fifty-seven American semiconductor producers, composed of both giant "captive" producers such as AT&T, IBM, and Digital Equipment, which manufactured for internal consumption, and "merchant" producers such as Texas Instruments (TI), which supplied other semiconductor-user firms. While in principle the SIA favored free trade policies, most member firms agreed that the United States was not obliged to extend this principle to the Japanese, whose pursuit of mercantilist strategies had placed the survival of American semiconductor industry in jeopardy.[5]

When it became clear that informal, ad hoc bilateral negotiations had failed to relieve the industry's plight, the SIA began to see the filing of a formal petition under U.S. trade law as a potentially effective measure to pressure Japan to change its policies. Thus in June 1985 the SIA submitted a Section 301 petition against Japan's unfair competitive tactics, which presented substantial evidence of market barriers in Japan: in 1984, the U.S. semiconductor industry captured 83 percent of sales in the American market, 55 percent in the European market, 47 percent in other (mostly Asian) markets, but only 11 percent in the Japanese market.[6] In the petition, the SIA sought to invoke the rhetoric of "fair trade" by pinning the blame for both the dumping and the market access problems squarely on the Japanese government. The association contended that the Japanese government, through a series of anticompetitive practices designed to promote an industry deemed essential to national development, had created a market structure highly discriminatory against foreign producers. As a result, according to the SIA, American firms, which commanded a dominant position in all other semiconductor markets, had seen their market share in Japan hovering at the same 10 percent since 1975.[7]

The SIA further charged that, by providing direct and indirect assistance to the domestic industry, the Japanese government helped reduce investment risks facing Japanese firms and encouraged their willingness to invest even during a recession, in effect promoting the dumping of semiconductors by Japanese firms. The SIA concluded that, since these Japanese policies denied American firms "fair and equitable market opportunities," it was imperative for the USTR to monitor Japan's predatory export behavior and market barriers and to take appropriate measures to counter the effects of Japan's industrial targeting practices. Specifically, it called on the USTR to press the Japanese government to encourage its firms to increase their purchases from American semiconductor companies, to strictly enforce U.S. antidumping laws against Japanese firms, and to undertake investigations of the Japanese firms' antitrust behavior.[8] Should Japan fail to substantially change its behavior, the SIA recommended sanctions against Japan.

The SIA's 301 petition was followed by several other industry complaints. Shortly after the SIA submitted the 301 petition, the small U.S. memory producer Micron Technology filed under U.S. antidumping laws a claim that Japanese producers (such as Fujitsu, Hitachi, NEC, Oki, Toshiba, and Matsushita) were dumping 64K DRAMS in the American market. In August 1985, the Justice Department initiated an investigation into possible predatory pricing by Hitachi. A month later, three more American firms—Intel, Advanced Micro Devices (AMD), and National Semiconductor—filed another antidumping complaint, alleging that Japanese producers were dumping high-density EPROMS, another memory device in which American producers still had a competitive edge.[9] Later, TI sued eight Japanese semiconductor producers for infringing various TI patents on semiconductor memory.

Tremendous industry pressure increased the imperatives for action on the part of the Reagan administration. In November 1985, the USITC issued a preliminary finding that Japanese firms had harmed American industry. At about the same time, a "strike force" set up by the Reagan administration recommended that the U.S. government initiate unfair trade complaints against Japan. Finally, in response to industry demands, the U.S. Commerce Department initiated a claim on behalf of American producers hurt by Japanese dumping in the 256K DRAMS and 1M (one megabyte) DRAMS markets. The Commerce Department's self-initiation without any industry petition was considered to be an unprecedented move. Since the Japanese dominated this product category, the threat of retaliation was intended to hurt the Japanese in the areas where they had the greatest strength.[10]

Meanwhile, the SIA stepped up the pressure on the administration to support its petition, writing letters to, and holding frequent meetings with, administration officials. It hired a public relations firm to expand media coverage and to draw greater public attention. The SIA also strengthened lobbying activities on Capitol Hill by organizing a support group of twenty congressmen, in the process gaining greater access to key administration officials. For example, through meetings with Secretary of State George Shultz arranged by the congressional support group, the SIA was able to convince him of the need to take firm action to respond to the Japanese challenge.[11]

The rising influence of the SIA and individual chip manufacturers ensured a relatively unified American position. The SIA moved early on to overcome possible resistance from other domestic players. In the first place, since the semiconductor industry was composed of firms that produced different types of chips (e.g., DRAMS versus EPROMS) as well as different types of companies (e.g., merchant versus captive producers), the SIA first of all sought to reconcile the different preferences that member companies might have regarding the trade conflict with Japan. The SIA invoked the common objective of gaining greater access to the Japanese market to unite manufacturers of both DRAMS and EPROMS. Captive firms such as IBM, while not particularly supportive of trade actions at the outset, eventually consented to the SIA's position under the organization's persuasion.[12]

More broadly, the SIA did not encounter any obvious domestic opposition in its persuasion efforts. Many American business groups outside of the semiconductor industry (such as the electronics, automobile, and machine tools producers), who were growing increasingly frustrated with continuing trade barriers and were disappointed with the slow progress achieved under trade agreements with Japan, were demanding tough action from the U.S. government to dampen the effects of unfair Japanese competition. For example, representatives of the U.S. electronics industry, who felt that the trade dispute with Japan ought to be given priority in the U.S. trade policy agenda, urged the U.S. government to retaliate against Japan's failure to open up its domestic market and to stop dumping on the world market. The AEA, a trade group representing over thirty-five hundred U.S. companies with $305 billion in global sales, launched a massive publicity campaign followed by lobbying efforts in Washington under the provocative banner "America's future at stake." AEA representatives contended that, as one of the nation's largest manufacturing industries and as an important foundation for the rest of the economy, the electronics industry directly impacted on the U.S. economic and military security. The AEA called for a strategic approach to trade policy that would break down trade barriers in Japan and safeguard the interests of American producers.[13]

In addition, since the AEA represented major semiconductor users who might potentially object to the petition due to the increase in chip prices that could ensue, cooperation from the AEA would have been essential to the success of the Section 301 petition. As a result, the SIA started early on to address the concerns of end users who might be adversely affected by the increases in chip prices in the United States. To compensate for American users, the SIA persuaded U.S. suppliers to agree not to push for additional quotas or floor prices on Japanese products as long as the Japanese were selling their products at prices above the individual firms' cost of production. As the negotiations with the Japanese proceeded, the SIA also engaged in frequent consultations with the AEA. The chairman of the SIA's public policy committee, George Scalise, worked particularly hard to secure AEA's endorsement of the Section 301 petition.[14] Like the U.S. merchant semiconductor firms, many major users of semiconductors had come to believe that the lack of fair market access in Japan would seriously jeopardize the interests of producers and users alike. Firms such as IBM and Hewlett-Packard indicated that they would not resist the semiconductor firms' trade initiatives, thus allowing the SIA to proceed with its 301 petition. Moreover, end users such as the American computer industry both lacked consensus among themselves and wielded far less influence than the semiconductor manufacturers.[15] This enabled the SIA to forge a consensus with the end users. In the end, the AEA produced a letter to USTR supporting the petition.

With Japan's increasing penetration of the American market negatively affecting so many sectors, no other U.S. business groups visibly opposed the SIA's trade initiative. When American negotiators later threatened to impose sanctions on Japan should Japanese firms fail to stop dumping and increase market share for American firms, most of the products on the sanction list were ones (such as electrical devices) that posed a competitive threat to American manufacturers. Since these American producers could benefit from the restrictions on Japanese products in the event that sanction threats failed, they did not have any incentive to resist the sanction threats but rather had reason to egg the SIA on.

If U.S. producers in industries (such as electronics) likely to be affected by trade sanctions were not opposed to the sanction threats, groups not directly affected by the Section 301 action (such as the automobile and machine tools industries) had even fewer reasons to interfere with the SIA's actions. U.S. auto producers, for example, had themselves felt victimized by the influx of more competitively priced, fuel-efficient Japanese auto imports, which drastically reduced American producers' share in their home market. Not surprisingly, they did nothing to obstruct the lobbying efforts of semiconductor producers.

In short, the SIA was able to advance its trade agenda without encountering any major domestic resistance. This unity across industry borders strengthened the credibility of the SIA's rhetoric. It also created irresistible pressure on the Reagan administration to provide trade relief through some form of government action. In the following sections, we will see how, under strong congressional and industry pressure, an administration ideologically committed to free trade veered toward government intervention and managed trade and how U.S. domestic consensus gradually started to elicit a Japanese response.

Reagan Administration Response to the Petition

Unlike in many other trade disputes, sanction threats against Japan won strong support from Reagan administration officials. That the free traders of the United States would resort to government intervention in negotiations with Japan was truly unusual. But the shift toward managed trade was hardly surprising when one took into consideration the magnitude of the threat that unfair Japanese competition posed to the very existence of a critical American industry. As the U.S. semiconductor industry faced the possibility of extinction, American policymakers were becoming increasingly concerned about the impact of Japanese industrial targeting on the ability of U.S. industries to compete effectively in international markets. That the semiconductor industry, one of the most dynamic sectors of the U.S. economy capable of producing state-of-the-art technology, was turning to the government for help not only suggested the seriousness of the problem but also signaled to the government the necessity of forging a close relationship with a critical domestic industry in an era when trade policy was having an increasingly important impact on industrial competitiveness.

For American policymakers, it had become clear that the Japanese government, through industrial targeting, was aiming to obtain comparative advantage in a range of high-technology sectors to ensure the continued international market dominance of the Japanese economy. The prevailing sentiment among administration officials was that the United States could not allow Japan to continue to capture the benefits of open international trade without also bearing the burden of competition in its own market. As Japanese companies were making substantial inroads at the expense of U.S. firms in a number of high-technology industries, including the semiconductor industry, U.S. negotiators felt that the American government could not leave the Japanese threat unchecked and had to come up with a policy response to Japan's protectionist policies.

It is important to note that the semiconductor conflict took place at a time when the gradual erosion of the American economy enhanced the appeal of the "strategic trade" argument among government officials. According to Judith Goldstein, the convergence of a number of factors strengthened the business community's appeal for government intervention: the fact that various domestic laws provided relief from some of the alleged unfair trade practices; the existence of a vocal coalition in Congress increasingly impatient with the disparities between the principle of free trade and persistent unfair foreign trade practices; and the ascendance of strategic trade advocates in the academic community, who argued that failure to adopt protective policies aimed at fostering strategic industries may seriously jeopardize national welfare. These domestic political realities both permitted and justified the shift in government policy away from principled support for free trade toward the managed trade approach.[16]

Recognizing the need to preserve a competitive U.S. industry, administration officials, particularly those in the Commerce Department, had adopted a proactive approach toward the semiconductor trade issue. Starting in the early 1980s, they had sought to exert strong pressure on the Japanese to create a level playing field for U.S. firms. Commerce officials such as Malcolm Baldrige and Clyde Prestowitz, who possessed prior industry knowledge and were fully aware of the depth of the problem, were known for their determination to save this strategic industry. Out of the belief that the industry's decline could have strongly negative implications for the competitiveness of the American economy as a whole, they had been engaged in a series of negotiations with the Japanese and had also taken a number of other measures to prevent the further slide of the semiconductor industry.

Also important in shaping the Reagan administration's policy orientation was congressional Democrats' attack against the Reagan team for its indifference to the ballooning trade deficit with Japan. In particular, the release by the Commerce Department in August 1985 of the United States' overall and bilateral trade deficit statistics for the first six months of the year immediately produced an uproar in Congress, resulting in the introduction of a good number of protectionist bills in Congress targeted specifically at certain priority countries (including Japan) or at certain sectoral issues. At the same time, the idea of reforming the trade system through omnibus trade legislation was gaining currency among a growing number of congressional members. Moreover, with the almost certain passage of the restrictive Jenkins textile bill in the fall, the president was faced with the difficult task of mobilizing enough support in Congress to sustain a presidential veto. Mounting congressional assertiveness on trade issues created an imperative for the White House to take some initiatives in order to preempt congressional challenge to executive authority over trade policy.[17]

Confronted with stepped up pressure from both Congress and industry groups, Reagan administration officials eventually forged a consensus on the need for an aggressive negotiation strategy despite some initial internal strains. To be sure, soon after the Section 301 petition was filed, senior Reagan administration officials came up with different responses. Officials at the USTR and the Commerce Department, seeing a vital American industry on the verge of demise, supported the petition. These agencies were afraid that, by failing to support the semiconductor producers' petition and by allowing the antidumping and unfair trade cases to proceed to final rulings, they would provoke Congress into passing retaliatory trade bills targeted specifically at Japan and supporting other highly protectionist trade legislation such as the Omnibus Trade Bill, which was then under consideration, thereby exacerbating the existing trade environment.[18] Officials at the Central Intelligence Agency (CIA) and the Defense Science Board, due to their concern about the growing dependency of the Defense Department on foreign suppliers, shared this view.

Initially, other departments such as State, Treasury, and the NSC were unwilling to see sanctions being imposed on the Japanese, insisting that problems of the U.S. industry partly resulted from poor management and that the Japanese government had taken some steps to eliminate barriers to semiconductor imports back in the 1970s. That Japan was both a friend and an ally of the United States further contributed to the reluctance of the State Department and the NSC to name it an unfair trader.[19] Agencies such as the Office of Management and Budget (OMB), the Council of Economic Advisors (CEA), and the Justice Department, because of their adherence to the free trade principle, objected even more strongly to the aggressive trade negotiation strategy endorsed by the Commerce Department and the USTR. For these offices, negotiating for a guaranteed market share not only would constitute a violation of GATT rules as well as U.S. and Japanese antitrust laws but would also interfere with the operation of dynamic markets, stifle technological development and innovation, and risk inciting a renewed trade crisis between the two countries.[20]

On the whole, however, the Section 301 petition received a sympathetic hearing from the Reagan administration. For one thing, the semiconductor industry was considered to be a high-technology sector having substantial spillover effects for the rest of the economy as well as important links to the defense industry. Besides having an important impact on competition and trade in the semiconductor industry, government intervention would also profoundly affect the competitive position of a number of related sectors.[21] For another, the SIA's petition "was in line with the administration's emerging stress on opening foreign markets, did not directly advocate closing the U.S. market, and would help mollify congressional critics who wanted a tougher Japan policy."[22] Personal contacts also strengthened the SIA's case at the USTR. Since the SIA's main counsel, Alan Wolff, had worked with both the new USTR, Clayton Yeutter, and his deputy, Michael Smith, these high-level contacts ensured that the petition would be given serious consideration at the USTR.

Thus the initial reservations that the State Department and the NSC had about the petition did not prevent Yeutter from proceeding with investigations of the SIA's charges. Under the lead of the USTR and the Commerce Department, the Reagan administration undertook a series of initiatives, including the establishment of a "strike force" to investigate Japanese dumping activities, in order to deal with unfair trade activities.[23] At this point, a small number of administrative agencies still had different opinions about the strike. At the crucial interagency meeting to consider whether to initiate the dumping case in October 1985, representatives from the NSC and the State Department voiced concerns that the investigation might jeopardize the United States' security relationship with Japan, particularly Japanese support for the Strategic Defense Initiative (SDI).[24] However, in view of the magnitude of the U.S. competitive reversals in the microelectronics market, they did not oppose the recommendation when it came up for a vote. The recommendation was thus approved by the president in December 1985.

As the investigations went under way in early 1986, several developments helped to dispel administration officials' lingering doubts about the threats against Japan. Importantly, the two champions of the U.S. semiconductor industry, AT&T and IBM, whose viability was considered key to the health of the U.S. semiconductor industry, were beginning to call on the government for help. Executives of these companies told Reagan administration officials that, because they had been forced by the decline of their equipment and materials suppliers to channel more resources into semiconductor development and, in the process, were becoming more dependent on the Japanese, it was imperative that the administration intervene in the semiconductor market "for the good of the nation."[25] The plea from these two semiconductor giants fully revealed the extent of the problem and helped administration officials to overcome their remaining doubts about the threats against Japan.

The sense of urgency voiced by these two giants was shared by other semiconductor manufacturers. In a document submitted to the USTR in October 1985, the SIA again presented overwhelming evidence of Japanese firms' collusive behavior, which excluded foreign producers from the Japanese market and undercut America's global competitiveness. The association further condemned the Japanese government for implicitly encouraging such behavior and called on the U.S. government to be an active "advocate of legitimate commercial interests" rather than merely "an impartial adjudicator" of the dispute.[26]

As an important component of its campaign, the semiconductor industry devoted considerable energy to convince the State Department of Japan's disproportionately small market for U.S. chips. In light of substantial and compelling evidence of dumping and of the continued difficulties American firms faced in accessing the Japanese market after repeated liberalization, the State Department and some other agencies that had traditionally come to the defense of Japan reached the conclusion that the Japanese market was effectively closed and that government action was necessary to ensure the survival of a critical industry. That addressing the problem through trade laws was not a viable alternative, as it would likely trigger legislative trade retaliation, increased the attractiveness of a hawkish posture. Moreover, mounting political pressure on Secretary of State Shultz and the state personnel to define American interests in both economic and political-security terms also led the State Department to reconsider its approach toward the trade dispute with Japan.[27] Thus, despite some initial resistance, the State Department and agencies more concerned with national security issues ended up supporting the Commerce Department and the USTR, thereby providing the latter with greater room for maneuver.

With a broad consensus in place, the Commerce Department and the USTR moved ahead with the dumping and market access negotiations. Incessant congressional and industry pressure prodded American negotiators to bargain even more aggressively, in the process forcing more Japanese concessions.[28] On July 30, 1986, the two governments reached the third semiconductor agreement. Formally signed in September, the agreement addressed all major American concerns with respect to both dumping and market access.[29] The Japanese concessions in the area of market access were perhaps most important, as the Japanese government not only committed itself to assisting American companies seeking to increase their sales in Japan and to coordinating the relationship between Japanese users and U.S. suppliers[30] but also, in a confidential side letter to the accord, explicitly undertook to increase foreign makers' share of the Japanese market to a 20 percent target within the five-year term of the agreement.[31] The 20 percent target, if achieved, would effectively double the foreign share of the Japanese market. Overall, the agreement clearly signaled the Japanese government's willingness to improve foreign firms' access to the Japanese market and, as a result, was widely hailed by SIA and government officials.

The 1986 semiconductor trade agreement was unprecedented for American trade policy in many respects. As authors such as Laura Tyson pointed out, not only was it the first time that the United States had threatened trade sanctions on Japan for failing to abide by the terms of a trade agreement, but it was also the first trade agreement the United States entered into in a high-technology, strategic industry aimed at improving market access and regulating trade in both Japan and the global market. In addition to setting the precedent for U.S. demands for "voluntary import expansion" (VIE), the agreement showed that the United States, out of concerns about the possible erosion of American leadership in strategic high-technology industries, was increasingly willing to abandon the principle of free trade in favor of aggressive unilateralism and managed trade.[32] The agreement therefore signified a fundamental change in the U.S. government's approach toward competition in high-technology industries.

Japanese Response to American Pressure

On the Japanese side, the semiconductor industry and the bureaucracy—the Ministry of International Trade and Industry (MITI)—were the major actors involved in the semiconductor dispute. Initially, U.S. pressure had elicited different responses from Japanese semiconductor manufacturers. On the one hand, some semiconductor firms did not mind if the negotiations failed and tariffs had to be imposed on Japan. Indeed, they even considered this outcome to be preferable to an agreement that would allow MITI to reinstate its control over prices and other requirements over the disclosure of propriety manufacturing-cost information. On the other hand, there also were firms that favored making some concessions in order to avoid American retaliation. Many of these firms were exporters of such products as electrical consumer goods that were concerned about the potential effects of U.S. retaliation on their exports to the United States. Thus the position of major firms on the appropriate response to the United States was conflicting, providing some possibility for an agreement.

The key objectives in this dispute—reaching a settlement and avoiding American retaliation—for MITI, the chief bureaucratic actor in this case, coincided with those of the prime minister and leaders of the Liberal Democratic Party (LDP). As Ellis Krauss argues, the institutional interests of MITI in this case contradicted those in the industry in favor of no agreement. In particular, MITI seemed to have an interest in using a trade agreement, with the powers and mechanisms that it would confer to the bureaucracy, to regain control over the semiconductor industry, an industry that was increasingly able to assert its autonomy. Krauss suggests that the fact that MITI had subsequently developed monitoring mechanisms with even broader coverage than the agreement would have warranted was fully consistent with such an interpretation.[33]

While Japanese exporters' preferences for agreement and MITI's interests in using an agreement to enhance its waning domestic power had left open the possibility for concessions, it was also important to notice that heavy-handed American pressure had figured prominently in the calculations of Japanese negotiators, compelling the Japanese to accede to American demands. Prestowitz, for example, reported that the Japanese were particularly concerned that the Americans were seriously considering naming Japan as an unfair trader and that they feared that if they were to get the "unfair trader" label this time, then they might get stuck with it in many other cases.[34] The imposition of sanctions against Japan in particular sensitized Japanese negotiators to the resolve of American industry and government officials to address the semiconductor problem. After the imposition of sanctions, a high MITI official reportedly told Prestowitz that MITI ought to have taken American demands more seriously sooner.[35] Other Japanese officials concluded from their interactions with their counterparts that the United States was indeed bent on punishing Japan for its trade infringements. For example, after his meeting with President Reagan in Washington, Shintaro Abe, leader of the LDP, commented that "there was no concrete indication that would suggest that the sanctions would be lifted" during Prime Minister Nakasone's upcoming visit to the United States and concluded that the political dynamics in Washington militated against any immediate action.[36]

In short, even though it took time for the Japanese to come to terms with American demands, the Japanese eventually realized that all major domestic actors in the United States were behind the threat and that some concessions had to be made to avoid retaliation or to get the Americans to lift it once it was in place. While Japanese negotiators did come up with bargaining tactics designed to minimize their losses during the negotiations, they were clearly aware of the tremendous pressure coming from the United States and had to reluctantly accept basic American demands.

The Imposition of Sanctions and the Effects of the 1986 Semiconductor Trade Agreement

Two years after the signing of the agreement, several semiconductor manufacturers complained that Japanese firms were violating the terms of the dumping agreement. Specifically, they were concerned that not only was Japanese dumping of EPROMS widespread in third-country markets,[37] but U.S. total sales in Japan were not improving either. Repeated Japanese violations of signed agreements presented American negotiators with no other option but to consider the imposition of sanctions. The lack of results after more than six years of negotiation and bargaining led most administration officials, including the president and some agencies with initial reservations, to embrace a more interventionist policy. Thus, in January 1987, the USTR threatened to retaliate with trade sanctions if Japanese firms failed to conform to the terms of the agreement by April 1. Meanwhile, in view of unmistakable evidence of Japanese violations and of the spiraling U.S. trade deficit with Japan, both houses of Congress passed resolutions urging the president to retaliate. The SIA also submitted a recommendation urging retaliation. To shore up U.S. credibility, a sub-cabinet-level interagency committee under the Economic Policy Council (EPC) proposed trade sanctions if the Japanese did not stop third-country dumping and improve market access for American firms. By the end of March, the EPC determined that Japan had violated the 1986 agreement and recommended that the president proceed with trade sanctions.[38]

With Congress's and the industry's unanimous condemnation, the president accepted the EPC recommendation and, on March 27, announced the imposition of 100 percent retaliatory tariffs on $300 million of Japanese electrical devices, including television sets, laptop computers, disk drive units, stereo equipment, electric motors, and other consumer goods.[39] Some of the retaliatory items on the list were ones for which American producers faced Japanese competition or were manufactured by the same corporations that were charged with violating the terms of the agreement (e.g., NEC, Fujitsu, and Hitachi). Since the sanctioned products were manufactured by a large number of American companies at competitive prices, they helped to prevent the large price hikes that otherwise would have occurred if trade between the two countries had been complementary. The choice of these products allowed American manufacturers competing with Japanese products to benefit from the increased prices of Japanese goods, thereby strengthening and broadening the coalition in support of retaliatory measures.[40] The announcement of sanctions suggested that U.S. trade policy had undergone dramatic shifts toward one that explicitly demanded results from Japan. The imposition of sanctions on a major friend and ally reflected both the depth of the trade problem and the perceived threat of the Japanese challenge to American industrial competitiveness.

To what extent did Japan respond to the sustained application of American pressure and comply with the semiconductor agreement? A number of studies suggest that the agreement played an important role in boosting the American (and foreign) share of the Japanese market and successfully stopped Japanese dumping in both the American and third-country markets, even though the Americans had to apply sanctions in order to get Japan to comply with the agreement on third-country dumping. Although the effects of the agreement were not particularly striking in the first few years after its signing, and the U.S. share of the Japanese market did not immediately reach the 20 percent target, the agreement played an important role in halting the sharp decline of America's competitiveness in the semiconductor industry and prevented Japan's monopoly of the global semiconductor market (see figures 5.1–5.3). Had the U.S. government refrained from the managed trade approach after 1985, Japanese producers "would probably have moved from a position of rough parity to virtual dominance."[41] American negotiators subsequently continued to press the Japanese to live up to their commitments and negotiated a new five-year bilateral agreement when the 1986 agreement expired in 1991.[42] Following the signing of the new agreement, unrelenting government and industry pressure succeeded in inducing Japanese companies to comply with an agreement that threatened their interests, as foreign share of the Japanese market reached the 20 percent target in 1992 and 30 percent by 1997. U.S. attempts at negotiating a semiconductor agreement thus produced significant gains that helped to consolidate American industry's position in the global market.

Super 301: Supercomputers, Satellites, and Wood Products

In the 1989–90 Super 301 investigations into Japanese practices in the supercomputer, satellite, and wood products industries, unified domestic support again turned out to be the key to enhanced credibility and effectiveness of U.S. sanction threats, allowing the United States to by and large achieve its negotiation objectives. Not only did American supercomputer, satellite, and wood products producers support the decision to designate Japan an unfair trader under U.S. law, but other key business groups, who felt injured and threatened by Japanese competition in their own industries, also favored threatening Japan with trade sanctions. Moreover, the U.S. executive, having tolerated policies advantaging the Japanese in the past, had by the mid-1980s become increasingly concerned about the effects of Japanese industrial targeting and trade restrictions on America's competitive position in the world economy. Out of concern for America's economic well-being and in response to congressional pressure, the Bush administration decided to resort to a high-profile trade weapon to dampen the effects of Japan's protectionist policies. The competitive nature of the trade relationship between the United States and Japan thus helped to unite major domestic actors. Domestic unity provided U.S. negotiators with added leverage in bilateral negotiations, allowing them to negotiate two trade agreements that yielded substantial benefits to American producers.

Supercomputers

In 1989, the United States initiated a Super 301 investigation into Japanese practices in the supercomputer industry on the grounds that Japanese policies designed to promote indigenous supercomputer production capabilities had excluded American producers such as Cray Research and Control Data Corporation, which were very competitive in world markets, from Japanese public procurements. Supercomputers drew the attention of U.S. negotiators both because of their important role in the most advanced research and development and because

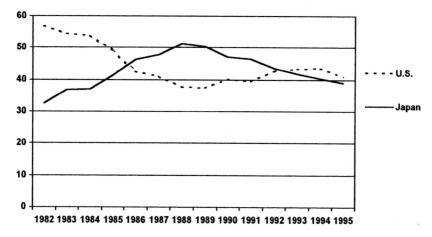

FIGURE 5.1. World semiconductor market, 1982–95 (selected years, in percentage of shares). (Data from Semiconductor Industry Association, available at <http://www.sia-online.org/pre_statistics.cfm>.)

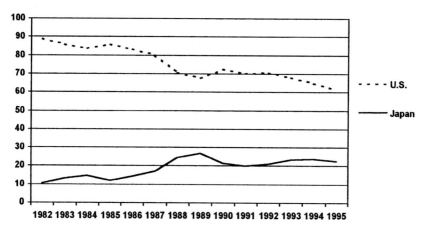

FIGURE 5.2. U.S. semiconductor market, 1982–95 (selected years, in percentage of shares). (Data from Semiconductor Industry Association, available at <http://www.sia-online.org/pre_statistics.cfm>.)

of the substantial government support that was needed for supercomputer development.

Early American attempt to address Japan's discriminatory procurement practices included the low-key Section 305 investigations and the Market-Oriented Sector Specific (MOSS) framework. Both initiatives were designed to tackle government procurement practices that allegedly discriminated against American producers and high dis-

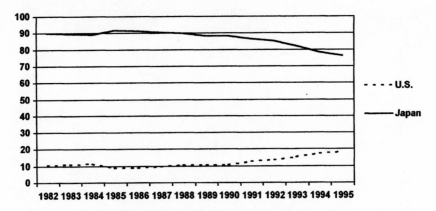

FIGURE 5.3.   Japanese semiconductor market, 1982–95 (selected years, in percentage of shares). (Data from Semiconductor Industry Association, available at
<http://www.sia-online.org/pre_statistics.cfm>.)

counts that Japanese producers offered to government institutions.
These initiatives and subsequent American pressure propelled Japanese authorities to come up with an emergency budget to provide public universities with increased funding for supercomputer procurement
and resulted in the purchase of two American computers by Japanese
public institutions. In August 1987, the negotiators reached a final
agreement on supercomputers that made the public procurement
process in Japan more transparent.[43] However, the agreement fell
short of addressing the discounting problem or establishing specific
performance criteria.[44] It was criticized also for its inability to break up
the preferential links between Japanese suppliers and their customers
in the public sectors or to substantially improve American firms' access
to the Japanese public market by altering the deeply entrenched structure of the Japanese public market.[45] Not surprisingly, U.S. manufacturers complained that they faced continued difficulties selling to public institutions in Japan. Cray Research, in particular, pointed out that
its share of the Japanese market was substantially lower than its share
in other parts of the world.[46] In light of American manufacturers'
difficulties of selling to the Japanese market, both Congress and the
industry urged the USTR to use the leverage provided by Super 301 to
enforce the market access agreement with Japan.

In early 1989, the supercomputer industry, citing the huge disparities
in their market access to Japan and other world markets, called on the

government to address the discrimination they encountered in the Japanese market. The announcement by NEC that it could now produce the world's fastest supercomputer and the exit of Control Data Corporation from the production of large-scale supercomputers in April 1989 heightened the sense of urgency felt by the supercomputer industry. Following the company's demise, Control Data representatives warned that, since supercomputers were important not only as a market in themselves but also as the means to developing other technologies and products, the United States would be in a very disadvantaged position to have to depend on its competitors for real value-added or product differentiation.[47] Other supercomputer manufacturers also felt that the United States would need to take effective measures in order to catch up with the Japanese.

At a congressional hearing, the Institute of Electrical and Electronics Engineers, Inc. (IEEE), an organization devoted to assisting the government and the public with evaluating technological progress and opportunities, alerted the administration to the vulnerability of the U.S. industry to the competitive threats from Japan, arguing that the "Japanese style of competition does present a significant threat to the U.S. high-performance computing industry through its systematic, targeted dominance of successive elements of the high technology 'food chain.'"[48] The organization contended that Japanese government support has been indispensable to Japan's acquisition of indigenous production capabilities. Industrial policy not only helped Japanese firms to break up the American monopoly of the supercomputer market in the early 1980s and to successfully penetrate the American market by the mid-1980s but also created formidable barriers in the Japanese market for U.S.–made supercomputers, which were clearly superior to Japanese machines in terms of both performance and availability of software. Reflecting the concerns of American supercomputer manufacturers, the organization complained that the Japanese did not notify their American counterpart of upcoming procurements, that Japanese producers were given deep discounts, that the Japanese government did not specify performance criteria in the bids, and that, even if they did, the specifications clearly favored Japanese producers.[49] The organization further argued that, since Japanese manufacturers had extensive financial resources and were willing to spend large sums and endure sustained losses to win market share, the United States must take the Japanese threat seriously and adopt new approaches to achieve an acceptable trading relationship with Japan.

Besides securing support from U.S. supercomputer manufacturers, threats to impose sanctions under Super 301 received positive responses from the business community as a whole. Many business groups within the United States felt victimized by unfair trade barriers and by Japan's one-way-street approach to trade, especially because so many of them competed with Japan in the production of a similar range of items. For instance, the AEA, one of the main actors in the semiconductor saga, testified before a congressional trade panel in favor of the Bush administration's decision to brand Japan an unfair trader under the 1988 trade law. Not only did the association have strong grievances against Japan's entrenched trade barriers that excluded foreign competition, including Japanese government procurement policies and preferential purchasing arrangements among Japanese firms, but it was also critical of Japan's restrictive trade practices, which enabled Japanese companies to capture an increasingly large share of the U.S. market and overtake American producers as the leader of technological advance. The AEA pointed to the semiconductor market as an example of a sector in which unfair Japanese trade policies worked to the detriment of the U.S. industry and welcomed the administration's move toward an aggressive negotiation approach with Japan.[50]

Many other business groups likewise supported the results-oriented approach included in the Super 301 provision and pressured the Bush administration to take a hard line in implementing Super 301. In a congressional hearing, the U.S. manufacturing community exhibited a broad willingness to stand by the stance adopted by the Bush administration, which they considered both responsible and pragmatic. The AEA, for example, expressed its satisfaction with the way the USTR dealt with the supercomputer issue. NAM testified that "the administration has done a masterful job" in enforcing American trade law. NAM supported the administration's decision to designate Japan a priority foreign country, indicating that it was concerned about the manufacturing component of the U.S.–Japan economic relationship and the serious Japanese rivalry facing American companies.[51] The U.S. Chamber of Commerce also approved of the sanction threat.[52] In a formal comment to the USTR, dated March 24, 1989, the U.S. Chamber of Commerce provided a list of "priority trade barriers and distortions," charging Japan with "targeting" a wide range of American industries through "administrative guidance, public procurement and restrictive business practices." Japanese officials, the American business organization argued, offered commercial "suggestions" and "advice" to businesses and public organizations over which they had regulatory jurisdiction. The Chamber of Commerce charged that, since the Japanese government possessed "broad authority to provide or deny loans," those official suggestions constituted "implied threats" to deny government benefits or impose new restrictions on businesses that did not accept the advice. The result of these government actions was that Japan imported fewer manufacturers than it would if its markets were as open as those of other developed countries.[53]

The business community's enthusiasm for trade sanctions dovetailed with the Bush administration's determination to pursue a fair trade outcome for the supercomputer industry. The administration's willingness to intervene was rooted in a number of considerations. First, the supercomputer industry was considered strategic because it could yield extremely high profits, produce beneficial spin-offs, and create knowledge that was useful to other sectors of the economy. As supercomputers were widely applied to solving problems involving complicated mathematical calculations such as weather and earthquake modeling, aerospace design, and crash analysis, failure to intervene to ensure the health and size of the industry could have broader implications for the U.S. economy.[54] Second, government action was considered necessary because of the supercomputer industry's importance to national defense and security. Supercomputers played an important role in a number of defense programs, including the Energy Department's nuclear weapons program and NASA's aerospace program. The undercutting of the supercomputer industry could therefore increase U.S. reliance on foreign supplies. Third, opening up the Japanese procurement market was considered essential for American producers to achieve maximum cost competitiveness and profitability and to head off Japanese competition in the United States and in the world market in the long run.[55]

In short, Bush administration officials believed that Japan's closed supercomputer market lent credence to the argument that Tokyo was targeting specific high-tech industries, keeping imports out to shelter domestic industries from the effects of foreign competition. They argued that if Washington waited until Tokyo succeeded in this endeavor to intervene, Japanese buyers would have already established stable relations with Japanese suppliers and, consequently, it would be even more difficult for American producers to gain a foothold in the Japanese market. While the United States had sought to establish a liberal trading order for most of the postwar period, the trade problem with Japan had become so intractable that many administration officials called for a new approach toward Japan. Moreover, in the presence of a large U.S. trade deficit with Japan and with many domestic actors from Silicon Valley to Capitol Hill calling for retaliation against Japan's one-sided trading practices that imperiled U.S. strength in key industrial and technological markets, the Bush administration felt compelled to respond with a more proactive trade policy. Thus, the designation of satellites and supercomputers under the Super 301 framework was perceived as a means for the United States to challenge Japan's strategy of building a protected home market in selected high-tech industries.[56]

To be sure, some administration officials were initially concerned about the political and diplomatic ramifications of citing Japan as an unfair trader. While the USTR and the Commerce Department urged the president to adopt an aggressive approach to enforce U.S. trade law, several other departments had some reservations about taking a harsh stance on trade with Japan. The president's chief economic advisor, Michael Boskin, and budget director Richard Darman, for example, warned that targeting Japan, one of America's most important trading partners and an ally in Asia, could lead to a trade war, damaging broader U.S. interests. Similarly, the State Department, the NSC, and the OMB warned that citing Japan for trade violations could harm the alliance relationship with Japan.

But trade officials and White House political advisers eventually managed to persuade the State Department and other agencies that were reluctant to designate Japan as an unfair trading partner to go along with a tough approach on trade. Their rationale was that, while citing Japan as an unfair trading partner could have some negative impact on relations with Japan in the short run, the action could produce some long-term benefits and indeed could help to strengthen ties between Tokyo and Washington by forcing the two sides to pay closer attention to enduring trade problems. These officials further cautioned about the potential of a direct confrontation with Congress, a scenario that could lead Congress to attempt to reduce executive discretion over the Super 301 process in the future and thereby undermine the Bush team's preference for consultation and compromise with the legislature on major public policy issues.[57]

Because of the trade officials' strong support for Super 301 designation, and in light of the festering trade problem with Japan, agencies such as the State Department and the NSC, which had previously spoken in favor of Japan, eventually consented to President Bush's decision. They came to realize, albeit with some reluctance, that some tough executive action was needed to placate Congress and that economic concerns were gaining prominence in foreign policy. In other words, the threat posed by Japan's unfair competition exerted sufficient pressure on officials concerned about the bilateral security relationship to modify their position on Super 301. With such a broad internal consensus, the Bush administration was able to proceed with the Super 301 designation. In May 1989, USTR Carla Hills announced the decision to designate Japanese government procurement as a priority practice under Super 301.[58] In June the USTR initiated an investigation under Section 302 of the 1988 Trade Act.

U.S. pressure, backed by a strong domestic consensus, soon began to elicit a positive response from the Japanese, as Tokyo agreed to limit academic discounts to government entities to 50 percent, to substantially increase the fiscal 1990 budget for public supercomputer procurement, and to convince the NEC to withdraw from a public bidding.[59] In March 1990, shortly before the scheduled deadline for designating Japan as a priority foreign country, the United States and Japan announced a new agreement on supercomputers that represented a significant improvement over the 1987 agreement.[60] The 1990 agreement was considered a partial success by U.S. supercomputer manufacturers, as it addressed structural barriers to the Japanese market, leading to short-term market-opening outcomes for American producers.[61] Importantly, of the nine public procurements Japan conducted under the supercomputer agreement between 1991 and 1992, Cray Research did not bid on four contracts, lost two to Japanese firms, and won three competitions.[62] According to some analysts, intervention by the Japanese government contributed to the temporary increase in Cray Research's share of the Japanese market.

The long-term effects of the 1990 supercomputer agreement might have been somewhat ambiguous, given the entrenched preferential arrangement between Japanese suppliers and their public-sector customers and the distinctive economic structure created by Japan's long-time promotional policies. Remaining concerns with Japanese practices in the supercomputer industry led the USTR in April 1993 to open a review of the agreement under Section 306 of the 1988 Trade Act that nevertheless found, on a positive note, that American firms had supplied six of the fifteen supercomputers Japan purchased between 1991 and 1992. Although Cray Research had lingering concerns about a number of Japanese public procurement practices and other problems with the implementation of the agreement, the supercomputer agreement had gone a long way toward sustaining the competitiveness of the supercomputer industry. On the whole, it is fair to say that the 1990 agreement yielded significant benefits to American producers.[63]

Satellites

Similar to the supercomputer dispute, the Super 301 case against satellites grew out of Japanese policies of industrial targeting in high-technology that allegedly denied American firms the benefits of a free market. In an attempt to reduce technological reliance on the United States, the Japanese government actively intervened in the market to promote an autonomous space industry. As part of this promotional strategy, the National Space Development Agency of Japan (NASDA) maintained tight control over market access by channeling all government satellite procurement to Japanese firms, prohibited the procurement of all kinds of satellites, and banned the procurements of Japan's telecommunications giant, NTT, despite the lower price and superior quality of foreign satellites.[64] Due to these policies, Japanese content in communications satellites increased from 24 percent in 1977 to 80 percent in 1988 and local content in broadcast satellites grew from 14 to 83 percent during the same period of time.[65]

But while the aforementioned policies contributed to the rapid development of an autonomous space industry, they also became a prominent source of trade frictions with the United States. Following the announcement of the "Long-Range Vision on Space Development" in 1983, which forbade procurement of foreign satellites, U.S. negotiators on various occasions expressed their concerns about Japanese government discrimination against U.S. aerospace firms.[66] While Tokyo made some concessions,[67] these gestures ultimately failed to placate American negotiators, who pointed out that Japan continued to ban government agencies from purchasing foreign satellites and that it was targeting space industries for commercial development.[68] These grievances led the Bush administration to consider designating Japan as a priority country under Super 301 in 1989.

The Bush administration provided the crucial impetus for the satellite designation. Because prior American pressure had already opened up a private market in Japan in favor of American firms, and aware that challenging Japan's strong commitment to space development would most likely lead to a political conflict, American officials might well have chosen to use bilateral discussions and private diplomacy to persuade Japan to further liberalize its public market. Nevertheless, the incoming Bush team eventually decided to invoke threats of sanctions under the Super 301 provisions of the Omnibus Trade and Competitiveness Act of 1988 for fear that Japan would use its closed domestic market as a strategic base to catch up to, and to eventually surpass, the United States in this strategically important high-technology industry.

As Michael Mastanduno points out, concerns about the possible erosion of the competitive edge of the U.S. space industry vis-à-vis Japan figured prominently in the Bush administration's decision to designate satellites as a Super 301 target. By the late 1980s and early 1990s, many observers had reached a consensus about the long-term threat that the Japanese government's promotional policies posed to the U.S. lead in the space industry. Through its active collaboration with Japanese firms and its support for research and development, the Japanese government effectively executed policies of industrial targeting, creating a captive government market that allowed its firms to reduce costs and diffuse technology. As Japan had pursued similar strategies in other sectors such as semiconductors, consumer electronics, fiber optics, and aircraft, there was a widespread fear in the United States that satellites could be one of the key industries in which Japan aimed for world leadership. To forestall the loss of market share and to prevent Japan from achieving greater gains than the United States, the Bush administration turned to Super 301 in an effort to preempt Japan's ascent in space development.[69] That Japanese barriers to satellite purchases were fairly transparent and constituted a clear violation of the rules of free trade provided greater justifications for government intervention. In addition, targeting satellites could also complement and reinforce American efforts to eliminate trade barriers in the multilateral negotiations in the Uruguay Round.[70]

Because of these considerations, the Bush administration was able to achieve remarkable cohesion on the satellite issue. The trade agencies, notably the USTR and the Commerce Department, strongly favored using threats of trade sanctions to protect the long-term economic interests of the United States and to enhance the credibility of the executive in the eyes of the Congress. The leading proponents of the satellite designation within the U.S. administration—Deputy USTR Lynn Williams, Assistant USTR Joseph Massey, and Commerce Undersecretary J. Michael Farren—saw the designation as providing an excellent opportunity to preempt Japanese targeting of an important high-technology industry in which the United States enjoyed a strong competitive advantage.[71] In a testimony before the Senate Commerce Committee in October 1989, Farren contended that

To the Japanese, satellites are not only an industry unto itself but a window on the whole space industry for the 21st century. Japan is emerging as a key participant in the global aerospace industry, a result of deliberate decisions aimed at establishing a world-class Japanese aerospace industry. Japan is looking to aerospace as a source for its future growth and prosperity. . . . Our National Aeronautics and Space Administration has pointed out in a recent report that space is a new economic frontier, and that space commerce is directly linked to American competitiveness in the global market.[72]

Similarly, Deputy USTR Williams argued that, in line with Congress's intent in drafting the Super 301 provision, eliminating the barriers in the satellite industry "would have the potential to increase U.S. exports significantly, both directly and by setting a precedent."[73] Trade officials thus recommended to the president that he take a hard line against Japan on the satellite issue. Although the State Department, with its characteristic concerns about the overall U.S.–Japan relationship, and agencies such as the CEA and the OMB, which were traditionally less receptive to the use of Section 301 provisions in general, were initially opposed to the designation of satellites, they eventually gave approval to the president's decision to go ahead because they too had concluded that Japanese government restrictions were so pervasive as to pose a real threat to America's industrial competitiveness.[74]

In short, as in the semiconductor case, the perceived threat of Japanese industrial targeting to the viability of the U.S. space industry was so grave that it overcame the considerations of the traditionalists and the defense personnel for political relations and free trade. In the end, even though the more free trade–inclined OMB and CEA insisted that they could not accept a managed trade approach specifying a certain market share for American firms, they came out in favor of using Super 301 to target Japanese government's discriminatory procurement practices. This internal consensus reinforced Congress's insistence on a tough line against Japan, substantially enhancing the credibility of the American action.

In this case, U.S. satellite makers reportedly refrained from openly pushing for Super 301 designation for fear of losing potential sales or leasing opportunities to the Japanese private sector and government institutions. Satellite manufacturers also seemed to be concerned about upsetting Japan's Ministry of Post and Telecommunications (MPT), which oversaw the licensing of satellite imports.[75] However, they obviously did not interfere with a decision promising substantially improved access to the Japanese market. Furthermore, the decision received overwhelming support from broad sectors of the U.S. manufacturing community that were also severely injured by Japanese competition. At a key Senate trade panel, groups representing a wide range of U.S. manufacturers asserted that the complex web of relationships among Japanese manufacturers, distributors, and retailers posed significant barriers to American producers' efforts to penetrate the Japanese market. NAM once again opined that Japan's distribution of goods and corporate buying policies presented one of the biggest obstacles to U.S.–Japan trade and welcomed the action on satellites, which in their view effectively signaled the government's determination to open up the Japanese market.

A large number of business organizations, all of which faced intense Japanese competition, favored invoking sanction threats under the Section 301 provisions of the Omnibus Trade and Competitiveness Act of 1988 to obtain a fair trade outcome. For example, the AEA, an organization representing over thirty-five hundred firms in the U.S. electronics industry, including components, computers, telecommunications, and software, went on record supporting administrative actions to designate Japan an unfair trader. The AEA argued that Japan's exclusionary business practices created tremendous barriers and distortions to U.S. electronics trade and referred to the United States' steadily deteriorating deficit with Japan in the electronics sector and the substantial damage done by Japan to various segments of the U.S. electronics industry as evidence of the structural problems in the U.S.–Japan relationship. The association urged the administration to resort to aggressive negotiation strategies to address such outright hindrances to free trade.[76]

NAM and the Chamber of Commerce expressed their strong support for Super 301 designation at the same hearing. NAM, which contributed 85 percent of employment in manufacturing and 80 percent of America's manufactured goods, asserted that it was essential that the administration name Japan a priority foreign country under Super 301 as a response to the profound Japanese challenge to U.S. international competitiveness. NAM representatives argued that Japan's ban on government procurement of satellites raised important questions for U.S. trade policy. They contended that, if Japan's "indigenous development objectives" could take precedence over free trade in particular products, then the United States needed to clearly identify its own "indigenous development objectives" and to ask how these development objectives could be affected by Japan's trade policies. Accordingly, NAM urged American negotiators to forcefully enforce existing trade law in order to defend U.S. trade interests.[77] Similarly, the U.S. Chamber of Commerce, taking into account the magnitude of trade distortions with Japan, called on the Bush administration to "more aggressively assert its legitimate trade rights," arguing that the aggressive use of Super 301 procedures would "benefit not only U.S. exporters but also exporters from third nations," as well as manufacturers and consumers "in restricted markets who pay higher prices as a result of trade restrictions."[78]

Also testifying at the hearing were the Automotive Parts and Accessories Association (APAA) and the United Automobile, Aerospace, and Agricultural Implement Workers of America (UAW). The APAA, representing various segments of the U.S. auto parts industry, welcomed the administration's more aggressive approach to redress the trade balance with Japan. Because APAA member firms, which were capable of producing competitively priced, world-class automotive parts, have long been afflicted with the deluge of exports of cars and parts from Japan, they supported Super 301 retaliatory action, which could demonstrate U.S. resolve and set the tone for future trade negotiations. In a similar fashion, the UAW recommended Super 301 trade retaliation, arguing that it would be the ideal forum in which to address the trade imbalance. The UAW contended that the United States should use the threat of retaliation to stimulate negotiations about other structural impediments to trade and that downplaying the Super 301 process would continue to expose American workers and manufacturers to the pernicious effects of Japan's unfair trading practices.[79]

Such overwhelming industry support lent greater credence to the Bush administration's threat of retaliation, clearly revealing Washington's willingness to apply existing trade remedies to force Japan to the negotiation table for serious, comprehensive negotiations. Enormous U.S. pressure left Japan with little room for maneuver but to gradually come to terms with U.S. demands. The satellite agreement that came into being in June 1990 reflected the extent to which sanction threats succeeded in opening Japan's highly protected domestic satellite market.

The 1990 satellite agreement was the product of several rounds of strenuous negotiations. The negotiations were rocky at times because the United States "basically was telling Japan that it had to give up its quest to become a competitor in the world market for applications satellite."[80] In other words, American demands were perceived as an outright encroachment upon Japan's sovereign right to develop an autonomous space program with noncommercial objectives. Nevertheless, Tokyo eventually agreed to such sweeping changes, even though many Japanese observers considered the 1990 agreement as representing "a complete acceptance of American demands."[81] Specifically, Tokyo undertook in the agreement to open its communications satellite and all other commercial satellite markets to U.S. imports. The loss of the communications satellite program was judged to be likely to entail substantial short-term costs for Japanese producers and to accentuate the difficulties Japan faced in developing key satellite technologies, as Japan was forced to cancel its plans for the development of the fourth series of its communications satellite program (CS-4). That the agreement applied not only to communications satellites but also to all commercial satellites led the MPT to the gloomy conclusion that the "severity of the settlement was beyond expectations."[82]

The 1990 agreement yielded substantial gains for American producers, as American companies such as Loral Space Systems, Hughes Space and Communications Group, and GE successively won bids to supply satellites to Japanese firms. Moreover, the agreement not only denied Japanese firms the benefit of a captive government market but also helped to maintain and strengthen American communications satellite manufacturers' dominant position in the global market.[83] American satellite producers were thus by and large satisfied with such an agreement that represented substantial fulfillment of U.S. negotiation objectives. In the words of a Hughes Space and Communications Group representative, the agreement "open[ed] a few more opportunities," and, more important, it prevented Japan from sheltering "an infant industry that might eventually become a world-class competitor."[84]

Forest Products

Initiated at the same time as the supercomputer and satellite cases, the Super 301 designation against Japanese practices in forest products was intended to address the entrenched market barriers in the Japanese wood products market. Throughout the negotiations, U.S. industry and government officials sought to pressure Japan not only to reduce its formidable array of nontariff, technical barriers (such as building codes, product standards, and testing and certification procedures), which clearly violated GATT principles, but also to significantly lower tariffs and to scale back subsidies to the Japanese forest industry.[85] The dispute was the natural culmination of a decade-long U.S. attempt to address the multitude of tariff and nontariff barriers that resulted in a highly skewed pattern of trade and consumption in the Japanese wood products market and turned out to be one of the largest Super 301 cases ever initiated against Japan.

Throughout the course of the negotiations, American producers repeatedly raised concerns that Japanese trade in forest products was strongly biased in favor of raw materials at the expense of finished products.[86] A related complaint was that, as the world's largest importer of wood products and as the largest wood products market for the United States, Japan nevertheless had the lowest per capita consumption of wood products among industrialized nations. American forest products manufacturers readily pointed out that, since Japanese production of fabricated products was highly inefficient, it would be difficult to explain Japan's unusually high ratio of raw to finished imports of wood products without taking into account the excessive trade and regulatory impediments that existed in Japan.[87] They further contended that, without those market barriers, American producers would likely accrue between $1 and $2 billion in additional income each year through increased exports of processed wood products to Japan.[88]

Of all the alleged market impediments, Japan's tariff structure in particular drew the ire of the U.S. industry, as Japanese tariff rates on wood products were positively related to the level of fabrication, resulting in a situation in which Japanese producers needed to pay no or little tariffs on the imported raw material but could nevertheless rest assured that they could easily survive foreign competition through the rents generated by high tariff levels on finished products. In other words, this escalation of tariffs led to rather high "effective rates of protection."[89] U.S. industry representatives maintained that, should Japan dismantle its tariff barriers, many inefficient Japanese producers would be forced to exit the industry, leading to substantially increased demands for imports. Besides tariff barriers, American industry representatives were concerned about a number of nontariff barriers, including discriminatory product standards, overly restrictive building and fire codes, government subsidies for inefficient producers, and lax enforcement of antimonopoly laws against cartels.[90]

Beginning in the late 1970s, American government officials began efforts to address wood products market barriers via both informal negotiations and more formal negotiation forums such as the MOSS talks. The MOSS talks in particular produced a bilateral "consensus" in January 1986 with some modest Japanese concessions.[91] Yet while American producers viewed these Japanese commitments as representing an important step in peeling off the onionlike layers of the Japanese market, they demanded even further progress along these lines.

Thus, in early 1989, both the forest products industry and Congress applied strong pressure on the Bush administration to designate Japanese wood product market barriers a priority under Super 301. As the association representing the vast majority of the forest products industry, the National Forest Products Association (NFPA) naturally became the leading advocate of the Super 301 case. NFPA's call for Super 301 designation was strengthened by strong support for government action stemming from congressional members of both parties. As representatives of major wood-exporting states, Senators Robert Packwood (R-OR) and Max Baucus (D-MT) were the two most vocal advocates of Super 301 designation in Congress. The two senators were able to bring their influence over trade policy, derived from their appointments as chairmen of congressional committees with primary jurisdiction over trade policy, to bear on the decision-making process. In April, Senator Packwood commissioned a study entitled *The Japanese Solid Wood Products Market.* The report, which provided a comprehensive survey of market impediments in the Japanese wood products market, concluded that it would be nearly impossible for the United States to liberalize the Japanese market short of a major trade initiative.[92] On May 16, Senators Baucus and Packwood sent a letter, signed by thirteen senators, to President Bush making a strong plea for a Super 301 case. Pointing to the substantial additional gains in exports that American producers would be able to capture through trade liberalization, the letter stated that the Super 301 procedures were designed precisely to deal with entrenched market barriers such as those posed by the Japanese practices in forest products. Throughout the rest of the negotiations, congressional members of both parties continually raised the specter of congressionally mandated retaliation should the Japanese fail to concede to the basic American demands. The Senate Finance Committee under Senator Baucus was particularly irate at Japan's neglect of American demands, threatening to initiate legislative bills authorizing retaliation against Japan if bilateral negotiations failed to produce any progress.[93]

Under strong industry and congressional pressure, USTR Carla Hills announced the decision to designate Japanese technical barriers on wood products that clearly discriminated against American exports and violated the GATT Agreement on Technical Barriers to Trade (also known as the Standards Code) as a Super 301 priority. Since the designation applied only to technical barriers to the exclusion of more transparent tariffs, which were a clear priority of the U.S. industry, it immediately spurred forest products manufacturers into active opposition. At a congressional hearing held in June 1989, the NFPA made a strong case for extending the Super 301 designation to cover nontariff as well as tariff barriers. The NFPA sought to persuade the USTR that, since Japan maintained multiple layers of protection for the forest industry and that peeling away one layer might simply expose another layer of protection, it was important for the United States to incorporate a multitude of objectives in the negotiations and to simultaneously tackle tariff and nontariff barriers in Japan.[94]

To back up its argument, the NFPA reiterated its concerns about Japan's high effective rates of protection on finished products as well as excessively restrictive and discriminatory Japanese building codes and Japanese product standards based primarily on design instead of performance criteria. The association strongly criticized the Japanese government's decision to offer more than $1 billion in subsidies to the domestic industry, a move that served to offset the liberalization effects of concessions offered during the MOSS talks. The NFPA once again brought to the attention of government administrators a variety of structural impediments maintained by the Japanese, ranging from anticompetitive practices, customs misclassification, land use and housing policies, to the distribution system.[95] Previously member firms within the NFPA held divergent views about what constituted the best strategy to liberalize the Japanese wood products markets due to the different export market niches they held. By the time of the Section 301 designation NFPA member firms had successfully reconciled their differences to reach a consensus on the desired negotiation tactics. Also supportive of the NFPA's negotiation position were other smaller industry associations or special organizations formed specifically in response to the Japanese challenge in the wood products sector such as the American Plywood Association, the Wood Products Sector Advisory Committee, and the Alliance for Wood Products Exports. Individual wood products manufacturers such as Georgia-Pacific Corp and Contact Lumber, which shared the same concerns about the Japanese forest products market as the NFPA, have similarly rendered active support for the NFPA's push for Super 301 designation.[96]

Other U.S. businesses outside of the forest products industry viewed the designation positively as well. As mentioned earlier, out of their frustration with Japan's increased penetration of the American market and with the difficulty of gaining a greater foothold in the Japanese market, many U.S. businesses regarded the Super 301 process as a key component of a more systematic approach to addressing foreign trade barriers. For instance, with many of its member companies severely battered by Japanese competition, NAM contended that the Super 301 process should put Japanese companies squarely in the spotlight. NAM representatives, believing that Japanese competition undercut America's position in the world market, stated that failure to name Japan "would have rendered the concept of priorities all but meaningless."[97] The AEA, with a steadily rising trade deficit with Japan reaching $20 billion a year in the mid-1980s, listed a wide array of structural barriers that American electronics manufacturers faced in the Japanese market. While the AEA supported the administration's decision not to target structural impediments in the Japanese electronics market as Super 301 priorities, it urged the government to use other means at its disposal to address structural problems and promised to work closely with the government to reach satisfactory solutions to the existing Super 301 issues.[98] The Chamber of Commerce, reflecting the interests of many of its member firms, urged the administration to name systemic, transsectoral trade barriers in an attempt to assert America's legitimate trade interests.

Congressional support for the results-oriented approach further bolstered the business community's advocacy for a tough bargaining approach. In particular, there existed a prevailing sentiment in Congress that the Super 301 process had been underutilized by past administrations and that failure by the executive branch to narrow the huge trade deficit with Japan would leave Congress with no choice but to implement independent legislative action. Constant congressional threat to legislate an even tighter and less discretionary Super 301 process also forced the Bush administration to accommodate business interests in the decision-making process to avoid an open confrontation with the legislature and to preserve the administration's overall preference for consultation and compromise with the Congress on major public policy issues.

With the U.S. industry and Congress running out of patience, the USTR accelerated the negotiations with the Japanese. An important tactic American negotiators adopted toward this end was to try to cultivate the support of Japanese ministries less hostile to American demands. For instance, they devoted considerable effort garnering support from the Ministry of Agriculture, Forestry, and Fisheries (MAFF) for relaxing the restrictions in the building code to allow the greater use of both domestic- and foreign-made wood products in construction projects. U.S. negotiators also pitched their message to Japanese consumers about the substantial benefits they would derive from less expensive and more aesthetic wood housing.[99]

Highly leveraged government and industry pressure prodded the Japanese into action. On April 25, 1990, shortly before the April 30 deadline that the USTR set for announcing Super 301 priorities for 1990, USTR Carla Hills announced the decision to refrain from naming Japan a priority country for a second time. While Japan's desire to avoid being named a priority country for a second time loomed large in its decision to capitulate at the last minute, unrelenting industry and congressional pressure made it all the more palpable that the United States would carry through with its threats to impose sanctions against Japan. The prospect of a trade war that would seriously hurt Japanese manufactured products as well as the U.S.–Japan economic and political relationship induced Tokyo to reluctantly concede to American demands.

In the agreement that the U.S. negotiators reached with Tokyo, Japan agreed to liberalize tariffs, in particular tariffs on high value-added products; address customs misclassifications; and reduce the tariffs on certain laminated products, concessions estimated to increase American exports by $100 million.[100] With respect to nontariff barriers, Japan agreed to accept the performance-based criteria in its building code, to acknowledge the validity of foreign test data in specifying new product standards, to increase the transparency and speed of the certification process, and to modify the building and fire codes so as to increase the volume of wood products being used in construction projects. In addition to these concessions, the agreement addressed the subsidy issue and provided for the establishment of technical committees both to monitor implementation and to facilitate dispute resolution.[101]

The 1990 agreement went a long way toward addressing industry and congressional concerns about Japanese market barriers in the forest products industry. U.S. industry officials were particularly pleased with the agreement's potential to substantially increase American exports to the Japanese market. Since the agreement provided a clearly spelled-out schedule of implementation, established special committees responsible for monitoring implementation, and created built-in mechanisms for coordinating building standards, industry and congressional reactions to the agreement were overwhelmingly positive. NFPA and the forest products' Industry Sectoral Advisory Committee viewed the agreement as representing a major step in America's drawn-out effort to pry open the Japanese market, even though they reminded the government to back up such actions with both multilateral and bilateral measures to tackle nontariff barriers in the Japanese market.[102] Senators Baucus and Packwood also applauded the agreement for opening markets and creating jobs for the United States. By the mid-1990s, American exports to Japan had picked up momentum. Consequently, American government and industry officials remained satisfied with the implementation of the agreement, although further improvements were considered necessary in several issue areas. Overall, they were cautiously optimistic about the potential for increased U.S. forest product exports to Japan.

Japanese Reactions to the Super 301 Process

In each of the Super 301 investigations described in this chapter, sustained and unified American pressure clearly conveyed to the Japanese the message that sanctions would be forthcoming if no concessions were made, thus forcing Japanese government and industry officials to reevaluate their optimal course of action and to make concessions that would have been unthinkable in the absence of foreign pressure.

Such dynamics were clearly to be found in each of the three sets of Super 301 negotiations. According to an insider's account of the negotiations over wood products, there existed "an unmistakable impression" among Japanese negotiators that American demands on the wood products issue enjoyed strong support from American log lobbyists.[103] An interview with a Japanese official involved in the talks suggested that the Japanese did take the American threat seriously in light of the overwhelming support for sanctions coming from both Capitol Hill and diverse quarters of the American business community. Given the impression that all U.S. actors were firmly behind the USTR, the Japanese consequently felt that it was important to relieve the pressure from the United States by resorting to a "crisis management" approach.[104] The negotiations over semiconductors and supercomputers illustrate this dynamic. As an official of the Ministry of Foreign Affairs involved in the negotiations put it:

> There was a consensus among the Japanese ministries to do the agreement to protect the U.S.-Japan relationship. SII [the Structural Impediments Initiative talks] did not go well. Trade figures were bad. It was crisis management. The United States threatened retaliation under Super 301; without that threat, many ministries would not have gone along.[105]

Thus, while the Japanese were concerned about the damage that the trade row could inflict on the U.S.–Japan relationship and were trying their best to contain the fallout of the dispute, their perception of a "crisis" stemmed above all from the strong U.S. resolve. Absent the perception that American trade officials both were intent on carrying out the threat and had the necessary domestic support to do so, the Japanese most probably would not have been able to reach a consensus to "do the agreement" in order to diffuse the crisis.

Moreover, as the Super 301 case coincided with the launching of the Structural Impediments Initiative (SII), Japanese politicians concentrated most of their attention on the SII talks, thus allowing the bureaucrats to take charge of the Super 301 negotiations. In addition, the media in Japan did not provide sufficient coverage of the Super 301 negotiations. That neither the politicians nor the media was actively involved in the Super 301 talks might have prevented the active use of strategies such as "participation expansion" to expand the "possible zone of agreement" for the Americans. Aware that some concessions had to be made, the Japanese strategy revolved around maximizing chances of obtaining a better deal by aggressively proposing alternatives and by taking a forthright position on most issues in order to establish better rapport with American negotiators.[106] But these strategies were clearly based on the assumption that some concessions had to be made and so represented only tactical moves by the Japanese to temper the repercussions of concessions.

Conclusion

The semiconductor and Super 301 cases described in this chapter demonstrate very similar political dynamics. In all four cases, not only were domestic interest groups united in support of sanction threats, but also the Reagan and Bush administrations showed a greater willingness to put aside the principle of free trade and to intervene on behalf of American industry. Such strong domestic pressure meant that the Japanese could no longer be secure in the knowledge that the United States would tolerate Japan's protectionist policies in the name of preserving the alliance relationship. Domestic unity strengthened the credibility of American threats, inducing Tokyo to make costly concessions that would threaten the interests of its powerful firms.

As we can see from table 5.1—which lists the position and impact of the exporters, import-competing interests, and import-users involved in each of these trade disputes—American threats to impose sanctions on Japan enjoyed wide support from domestic interest groups. Most importantly, American semiconductor, supercomputer, satellite, and

TABLE 5.1. Profiles of Main Actors Involved in U.S.– Japan Semiconductor and Super 301 Cases

	Companies and Associations	Position	Impact
Semiconductors			
Directly Affected Exporters	Semiconductor Industry Association (representing firms such as AT&T, IBM, and TI)	Contended that Japan's protectionist and promotional policies denied American firms "fair and equitable market opportunities." Called on the USTR to use trade sanctions to correct Japan's predatory export behavior and market barriers and to stop Japanese dumping in the American market.	Were instrumental in initiating the dispute; their aggressive pursuit policy demands increased the pressure U.S. policymakers felt to act.
Exporters Not Directly Affected	Many of these are also import-competing interests, including producers of electronics, automobiles, and machine tools; American Electronics Association	Frustrated with entrenched market access barriers in Japan; supported trade sanctions that would help U.S. firms pry open the Japanese market.	Helped bolster the SIA demand.
Import-Competing Interests	Producers of electronics, automobiles, machine tools; American Electronics Association	Faced stiff Japanese competition and demanded tough action from the U.S. government to dampen the effects of unfair Japanese competition.	Their support for tough negotiation tactics reinforced the appeal of semiconductor manufacturers' policy demands.
Import-Using Interests	Semiconductor users represented by AEA	Concerned about the price increases that trade sanctions would produce.	Eventually endorsed semiconductor producers' position.
Supercomputers, Satellites, and Forest Products			
Directly Affected Exporters	Supercomputer manufacturers (Cray Research, Control Data Corporation); Institute of Electrical and Electronics Engineers; satellite manufac-	Charged that Japan, through policies designed to cushion domestic industries from foreign competition, excluded U.S. producers from the	Were instrumental in initiating the dispute; their aggressive pursuit of policy demands increased the pressure U.S. policymakers felt to act.

(continued)

TABLE 5.1.—*Continued*

	Companies or Associations	Position	Impact
	turers; forest products industry (represented by the National Forest Products Association, American Plywood Association, and Alliance for Wood Products Exports, etc.)	Japanese market; advocated trade sanctions to open the Japanese public sector market.	Bolstered the case for Section 301 action.
Exporters Not Directly Affected	Many of these were also import-competing interests; representative organizations included the American Electronics Association, National Association of Manufacturers; U.S. Chamber of Commerce; Automotive Parts and Accessories Association	Faced considerable market access barriers in Japan; supported aggressive market opening policies in general.	
Import-Competing Interests	American Electronics Association (representing over 3,500 firms in U.S. electronics industry, including components, computers, telecommunications, and software); National Association of Manufacturers; U.S. Chamber of Commerce; Automotive Parts and Accessories Association; United Automobile, Aerospace and Agricultural Implement Workers of America	Urged American negotiators to forcefully enforce existing trade law in order to defend legitimate U.S. trade interests and to correct the effects of unfair Japanese competition.	Their support for tough negotiation tactics reinforced the appeal of super-computer and satellite manufacturers' policy demands.
Import-Using Interests	—	—	—

forest product producers, whose competitiveness was directly threatened by Japanese government's protectionist and promotional policies, were not the only groups in the United States supporting the aggressive use of threat tactics. Since trade relations between the United States and Japan are highly competitive, a large number of American manufacturers faced strong Japanese competition. Not surprisingly, the majority of business groups, even including those targeted by Japanese counterretaliations, welcomed sanction threats that would allow them to enjoy the benefits of a protected home market and to gain an advantage over their Japanese competitors. In all four cases, unity among interest groups contrasts sharply with divergent business interests in the China cases, contributing to the success of threat tactics.

Equally important to the enhanced effectiveness of American threats was the consensus the two government institutions were able to forge with regard to the appropriate trade strategy toward Japan. Faced with Congress's call for tough action to deal with the spiraling U.S. trade deficit with Japan and with Japan's anticompetitive trade policies, the U.S. executive could have, as in the China cases, chosen to emphasize America's broader security and economic interests. However, that Japan's unfair trade practices in a wide assortment of industries posed a grave threat to the survival of competitive U.S. firms precluded dispute resolution through broad discussions. Cases involving high-tech industries in particular had created a strong incentive for the free traders of the United States to adopt a managed trade policy to counter the effects of foreign government's protectionist policies.[107] In such cases, consideration for America's long-run economic well-being and security needs convinced both the Reagan and Bush administrations, including even those administrative agencies more sensitive to U.S.–Japan political relations, of the need to adopt more aggressive tactics in dealing with Japan. With threats being ratified by both government institutions, Japan became aware of the U.S. determination to obtain a fair trade outcome and, as a result, offered concessions that would have been unimaginable in the absence of American pressure.

Unity among domestic constituents and the two government branches thus substantially increased the credibility of American threats, facilitating the achievement of American objectives in these negotiations. American pressure halted Japan's competitive onslaught in the semiconductor case and helped U.S. supercomputer, satellite, and forest products manufacturers secure a foothold in the Japanese public-sector market. The gains to American producers were by no means inconsequential.

CHAPTER 6

U.S.–China "Trade Peace": Intellectual Property Rights and Textiles

Through detailed case studies, the previous two chapters suggest that U.S. sanction threats are far more credible and effective against countries such as Japan than against countries such as China. Trade structure has been found to be an important determinant of the degree to which interest groups in the United States can maintain a cohesive position with respect to the sanction threats, and hence the variations in threat effectiveness. Since trade structure exerts such a significant impact on the level of domestic unity, which is also a key factor affecting the likelihood that two parties will escalate their dispute to the level of a trade war, it seems reasonable for us to expect a positive causal linkage between trade structure and the probability of trade war. A highly competitive trade relationship is likely to enhance domestic support for sanction threats, thereby producing stronger pressure for brinkmanship and for trade war, while a complementary trade structure is likely to produce the reverse. The importance of this variable is likely to overwhelm the potential effects of regime type that might lead one to expect a "democratic peace" in trade relations.

The two chapters that follow extend the insights gleaned from analyses of the variable degree of threat effectiveness to examine the pattern of trade war, contrasting the overall pattern of "trade peace" between the United States and China, which involves bargaining between a democratic and an authoritarian state, with the frequent occurrences of trade wars between the United States and its democratic trading partners such as Europe and Canada. This comparison will reveal that despite the absence of democratic norms of peaceful dispute resolution that presumably mute conflict, trade disputes between the United States and China have rarely resulted in mutual retaliation. Without disaggregating the impact of trade structure on domestic politics in the sender of threats, it would have been difficult for us to explain this paradoxical outcome.

U.S.–China Trade Disputes over Intellectual Property Rights

Besides the highly acrimonious MFN debate described earlier, the United States and China have also been involved in endless bickering over Beijing's protection of American intellectual property products. Since the early 1990s, the United States has three times (in 1991, 1995, and 1996) threatened to impose sanctions on China under Section 301 should Beijing fail to provide more adequate protection for U.S. intellectual property–related products. However, on all three occasions the United States managed to reach last-minute agreements with Beijing and withdrew the threatened sanctions against Chinese exports.

The extended negotiations between the United States and China over IPR issues lend support to my key contentions. First, as in the other U.S.–China trade disputes described in chapter 4, U.S. pressure on China to provide more adequate protection for American IPR products was at best only partially successful. Although, in the negotiations prior to 1996, Beijing agreed to U.S. demands on paper and also made genuine efforts to transform its legal regime for IPR protection, it repeatedly failed to follow through with enforcement. As a result, the United States had to constantly prod the Chinese to change their policies and practices. In the 1996 negotiations, the United States even withdrew the threat of trade sanctions with no concessions from China. On the whole, it seems fair to say that the United States has by and large failed to achieve its objective of obtaining improved IPR protection for American industries, a pattern that is consistent with the findings reported in chapter 4 about the futility of American pressure against China.

The history of the IPR disputes provides further support to my hypothesis about the relationship between trade structure and the probability of trade war. Despite Washington's deep frustration with China's poor record of IPR protection and its repeated vows to cut off Chinese imports, it has consistently failed to make good on its threats. In each of the negotiation episodes, the United States issued sanction threats, raising the specter of a trade war, but always backed down at the last minute and accepted Chinese promises of enhanced enforcement effort. Why was the United States willing to withdraw sanction threats and to resolve the IPR dispute cooperatively with China? Why did China's repeated failure to abide by the terms of signed agreements fail to provoke a more confrontational U.S. response?

As in previous chapters, the following analysis will draw on the two-level game approach and explain the ability of the United States to stave off trade war with China in these cases by illustrating the divisions in U.S. domestic politics created by trade structure. Some reports and analyses seem to portray the intellectual property industries and the U.S. government as being more united in pursuit of fair trade outcomes in the IPR case than in the MFN case.[1] But while domestic opposition to sanction threats seemed less vociferous in the IPR dispute, it did constrain domestic interests in the United States from emerging as a homogenous entity. As in the MFN debate, highly complementary trade relations between the two countries generated considerable opposition to escalation, in the process undermining the USTR's negotiation position. In this case, American industries adversely affected by Chinese piracy were the only group calling for trade sanctions against China. Instead, much of the U.S. manufacturing community, including both importers of labor-intensive products made in China and exporters seeking expanded market access in China in areas less affected by IPR issues, opposed attempts to close the American market to the Chinese. Furthermore, although certain administrative agencies (notably the USTR) seemed to favor protecting the IPR industries from unfair trade practices, heavy pressure from import-using groups interested in maintaining a steady flow of Chinese imports and other groups with a vested interest in the China trade compromised the USTR's position. The belief that efforts aimed at seeking trade relief for particular industries should not jeopardize American economic and political interests in China also prevented the executive branch from pursuing an overly aggressive trade strategy.

Thus, similar to the MFN debate, the dispute over intellectual property protection exposed a fundamental dilemma in U.S. trade policy toward China: the United States could not punish China for its misbehavior without negatively affecting many powerful and active domestic constituents. The following analysis of the political forces that actively shaped the IPR debate further illustrates this point.

Explaining the U.S.–China IPR "Trade Peace"

As in the MFN debate, American threats to impose sanctions against China for its inadequate protection for IPR products suffered from factional conflict at the domestic level. Due to the complementary trade structure between the United States and China, the prospect of a trade war created a deep schism between American industries that focused on intellectual property as a means of expanding their share in the Chinese market, on the one hand, and American importers and retailers, on the other. Resistance by those industries insisting on market access alone without any concerns about the existing intellectual property practice in China further enhanced the power of the opposition. Although associations of copyright producers such as the Recording Industry Association of America (RIAA), the International Intellectual Property Alliance (IIPA), the Business Software Association (BSA), the Motion Picture Association of America (MPA), and the International Federation of the Phonographic Industry (IFPI) consistently pushed for trade sanctions, they were counterbalanced by other segments of the business community, most notably importers of labor-intensive products who have developed a high degree of reliance on the Chinese market. In this case, manufacturing industries such as automobile and aircraft manufacturers also advocated a position that conflicted with that of the copyright industry. The absence of solid support from the business community not only weakened the hands of the U.S. negotiation team but also impeded American negotiators' ability to escalate the dispute.

U.S. copyright industries were the most forceful proponents of Special 301 investigations against China. For instance, the IIPA, an umbrella organization representing filmmakers, book publishers, the music industry, and computer software manufacturers, pointed to the estimated $1 billion in annual losses the American industries incurred due to Chinese piracy[2] and strongly advocated placing China on the list of priority countries that would face retaliatory actions by the United States. The IFPI, irritated by China's illegal production and export of fake CDs, which had displaced legitimate U.S. CD exports in world markets, also backed the use of Section 301 in order to halt China's illegal CD exports.

Computer software industries were similarly concerned about rampant software piracy in China. The BSA, a trade group in Washington representing large U.S. software publishers, together with organizations such as the Computer and Communications Industry Association, voiced support for strong government action designed to secure adequate IPR protection in China that would provide U.S. firms with genuine access to the huge China market.[3]

But although the motion picture, recording, and software industries waged an impressive lobbying campaign to punish China for its IPR infringement, a greater number of industries protested the United States' threatened sanctions that would likely jeopardize one of their most important sources of imports. Since the Chinese products targeted for sanctions included almost all of the most popular U.S. imports from China, such as textiles, toys, and electronics, American importers and retailers that have become dependent on the Chinese market opposed the imposition of sanctions. In public hearings in January 1995, major U.S. importers, retailers, and manufacturers complained that they would be unfairly harmed by Washington's use of punitive tariffs to force China to crack down on infringement of IPR. For example, the National Retail Federation, representing the largest U.S. retail chains, argued that Washington's pursuit of fair trade should not come at the expense of American consumers.[4] The federation asserted that the punitive tariffs, if imposed, would force U.S. retailers to raise prices to make up for the costs of purchasing the goods from elsewhere. Because some Chinese goods were so inexpensive or they were unavailable elsewhere, U.S. retailers would have to bear the costs of stiff tariffs in order to replenish their stocks. For example, it was estimated that the sanctions, if carried out, would raise the price of children's bicycles by 8 to 29 percent, increase the price of telephone answering machines by 31 percent, and nearly double the cost of a Chinese-made phone.[5] The federation further complained that textiles and apparel had been targeted "for the benefit of Hollywood moguls" and that sanctions would add $100 million to America's clothing bill.

The American Association of Exporters and Importers agreed that USTR Mickey Kantor's proposed sanctions would negatively affect various U.S. business interests, including retailers. The association warned that it would be difficult to reverse trade retaliation once it was in place and urged Washington to give Beijing more time to develop an effective system for IPR protection.[6] In a similar vein, the International Mass Retail Association argued that, since the punitive tariffs targeted kitchenware, lighting supplies, sporting goods, and consumer electronics products, for which China was a major supplier, the threatened sanctions, if implemented, would inflict severe pains on U.S. retailers.[7]

Besides the retailing community, American toy makers actively opposed the sanction threats. Toy manufacturers, who sourced most of their products from China, contended that the proposed trade sanctions would negatively affect the U.S. toy industry. The Toy Manufacturers of America asserted that, since virtually the entire toy industry was based in China, it would be very difficult to replace toy imports from China. Because Chinese toy production accounted for half of the world's total and Chinese toy exports to the United States reached $5.4 billion in 1995, toy makers remained apprehensive that sanctions would invite Chinese retaliation and would shut off America's toy imports from that country.[8]

U.S. footwear manufacturers were concerned about the effects of retaliatory measures as well. Since China was the top supplier of footwear imports to the United States, shoe manufacturers had been campaigning to make sure that footwear would not be included in the U.S. hit list. A group of shoe manufacturers submitted a letter to the White House warning that higher tariffs on footwear imported from China would lead to a steep price hike for U.S. consumers.

In addition, some small U.S. businesses that were targeted by the USTR's sanction threats in 1995 felt particularly vulnerable to a trade war. A number of U.S. greeting card companies and bicycle importers, for example, pleaded with U.S. negotiators to withdraw the sanction threats, arguing that businesses dependent on low-cost imports from China would be hit hardest by a trade war and would have to bear the brunt of the costs of retaliation if it occurred.[9]

Even the electronics industry itself was split about the USTR's choice of trade weapons. Some members of the Electronic Industries Association (EIA) were high-technology companies whose products were being pirated in China. But other companies such as AT&T regularly imported consumer electronics products such as telephone-answering machines, microphones, and magnetic-tape recorders from China. The EIA, therefore, complained that such products had been "disproportionately, if not unfairly, targeted for retaliation," warning that a sharp increase in duties on these products could cause "severe business disruption" and negatively affect U.S. production.[10]

The American Forest and Paper Association and power tool manufacturers, which made extensive use of raw materials from China, voiced similar concerns. For example, power tool manufacturers argued that the threatened sanctions would sharply raise the price of one of its most important inputs, thus giving Japanese competitors an advantage in world markets. Importers of electronic gear from China also opposed sanctions. They argued that, while they could find alternative sources to build their products, the cost would be significant and would have a major impact on U.S. sales.

To be sure, sanction threats did generate some mixed feedbacks from the American textile and apparel industry. While textile and apparel retailers opposed sanction threats, textile manufacturers and labor unions, which were less tied to Chinese production, took the opposite position. On the one hand, some locally based companies that relied heavily on imports from China to fill out their lines pointed out that, since China is the United States' largest source of apparel imports, followed by Hong Kong, the threatened sanctions would lead to higher prices and to scarcity of some goods. Although apparel manufacturers were not the primary victims of China's widespread IPR violations, they expressed fear that the escalation of hostilities would have a very negative effect on U.S.–China textile trade. According to the American Apparel Manufacturers Association, the United States imported $3.5 billion of clothing made in China, or roughly 10 percent of all imported apparel. Certain items could be found only in China. Silk distributors, for example, were almost 100 percent dependent on China. These groups, therefore, argued that the implementation of trade sanctions against Beijing for its failure to protect American copyrights and trademarks would have devastated "hundreds of small American companies and thousands of workers."[11] The National Apparel and Textile Association commented that the association had no interest in waging a battle with China over IPR.[12] The U.S. Association of Importers of Textiles and Apparel also voiced concerns that the threat would be very disruptive to people doing business in China and would make life more uncertain for importers. The association urged the administration to look more carefully at the impact of trade sanctions on the American manufacturing, retailing, and consuming community when making its final decisions.[13]

On the other hand, however, another segment of the American textile industry, which was less dependent on Chinese imports, supported retaliation. Trade groups such as the American Textile Manufacturers Institute and the California Fashion Association, whose members' products competed with cheap Chinese goods to which the punitive tariffs would be applied, welcomed the action that could help them boost their sales by forcing price increases on imports.[14] Textile manufacturers in the American South, including those in key electoral states, have been hurt by imported goods produced in low-income countries. As potential beneficiaries of the threatened sanctions, they adopted a position in favor of the aggressive bargaining strategy.[15]

But, despite textile manufacturers' support for threats to impose sanctions against China, the U.S.–China copyright dispute exposed a fundamental dilemma for U.S. trade relations with China. While the United States would like to have ensured more adequate protection for

American IPR through aggressive market-opening actions, it also was not willing to expose the labor-intensive manufacturing sectors to the effects of countersanctions. Moreover, due to the high level of trade complementarity between the United States and China, there was a particularly large constituency reluctant to see sanctions imposed on China. This import-using constituency's active opposition to sanction threats did not help the U.S. position. It only served to diminish the credibility of American threats in the eyes of the Chinese.

Opposition from American exporters and investors further eroded the American credibility. The three largest automobile manufacturers, for example, were strongly opposed to any measures that would upset the U.S.–China trade relationship. They were worried that sanctions, if carried out, would curtail their investments in joint ventures in the short run and would reduce their access to a potentially lucrative market in the long run. Ford Motor Company, one of the auto manufacturers with extensive investments in China, urged the administration to undertake high-level negotiations with China to find a solution to piracy that would avert sanctions.[16] Similarly, GM, which was negotiating an investment project worth $2 billion in an automobile manufacturing venture in China, expressed the concern that a trade war might jeopardize both current and future investments.[17] The big three auto manufacturers, which feared that they could be frozen out of one of the highest potential markets in the world, thus became outspoken opponents of sanction threats in the IPR dispute.

Aerospace companies, whose main concern was capturing a bigger share of the Chinese aerospace market, which now ranks third behind the United States and Japan, also did not want to see sanctions imposed on China. Aerospace giants with heavy investments in China, such as Boeing, were concerned that they might become the target of counterretaliation in a trade row. These companies argued that, in the event that sanctions were carried out, China could easily turn to competitive European companies, causing a major setback to their own attempt to gain a greater share of the Chinese market. With access to the China market at stake, the aerospace companies vigorously opposed the Clinton administration's sanction threats.[18]

More generally, executives of major U.S. industries expressed concern that the administration's tough approach over Chinese piracy could lead to a wider trade conflict and endanger their ability to compete in the vast Chinese market, especially in view of the Chinese government's threat to suspend U.S. investment projects in China. The U.S.–China Business Council, an organization of chief executives from one hundred of the nation's largest companies, warned the administration that it should not allow differences with Beijing over piracy to poison the broader political and economic relationship between the two countries. Since most American companies saw China as one of their most promising foreign markets, they were worried that a trade confrontation with China would yield market share to European and Japanese competitors. Many company executives argued that imposing sanctions on China could backfire by making it harder for the United States to use its economic influence to bring about commercial, social, and political change in that country.[19] The prevailing view was that in fighting for Hollywood and Silicon Valley the United States would be putting the U.S.–China commercial relationship in jeopardy for a narrow and limited segment of U.S. business in China.

States and regions with heavy trade with China were likewise leery of the sanction threats. In 1992, when the United States threatened to impose sanctions for China's IPR infringement, the Washington State China Relations Council, representing more than one hundred companies in the Northwest that export to China, wrote a letter to USTR Carla Hills warning that "punitive measures imposed by the U.S. government and subsequent Chinese counter-retaliation would cost American companies hundreds of dollars in one fell swoop."[20] The council stated that American companies would emerge as the major victim of trade retaliation, as the Chinese would not find it too difficult to replace exports from Washington State with products from other countries. The council urged American negotiators to reach a compromise settlement with the Chinese through negotiations.

As in the MFN debate, therefore, the Clinton administration was learning that it could not punish China for its misbehavior without encountering opposition from other segments of the business community. Highly mixed feedback from American companies and business associations weakened the position of USTR Mickey Kantor, making it more difficult for him to convince Chinese authorities of the U.S. determination to carry out the threat if China failed to satisfy U.S. demands. Acting on the assumption that the USTR himself was reluctant to impose sanctions, the Chinese delayed most negotiations until the last moment. With the deadline approaching but no agreement in sight, the USTR was placed in the disadvantageous position of having to find a quick solution to the dispute. Having no other alternatives, he had to accept Chinese guarantees of better IPR enforcement.

In terms of the policy preferences of the executive, it seems that the USTR initiated the Special 301 investigations out of a genuine concern about the harm that rampant piracy in China caused to American business interests. At first glance it appears that the administration adopted a sufficiently tough stance on the IPR issue in order to protect American jobs and economic interests. But a more careful analysis would suggest that the White House did not really want to see a trade war with China and that it threatened sanctions on IPR in part to defuse the broader movement in Congress to terminate China's preferential trading status. Indeed, as the negotiations over IPR unfolded, the administration came under strong pressure from large segments of the business community to soften its position. Broader economic and strategic concerns also constrained the administration from adopting an overly punitive measure. Hence, despite its tough rhetoric, the White House had strong incentives to avoid confrontation with China.

In the first place, as various domestic constituencies raised their complaints about trade barriers and other anticompetitive actions they faced in China in the Special 301 petition process, the homogeneity of the U.S. negotiation position was sharply reduced. The increase in the number of interested parties with different views placed a larger set of constraints on the principal negotiators of the United States. The executive was forced to find a compromise deal that could be ratified by all the major constituents involved in the dispute. Unwilling to expose importers and users of labor-intensive manufacturing products made in China to the effects of countersanctions or to see exporters lose out to Japanese and European competitors in the China market, the Clinton administration had to put together a package deal that would advance the agendas of all the groups without satisfying any one completely. The outcome of the IPR negotiations reflected such a package deal: the United States refrained from carrying out the threatened sanctions, much to the relief of the import-using interests in the United States, and China modified its copyright laws, partly satisfying the copyright industries. In each round of the IPR negotiations, the United States obtained concessions from China not large enough to fully satisfy the copyright industries but sufficient to show Congress and the general public that progress was being made and to avoid imposing sanctions.[21]

Considerations for the overall U.S.–China relationship complicated the decision-making process. For example, after the USTR threatened to impose sanctions on China in 1996, a number of Clinton administration officials expressed concern that the imposition of trade sanctions on China could jeopardize other vital U.S. interests. In particular, the State Department, a vocal advocate of a "soft line" toward the

Chinese throughout the IPR dispute, argued that a trade war with China would endanger important U.S. interests such as the security of Taiwan, the termination of the sale of Chinese missile and nuclear weapons technology to Pakistan and the Middle East, and the improvement of China's human rights record.[22] Administration officials were concerned that trade sanctions would merely reinforce Chinese intransigence. Since U.S.–China trade was becoming more important, they were wary of having that relationship disrupted.[23]

Thus, while Chinese piracy of American intellectual property products posed a threat to legitimate American interests, the White House did not consider it worthwhile to compromise broader American economic and strategic interests over a single trade dispute. In the process of addressing different constituency demands, the American negotiating team refrained from carrying out trade sanctions against China and ended up with incomplete solutions to the main problem—better copyright enforcement in China.

Chinese Perceptions

Despite the substantial pressure exerted by American negotiators on the IPR issue, Beijing held out against the American demands in part because it was cognizant of its bargaining leverage vis-à-vis the Americans. On the one hand, as the Chinese learned from media reports and congressional hearings about importers' staunch opposition to sanction threats, they became less apprehensive that the United States would actually impose sanctions and more confident that a trade war would inflict significant damage on both American importing and exporting interests. For example, when the United States threatened to impose import tariffs worth $1.08 billion against Chinese production in 1995, MOFTEC minister Wu Yi responded, "There is nothing terrible [about this threat]. . . . China can simply turn elsewhere. . . . There are countless markets abroad for Chinese products. This is nothing that we cannot deal with." Referring to other partners' willingness to fill any void resulting from the possible disruption in U.S.–China trade, Wu Yi stated even further that "Other countries are happier about this."[24] During the 1996 piracy dispute, Wu Yi again proclaimed that, in the event that the United States imposed sanctions, China would not "be the only victim" and that the Americans "would also have to suffer."[25]

On the other hand, well aware of the importance of the China market for American exports and investments, Chinese negotiators regularly threatened American companies such as AT&T, Boeing, and Chrysler as well as the Midwestern farmers with lost sales and investment if U.S. demands for IPR protection became too stringent. As Zhou Shijian, of China's International Trade Research Institute, explained, "The United States could gain nothing from retaliation" because by imposing sanctions "the United States is risking losing an emerging new market for both U.S. products and capital."[26]

The general perception in Beijing was that the U.S. industry was far more divided than what American negotiators portrayed and that Hollywood and Microsoft could be pitted both against importers eager to maintain their steady supply of labor-intensive products from China and against investors and exporters (such as Boeing, Ford, and GM) wanting to maintain expanded access to the Chinese market. These divisions in American industry were both real and palpable. They help to explain why Beijing's position seemed to stiffen a bit more with each annual cycle of American threats and counterthreats. Indeed, with each Sino-American trade row, the Chinese were becoming increasingly adept in their counterretaliation threats. In 1996, when Washington issued threats of sanctions valued at $2 billion, followed swiftly by Beijing's vows to counterretaliate, Beijing's official newspaper, the *China Daily,* boasted that China's sanctions would be of higher value than the U.S. list because they would affect U.S. imports as well as U.S. investment in China.[27] Confident that the United States would not go so far as to actually implement the threats due to conflicting domestic interests, Beijing was less than enthusiastic in complying with American demands.

Summary

In several rounds of U.S.–China IPR negotiations, U.S. negotiators repeatedly refrained from carrying out the threatened sanctions due to highly contradictory domestic pressure. The IPR negotiations revealed to American negotiators that trade sanctions were essentially a double-edged sword that could not be imposed on Chinese producers without also inflicting pains on this side of the Pacific. The negative repercussions of the sanctions would include increased duties on some U.S. importers, higher prices for consumers, and shortages of goods that could not be easily replaced. Even importers that could find alternative sources of supply would likely face higher prices for those goods. As diverse U.S. business interests voiced their opposition to the sanctions, they not only diminished the credibility of American threats but also reduced the cohesiveness and persuasiveness of the IPR lobby and constrained U.S. negotiators from carrying through the threatened sanctions. In this sense, divided domestic politics created by complementary trade relations proved to be a key factor mitigating the propensity for trade war between the United States and China. In the U.S.–China textile and apparel disputes described in the next section, trade complementarity again spurred textile and apparel importers and retailers into active opposition, reducing the chances for a full-scale textile trade war between the two countries.

The U.S.–China Textile Wrangle

An Overview of U.S.–China Textile and Apparel Trade Disputes

Textiles have been a frequent source of friction in U.S.–China trade since the early 1980s, when the reorientation of China's development strategy away from autarky in favor of the development of labor-intensive, light-manufacturing sectors began to stimulate the rapid growth of China's textile industry. The resulting surge in Chinese textile and apparel exports caused considerable disruption to American manufacturers, resulting in charges that Beijing resorted to unfair and often illegal measures to evade U.S. textile quota restrictions. Although in September 1980 the two sides managed to enter into a formal bilateral textile agreement in which the United States relaxed some quota restrictions, the agreement did not appease Chinese manufacturers, who continued to complain about what they perceived as overly stringent U.S. quota restrictions. Chinese producers' search for export expansion subsequently led to a surge in China's exports of textile products not covered by the agreement.[28] Thus, beginning in 1982, American textile manufacturers pressured the U.S. government to undertake investigations of China's export practices and to strictly enforce U.S. trade laws if Chinese textile manufacturers were found to have violated the agreement. When Beijing refused to accept the 1 percent cap American negotiators sought to place on the growth rate of a greater number of Chinese textile exports, Washington in January 1983 unilaterally imposed rules increasing the number of Chinese textile product categories subject to quantitative restrictions to thirty-two and reducing China's total quota allowances by 16–45 percent, inviting Chinese retaliation against American agricultural products.[29] China did not withdraw these retaliatory measures until July 1983, when the second textile trade agreement went into effect.[30]

Throughout the rest of the 1980s, U.S. textile trade policy toward China became increasingly protectionist. What became particularly frustrating to American officials was China's inability to comply fully with the terms of the bilateral textile agreement, as Chinese textile producers increasingly adopted illegal means, such as forging fraudulent country-of-origin certificates, to bypass U.S. quota restrictions. As illegal transshipment of Chinese textile products via third countries became the focus of U.S.–China textile disputes in the 1990s, the United States has several times (in 1991, 1994, and 1996) threatened to cut back China's textile quotas in retaliation against continued Chinese transshipment of textiles and apparel. However, U.S.–China textile disputes have become less confrontational over time. In each round of negotiations, Beijing protested the U.S. action with its own retaliatory threat but nevertheless backed off right before the threatened deadline with the signing of a new textile agreement in which both sides made compromises. The only exception took place in 1994, when the United States carried through with threats to impose unilateral quota restrictions on Chinese textile exports in retaliation against continued Chinese transshipment of textiles and apparel via Hong Kong.

However, even though the United States did adopt unilateral quota restrictions in the 1994 textile dispute, it is important to note that this measure was primarily intended to correct Chinese practices that clearly violated U.S. trade law. Unlike other U.S.–China cases described in chapter 4 that concerned U.S. exports to the Chinese market, the textile dispute mainly involved U.S. imports from China. In such import-related cases, protectionist forces have generally played a more important role in the policy process. Moreover, the textile restrictions against China took place against the backdrop of tightened U.S. textile import policies from other developing countries in general. Nor did U.S. trade restrictions invite Chinese retaliation. Therefore, the relatively less tranquil history of U.S.–China textile dispute as compared to other trade confrontations between the two countries may need to be viewed in relation to the issue dimension.

Nevertheless, even though they concerned an import-related issue and so were more susceptible to protectionist pressure, the textile trade disputes created divisions among domestic groups in the United States. Although American textile manufacturers had a strong interest in restricting Chinese textile exports to the American market, American importers and retailers of textile and apparel products lined up against

the sanction threats. As in other U.S.–China cases, the active opposition of the import-using constituency muted incentives for confrontation. This pattern of domestic interest alignment was easily discernable
in the late 1980s and 1990s, after China established its position as
America's largest supplier of textiles and apparel. During this period,
opposition from textile importers and retailers undercut the effectiveness of textile manufacturers' efforts to obtain trade relief. In the early
1980s, U.S. importers, as they had in the textile wrangle in the subsequent decade, also voiced opposition to the threatened sanctions.
However, since Chinese textile exports had not yet achieved the prominence they later attained, U.S. import-using interests were far less powerful and active and hence did not prevent the U.S. government from
responding to the powerful, protection-seeking manufacturing interests. The following sections will compare the earlier U.S.–China textile
dispute with the negotiations that unfolded in the 1990s, highlighting
the importance of a strong import lobby in ameliorating protectionist
pressure.

Textile and Apparel Trade Dispute: The Early 1980s

American textile and apparel manufacturers started to press the government to restrict textile imports through various bilateral and multilateral arrangements as early as the 1960s. As textile trade between the
United States and China expanded rapidly after the conclusion of the
first bilateral textile treaty, threatening the dominance of U.S. textile
manufacturers in the domestic market,[31] it drew the immediate attention of American textile producers. Textile and apparel manufacturers
were concerned that, as the fastest-growing exporter to the United
States, ranking only behind Hong Kong, South Korea, and Taiwan,
China's huge export capacity would disturb the existing market balance. As a result, they increasingly sought consultations with China to
maintain orderly trade.

In August 1982, U.S. textile producers submitted two petitions to
the Commerce Department and the USITC, charging Chinese companies with dumping in the U.S. market and seeking penalty duties on
Chinese-made fabrics. The textile industry clearly hoped that the trade
complaint would send a clear message to the administration about the
growing Chinese threat to the U.S. industry. In both cases, Chinese
producers were found to have dumped in the American market. In
October 1982, under intense pressure from both textile and apparel
producers, American negotiators sought to reduce China's textile

export growth in negotiations with Beijing. By the end of 1982, frustrated with the slow progress of bilateral negotiations for a new textile agreement to replace the 1980 treaty, U.S. chief negotiator Peter Murphy threatened to impose unilateral quota reductions against imported Chinese textile products.

Textile producers' attempt to tighten import restrictions on China met with strong resistance from importers of textiles and apparel from the very beginning. In November 1982, textile and apparel importers filed a suit with the United States Court of International Trade against the government's stringent import control program, claiming that the restrictive measures against textile imports, often taken without valid finding of market disruption, had frequently forced importers and retailers to pay higher prices, to face delays and embargoes of goods, and to deal with alternative, less reliable suppliers.[32] While the suit was directed at the government's tight import control policy in general, it specifically challenged the U.S. textile policy toward China.

The Reagan administration, despite its ostensibly free trade rhetoric, insisted on maintaining tight controls on textile imports. One of the key objectives of the Reagan team's textile policy was to peg overall textile imports to the United States from low-cost suppliers to the growth of the domestic market, pursuant to the guidelines of the Multifiber Agreement. But Washington's target of a 1.5 percent annual growth rate, which was far below the 6 percent growth rate called for by Beijing, exacerbated the difficulties of reaching an agreement. In January 1983, when talks failed to reach a successful conclusion, the United States announced the decision to impose unilateral quotas on Chinese textile imports. China reacted to the U.S. restrictions by immediately suspending imports of cotton, synthetic fibers, and soybeans from the United States, items that were among the most important U.S. exports to China.

The outbreak of a U.S.–China "trade war" over textiles presents an anomaly to the overall pattern of "trade peace" between nations with complementary trade relations posited in chapter 3 but is explicable in terms of the United States' overall textile trade policy and of the lower level of China's textile exports to the United States in the early 1980s. In the first place, it should be noted that, while the executive branch of the U.S. government had been traditionally a key advocate of liberal international trade policy, it had afforded special protection to the textile and apparel industry on several occasions to satisfy the large domestic constituency represented by the industry. Although the textile and apparel industry had suffered long-term structural decline and was facing major difficulties in remaining competitive in global markets, it was able to provide critical support in presidential elections because of its size and concentration in key regions. Domestic pressure, reflecting the combination of industrial alliance strength and the degree of institutional access, had in the past forced U.S. policymakers to provide trade relief to textile and apparel manufacturers despite their professed ideological inclination toward free trade.[33]

The Reagan administration, in spite of its endorsement of free trade principles, was not insulated from protectionist pressures. Previous studies of American trade policy found that, in part due to its institutional setup, the Reagan administration had developed a pattern of embracing free trade in principle but tightening protection in practice. Between 1981 and 1984, the Reagan administration in several cases failed to mobilize countervailing interests against the protectionist forces in the early stages of the industry's trade-relief campaign, thus allowing the powerful textile manufacturing interests to define the issue.[34]

In the textile trade dispute with China in the early 1980s, the powerful and organized protection-seeking textile manufacturers enjoyed an advantage over importers and retailers, who were driven by prospects of direct economic losses to oppose the protectionist forces. Since Chinese low-cost exports at that time had not penetrated the U.S. market as extensively as they had by the 1990s, sanction threats did not mobilize as wide a segment of the U.S. importing and retailing community into active and effective opposition. An early study of the relative strengths of the pro- and anti-protection forces in the 1983 textiles case found that the anti-protection potential of importers and retailers, measured by the employment figures of these directly affected sectors, was merely 21 percent of the proprotection potential of textile and apparel manufacturers.[35] As the first group to begin working on textile trade policy toward China, the textile lobby was able to derive significant benefit from the policy process. As a result, resistance by importers and retailers of textiles and apparels, which were not yet organized at this time, did not undermine the ability of textile manufacturers to achieve their political objectives.

Developments in 1983 did nothing to dispel the tension in U.S.–China textile trade disputes. In March 1983, as the United States and China resumed negotiations toward a new textile agreement, textile producers launched a more intensive lobbying effort against liberalizing textile trade with China. In the same month, the International Ladies Garment Workers Union initiated a "spring offensive" against garment imports, calling on Congress to reduce the share of garment imports in the domestic market by 41 percent.[36] Textile producers also released reports emphasizing the need for protection in order to sustain their international competitiveness.

Retailers, meanwhile, protested textile producers' demand for import restrictions. Uncertain about clothing supplies, retailers claimed that the Reagan administration's tight import restrictions would raise retail prices of inexpensive clothing by nearly 20 percent. They argued that the unilateral quotas on Chinese textile imports violated the Multifiber Agreement's provisions regarding quotas for textile-exporting countries. The retail industry further charged that the restrictions constituted "unprecedented . . . protectionist actions" very disruptive to the entire import and retail trade.[37]

Consumers and farm interests entered the debate on the side of importing and retailing interests. Consumer groups complained to their representatives that it would be difficult for a large number of low-income families to find affordable clothing in the absence of inexpensive products from abroad. Agricultural groups, having already suffered more than $500 million in lost sales by mid-1983 because of Chinese retaliation, also started to press the executive to negotiate new quota levels with China. Agricultural producers brought in Senator Robert Dole from Kansas to counter Congressmen Jesse Helms and Strom Thurmond, two major textile industry champions. As a result of these conflicting domestic pressures, the Reagan administration reached an agreement on new quota levels with China in August 1983, allowing Chinese textile exports to increase by 3 percent a year rather than the 1.5 percent originally demanded by the United States.[38] China withdrew the restrictions on American agricultural products shortly after the conclusion of the agreement. The issue was thus reached to the satisfaction of American agricultural interests but left U.S. textile and apparel producers disgruntled. Industry organizations such as the American Fiber, Textile, and Apparel Coalition and the Federation of Apparel Manufacturers reacted particularly strongly against the agreement and the large cumulative increase of Chinese textile imports that it would generate by 1987.[39]

Unwilling to accept the terms of the new agreement, textile manufacturers started another round of concentrated lobbying effort in September 1983. In a surprise move, the ATMI, the International Ladies Garment Workers Union, and the Amalgamated Clothing and Textile Workers Union submitted a petition to the Commerce Department charging that the Chinese government's subsidization of textile and apparel export production had caused substantial material injury to the domestic industry and was actionable under U.S. countervailing duty (CVD) law. The textile manufacturers contended that the Chinese government, by allowing its export-oriented enterprises to enjoy a more favorable exchange rate than the official exchange rate, in effect subsidized its textile exports. They pointed to a number of other Chinese policies such as preferential access to raw materials, foreign-exchange loans, and preferential tax policies as additional evidence of government subsidization. The textile manufacturers argued that, since the U.S. government in the past had levied CVDs against government subsidies by other countries, the Chinese case should be adjudicated according to these precedents.[40] The petition was significant because it was the first time that U.S. textile manufacturers had invoked the CVD statute against exports from nonmarket economies.

Divergent views about the wisdom of applying the CVD law against China were expressed at a public hearing in November 1983. American importers and retailers of Chinese textile and apparel products were the major actors opposing the application of CVD law to a nonmarket economy such as China. Large textile retailers that depended on apparel imports from China, represented by the American Association of Exporters and Importers (AAEI), strongly objected to the textile manufacturers' position. By the early 1980s, China was already the world's largest textile producer and the fourth-largest exporter of textiles and clothing to the United States. Due to the competitive prices of Chinese exports, most major U.S. department stores and specialty stores carried products made in China. Some retailers even had clothing produced in China to their specifications. Swelling Chinese exports, therefore, drove them into action.

Importers and retailers argued that unlike antidumping laws, which contained specific language with regard to application to nonmarket economies, the CVD statute did not incorporate such provisions. Moreover, conceptual and measurement problems would exacerbate the difficulties involved in the application of law. The countervailing duties, if implemented, would also have substantially raised merchandise costs. Applying the CVD law to Chinese textile exports, the importers concluded, would be neither a realistic nor a feasible option. Large retailers such as Sears, Kmart, and J.C. Penney, all members of AAEI, contended that the proposed quota restrictions would disrupt merchandise delivery schedules and increase the price they would have to pay for Chinese products. In addition, they pointed out that, since the data upon which the U.S. quota system depended were obsolete, the import restrictions the U.S. government was trying to negotiate was not entirely reasonable.[41] Also, the Retail Industry Trade Action Coalition (RITAC), another major opponent of the textile lobby representing such companies as Sears and J.C. Penney, went on the offensive, arguing that current import restrictions would cost domestic consumers up to $27 billion a year.

A number of other groups relying on inexpensive Chinese products supported the contention made by the AAEI. The National Retail Merchants Association, Kmart Corporation, Federated Department Stores, the U.S. Wheat Associates, and the National Council on U.S.-China Trade were among the groups that opposed the textile manufacturers' petition. As China's low-cost manufacturing exports to the United States rose, U.S. importers and retailers became increasingly wary of trade sanctions that threatened to cut off their access to an inexpensive import market.

The dividing line in U.S. politics in this case was thus clear. On the one side were U.S. producers of apparel, textiles, and textile fibers and their industry unions, which resolutely sought protection from imports. On the other side were American retailers, which strongly believed that it was in American consumers' interests to have access to inexpensive imports. Producers' and importers' views on the issue were contradictory.

The textile producers' petition elicited heated debate among U.S. policymakers. Commerce Secretary Malcolm Baldrige and White House advisors Edwin Meese and James Baker, with an eye to the upcoming elections, supported going ahead with the sanctions. However, Secretary of State George Shultz, due to his concern about the broader U.S.-China relationship, and USTR Bill Brock, out of a reluctance to provide protection to a fading domestic industry at the expense of exporting interests, opposed the action. President Reagan— faced with substantial pressure from an industry considered by some to be "the most aggressive, vicious, demanding lobby in the country" and following the pattern of bilateral textile negotiations established by previous negotiations[42]—eventually opted to overrule the majority of his cabinet and in December 1983 announced decisions to enforce strict controls on Chinese textile imports through executive order.[43] Under the executive order, the interagency Committee for the Implementation of Textile Agreements (CITA) was authorized to engage in bilateral consultations with the Chinese government with regard to textiles and apparel products and to implement new restrictions if Chinese import penetration reached a certain level. China allegedly failed to comply with the terms of the 1983 agreement. This not only hampered the ability of CITA to fully implement the executive order but also left textile trade a major contentious issue throughout the rest of the 1980s and well into the 1990s.

U.S.–China Textile Trade Dispute in the 1990s

Chinese textile and apparel exports to the United States remained a focus of disagreement in the 1990s as American textile and apparel makers increasingly shifted their concern to illegal Chinese transshipment of textile products through third countries with extra quota allowances (such as Hong Kong and New Zealand) in order to increase sales of Chinese textiles to the American market. American textile manufacturers alleged that illegal Chinese transshipment in the early 1990s far exceeded the $4.5 billion specified in the bilateral agreement, amounting to $2 billion annually and costing more than fifty thousand American jobs.[44] To ensure U.S. producers' share of the American market, the United States threatened to substantially reduce China's textile quotas unless the Chinese government took measures to address the problem.

For its part, Beijing acknowledged the existence of the transshipment problem but questioned the U.S. estimate of the amount of illegal transshipment, contending that the lack of effective control over the behavior of nonstate enterprises and trading companies accounted for the difficulties of eliminating the problem. It was against this backdrop that the United States in 1994 and 1996 twice again threatened to restrict unilaterally Chinese textile and apparel imports. However, as mentioned earlier, the two rounds of negotiations that followed did not spark a trade war, as the two sides managed to conclude eleventh-hour agreements. The ability of the two sides to avert the trade war outcome could be explained by vociferous opposition from American textile importers and retailers that substantially weakened the case of textile producers, making it more difficult for U.S. negotiators to carry out the threat.

For example, when USTR Mickey Kantor announced on January 6, 1994, that the United States would cut China's textile quotas by 25–35 percent if a new bilateral agreement could not be signed by January 17, reaction from domestic interest groups was highly contradictory. Apparel manufacturers naturally supported the action, which in their view would help to lessen the impact of competition they faced from Chinese products and would preserve some American jobs. Textile manufacturers and unions, having lost market share due to swelling exports from China and other developing countries and disgruntled over the Clinton administration's failure to win them the long-term protection they had sought in the recently concluded global trade talks, also welcomed threats to limit the imports of clothing and fabric from China. Protectionist pressure from the U.S. textile industry and some members of Congress thus bolstered the case for a more confrontational approach to trade.

But the Clinton administration's toughened stance also encountered criticism from American textile retailers, which were becoming progressively more dependent on China's low-cost textile output. Retailers urged the administration to reach a negotiated settlement with Beijing on the grounds that sanctions would substantially raise the prices of their goods in the United States. The share of Chinese textile products in the U.S. market had increased substantially by the early 1990s. While in 1988 China was still the fourth-largest supplier to the United States, by 1993 it had become the largest supplier to the American market. Chinese textile exports to the United States increased from $1 billion in 1983 to $7.3 billion in 1994, supplying 20–25 percent of all the textiles and apparel sold in the United States.[45] The threatened cuts, if carried out, would have cost U.S. importers and retailers $300 million in Chinese-made clothing. The textile dispute, therefore, pitted the politically influential textile industry against major U.S. retailers such as J.C. Penney, Gap, Sears, and Wal-Mart, all of which relied on low-cost Chinese textile products.

U.S. importing and retailing associations spearheaded the lobby effort against trade sanctions. AAEI, a main protagonist in the 1983 dispute, once again emerged as one of the most forceful opponents to the sanction threats. The association criticized the administration for exaggerating the magnitude of the transshipment problem, contending that most textile importers would suffer directly in the event of a trade war, as they would be forced to absorb the losses incurred from trade restrictions and the resulting political uncertainty. According to importers, although sanctions may not be devastating to most wholesalers, which had diversified sources of supply, they would force them to search for alternative sources of supply in other textile-producing countries and regions, where labor rates would be much higher or where U.S. importers would be required to make long-term commitments.[46]

The National Federation of Retailers further charged that evidence on the scope of the transshipment problem was inconclusive. The federation warned that, if the United States made good on its threats, it would restrict its access to an "important supplier of moderate-priced consumer apparel."[47] The federation pointed out that American consumers would be the real losers in such an event. It further commented that, although American makers could theoretically fill the gap, they would not be able to do so "at the same quality and price."[48]

USTR Mickey Kantor's threat of trade sanctions brought cries of outrage from a number of other organizations and companies as well. The National Apparel and Textile Association, a Seattle-based organization representing a fair number of textile importers, argued that big retailers that depended heavily on China would suffer heavy losses if the sanctions were carried out. The U.S. Association of Importers of Textiles and Apparel, based in New York, made the familiar allegation that the United States had not offered sufficient evidence to back up its claims about the transshipment problem and criticized the Clinton administration for "playing with fire" through the threatened sanctions. Companies such as Gap cautioned that the cutback would strain the production capacity of apparel factories in other Asian countries and would raise the prices for American consumers, particularly low-income consumers.[49]

Business associations directly involved in U.S.–China trade joined textile manufacturers and retailers in the battle against the quota reductions. The U.S.–China Business Council cautioned that, since textiles accounted for a large portion of U.S.–China trade, a major trade confrontation in this area would have far-reaching implications for overall economic and trade relations between the two countries. Echoing the concerns of export-oriented groups, the council stressed that U.S. brinkmanship might also induce Chinese retaliation against leading U.S. exports to China such as aircraft, computer, telecommunications, and grain exports.[50]

A senior U.S. Treasury official reportedly commented on the 1993–94 textile negotiations that "one of the things the Chinese need to understand is that for the first time in seven years, Washington is speaking with one voice."[51] But even with one voice, it was sending highly contradictory messages. With importers and retailers calling positively for an amicable settlement of the dispute, the USTR was placed in the middle of a dispute involving two politically active groups and had difficulty justifying the decision to impose the sanctions.

This pattern of interest group alignment repeated itself in 1996 when the United States again threatened to impose sanctions on Chinese textile and electronic goods for China's violation of the 1994 textile agreement. On the one hand, the ATMI, representing textile manufacturers, whose market share had undergone a steady erosion due to the huge inflow of Chinese goods, charged that China had counterfeited textile designs and trademarks, illegally transshipped $2–4 billion of textile and apparel products to the United States each year, and kept its market closed to American products. On the other hand, American importers and retailers had mounted a strong counteroffensive against the textile producers' position. The U.S. Association of Importers of Textiles and Apparel, for example, questioned the government's estimate of the magnitude of the transshipment problem and criticized the Clinton administration for targeting textile imports to appeal to the powerful textile interests in a presidential election year. Importers asserted that the sanctions would make life more uncertain for them and urged the administration to more fully take into account the impact of the sanctions on the American manufacturing, retailing, and consuming community.[52] Although the U.S. government claimed that most of the sanctions would be imposed on goods available from sources other than China and therefore would incur minimal costs, importers pointed out that the sanctions would cause considerable difficulties to small manufacturers that simply could not afford to shift production. Particular sectors of the apparel industry (such as the silk apparel sector) were especially worried about the possibility of Chinese retaliation due to their high vulnerability to restrictions on Chinese silk exports. The industry moved quickly to publicize its vulnerability to Congress and the USTR, emphasizing in particular the importance of a steady silk supply to the maintenance of jobs and stable price.[53]

While the sanction threats brought importers into the fray, they energized export-oriented interests (including auto, wheat, and aircraft producers), who also feared the consequences of Chinese retaliation. As in the 1994 disputes, export interests argued that sanction threats might provoke Chinese retaliation, placing major U.S. exporting items to China in jeopardy. Given the prospect of a rapidly expanding China market, exporters urged U.S. negotiators to be more prudent in their choice of trade weapon. These countervailing forces in U.S. domestic politics, stemming from importers' and exporters' concerns about potential economic losses, therefore placed a major constraint on American negotiators' actions.

Chinese Negotiation Strategy

The Chinese detected the divisions among domestic actors in the United States early on and adroitly manipulated these divisions to advance their own negotiation objectives. Beijing's threat to target

TABLE 6.1. Profiles of Main Actors Involved in U.S.–China Negotiations over Intellectual Property Rights and Textiles

	Companies and Associations	Position	Impact
U.S.–China Intellectual Property Rights			
Directly Affected Exporters	International Intellectual Property Alliance; Business Software Association; Recording Industry Association of America; Motion Picture Association of America; International Federation of the Phonographic Industry	Alleged that rampant piracy in China impeded American industry's attempt to gain genuine market access.	Successfully brought the issue of IPR protection onto the policy agenda.
Exporters Not Directly Affected	Automobile and aircraft manufacturers; U.S.–China Business Council; Washington State China Relations Council	Concerned that sanctions would curtail American manufacturers' investments in the short run and reduce their access to a potentially lucrative market in the long run.	Joined import-using interests to oppose sanction threats; very influential.
Import-Competing Interests	—	—	—
Import-Using Interests	National Retail Federation; American Association of Exporters and Importers; International Mass Retail Association; American Apparel Manufacturers Association; National Apparel and Textile Association; U.S. Association of Importers of Textiles and Apparel; Toy Manufacturers of America; footwear manufacturers; Electronic Industries Association; American Forest & Paper Association; power tool manufacturers	Argued that Washington's pursuit of fair trade should not come at the expense of the American importing and retailing community. Sanctions would increase the price they pay for imports.	Very influential in opposing sanction threats; provided an important counterbalance to the IPR industries.

U.S.–China Textiles

Directly Affected Exporters	—	—
Exporters Not Directly Involved	National Council on U.S.–China Trade; U.S. Wheat Associates; auto, wheat, and aircraft manufacturers	Argued that sanction threats might provoke Chinese retaliation, placing major U.S. exporting items in jeopardy. Urged U.S. negotiators to be more prudent in their choice of trade weapon. Were one of the most outspoken opponents of sanction threats. Their active opposition in the early 1980s played an important role in removing the sanctions.
Import-Competing Interests	American Textile Manufacturers Institute; International Ladies Garment Workers Union; Amalgamated Clothing and Textile Workers Union	Argued that China's rapid textile export growth and illegal quota evasions caused market disruption. Advocated more stringent quota restrictions. Supported highly protectionist policies; exerted considerable influence in the textile trade dispute.
Import-Using Interests	American Association of Exporters and Importers; National Retail Merchants Association; Kmart Corporation; Federated Department Stores; National Federation of Retailers; National Apparel and Textile Association; U.S. Association of Importers of Textiles and Apparel	Called for policies that would guarantee their continued access to inexpensive imports. Actively opposed textile manufacturers' attempt to impose quota restrictions on Chinese imports.

businesses that desired either cheap imports from China or access to the Chinese market reflects Beijing's savvy about how to take advantage of the opportunities created by its complementary trade relationship with the United States so as to exploit the different policy preferences of interest groups within America. Consequently, the well-financed, politically powerful U.S. apparel retailers and agricultural interests became the most reliable partners of China in the 1983 textile dispute. Their opposition to the retaliatory measures soon forced Washington to reverse its decision and to withdraw the sanctions being imposed on China.

In June 1995, in response to the U.S. quota "charge back" decision, Li Dongsheng, director of the Trade Administration of the Ministry of Foreign Trade and Economic Cooperation, stated that the U.S. quota "charge backs" against China caused the United States nearly $100 million in losses and "great economic losses to U.S. importers, retail dealers and consumers."[54] During the negotiations over textiles in September 1996, Li again announced that U.S. plans to reduce Chinese textile quotas not only "seriously violated the Sino-U.S. textile agreement" but also "met opposition from American businessmen who are engaged in U.S.–China trade, according to American press reports." He further opined that some Americans have criticized the charging move as "politicising trade issues and political maneuvering in a presidential election year."[55] These comments by the Chinese negotiator reflected Beijing's expectation that domestic divisions within the United States might still help to reverse the decisions of the U.S. government and that latent support within the United States for its own case obviated the need for taking American demands seriously. Such perceptions allowed Beijing to continue to flout American pressure without having to make substantial changes in its practices in the textile sector.

Conclusion

In both U.S.–China intellectual property and textile trade negotiations, American negotiators failed to make good on threats to impose sanctions on Chinese products primarily because of opposition from the U.S. importing and retailing community. Some analysts may contend that, unlike in the MFN debate, U.S. business interests enjoy a much higher level of unity in both of these cases. But while opposition interests in these cases were far less vocal and prominent than in the

MFN case, they nevertheless influenced the policy orientation and position of the executive in a way that made an open trade confrontation less likely. Despite efforts by U.S. IPR-related industries and textile manufacturers to penalize China for its trade infringements, active opposition from a large constituency dependent on low-cost, labor-intensive products made it far more difficult for these industries to achieve their negotiation objectives in China. U.S. importers and retailers of such products as footwear, toys, apparel, and consumer electronics made the familiar argument that they would suffer severely if restrictions were placed on these Chinese imports, in effect constraining the IPR industries and textile manufacturers from escalating the conflict to a trade war. Table 6.1 presents a profile of the major U.S. interest groups involved in the U.S.–China negotiations over IPR and textiles.

The mutual imposition of sanctions in the textile case in the early 1980s constitutes an exception to the general pattern described here. But it can be explained in terms of the relatively low level of Chinese textile and apparel exports to the United States and hence the absence of organized political opposition on the part of textile importers and retailers during that period. As the volume of Chinese textile exports to the United States rose rapidly in the 1990s, textile importers and retailers became a more active political force in opposing the threats against China. In a context of generally protectionist U.S. textile policy, such opposition at least prevented U.S. negotiators from pursuing overly aggressive trade policies, lessening the chances of trade war between the United States and China. Due to these domestic divisions generated by trade complementarity, U.S.–China trade disputes have preserved a degree of cooperativeness.

The finding that U.S.–China trade disputes have not evolved into bruising trade wars is particularly salient in view of the fact that trade conflicts between the United States and China were not governed by democratic norms of conflict resolution, which, from the perspective of the "democratic peace" theory, would likely aggravate misunderstandings or otherwise increase the risk of a trade war. That the exact opposite of the pattern predicted by the democratic peace thesis has come to characterize U.S.–China trade negotiations suggests that institutional qualities of states, such as whether they are democracies or not, are not as relevant to trade bargaining outcomes as some analysts have assumed. Even in the absence of democratic institutions and norms, states' trading relationships can be considerably resilient if they are structured in a way that cushions the influence of domestic rent-seeking groups.

CHAPTER 7

Democracy and Trade Conflicts

The previous chapter reveals how the complementary trade relationship between the United States and China, by creating such deep divisions in U.S. politics, decreases the probability of trade war between the two sides. Although, according to the literature on crisis bargaining, trade conflicts between democratic and authoritarian regimes should more frequently escalate into trade wars, complementary trade relations between many of these dyads structure domestic politics in the sender of threats in a way that dampens the incentives for brinkmanship in bilateral trade disputes. Domestic division on the democratic side of the dispute compensates for any possible aggravation of relations caused by the inferior signaling capabilities of authoritarian states, preventing trade disputes between autocracies and democracies from escalating into trade war.

This chapter contrasts the "trade peace" between authoritarian and democratic regimes (such as that between the United States and China as described in the previous chapter) with the greater frequency of the imposition of retaliatory measures between democratic dyads. Through detailed analyses of the trade dispute between the United States and the EC over EC enlargement and U.S.–Canada timber trade conflicts, this chapter highlights how trade competitiveness between democratic regimes creates stronger domestic pressure for the use of threat tactics, increasing the risk of trade war. In both the U.S.–EC and the U.S.–Canada cases, sanction threats enjoyed widespread domestic support. In the enlargement case, since a wide range of U.S. agricultural interests faced the effects of unfair EC competition, both U.S. interest groups seeking to eliminate the newly erected trade restrictions in the Iberian markets and those facing import competition lent their support to the sanction threats. Unlike trade negotiations between the United States and China, there was a particularly large import-competing constituency in the United States that welcomed sanction threats promising to restrict the imports of products that they had been trying to keep out of the U.S. market. Similarly, in the U.S.–Canada timber trade conflict, softwood lumber producers' campaign for protection won the support of diverse segments of the forest products industry threatened with growing Canadian penetration of the U.S. market. Competitive trade relations solidified domestic industries' support for sanction threats, exerting strong pressure on the executive branch of the government to provide relief for domestic industry. Such unified domestic support for sanction threats overwhelmed the constraints imposed by democratic norms of conflict resolution, thus lowering the threshold for trade wars and leading the United States to opt for retaliatory measures in both cases.

EC Enlargement

The dispute over EC enlargement was the natural outgrowth of a series of U.S.–EC confrontations in the farm sector. Ever since the formative years of the EC, the U.S. government and agricultural producers have been irritated by the EC's highly protectionist agricultural trade policy. American farm interests argued that the EC's Common Agricultural Policy, by shielding European farmers from market competition, threatened the survival and competitiveness of the U.S. agricultural sector. Although in the 1960s and 1970s both sides sought to limit the scope of trade frictions to prevent disruptions to the Atlantic relationship, they found it difficult to avoid trade wars even then due to diametrically opposed domestic interests. Consequently, the Americans and the Europeans have found themselves engaged in tit-for-tat retaliation over EC policies discriminating against imports of chicken and turkey from the United States, alleged EC practices in third markets that displaced American producers from their traditional agricultural markets, and the EC's preferential trading system that granted lower customs duties to citrus fruit exports from a select group of Mediterranean countries.[1]

The U.S.–EC trade spat over the accession of Spain and Portugal into the EC similarly took place over U.S. concerns about the EC's protectionist policies excluding American farmers from the Iberian markets. When Spain and Portugal acceded to the EC in March 1986, the EC implemented new trade restrictions against agricultural imports from third countries, particularly feed grains. Under the accession agreement, the EC raised Spanish tariffs on feed grains from 20 to

100 percent, imposed new quotas on soybean and soybean oil imports, and reserved 15 percent of Portugal's grain import market for EC members. The United States, charging that these restrictions violated the spirit of the GATT since they disproportionately favored European farm interests at the expense of U.S. exporters of corn, sorghum, and soybeans, demanded that the EC rescind the quotas and provide U.S. producers with full compensation or else face retaliatory tariffs on roughly $1 billion of EC exports. In April, the EC threatened counter-retaliation and targeted politically active U.S. groups such as producers of corn gluten feed, wheat, and rice. When bilateral negotiations were still going on, the United States imposed nonbinding quotas in retaliation against the Portuguese restrictions on U.S. soybeans and soybean oil. The Portuguese quotas on oilseeds and the U.S. retaliatory quotas remained in effect until 1991.[2] Although the Reagan administration later refrained from carrying through with threats to retaliate against the Spanish restrictions, that both sides decided to go ahead with retaliatory measures in the Portuguese case indicates the intensity of the conflict.

The frequent escalation of U.S.–EC agricultural trade conflicts into trade wars, as the few episodes cited previously illustrate, can be explained in terms of the competitive trade relationship between the United States and the EC and the effect of this trade structure on the level of domestic support for aggressive negotiation tactics. A broad spectrum of U.S. farm groups, which competed with European farm products, had for years decried the EC's anticompetitive trade practices. As a result, threats of trade retaliation garnered support both from groups seeking enhanced market access in Europe and in third markets and from groups that had to compete with European imports in the U.S. market. For example, in the U.S.–EC trade war over export subsidies mentioned earlier, most American agricultural groups saw subsidies as an effective instrument with which to correct the market distortions caused by the EC's protectionist agricultural policies. Wheat producers, the main protagonists in this dispute, naturally advocated an aggressive negotiation strategy. But other major agricultural groups such as corn and gluten feed producers also endorsed a proactive trade policy, which in their view provided the single most effective means to alleviate the competitive onslaught they faced in the domestic market. Domestic opposition to the export subsidy program was thus muted, permitting a united front among U.S. producers.

Moreover, on most issues related to agricultural trade with the EC, both the Reagan and Bush administrations favored a considerably tough posture. From the executive branch's point of view, agriculture was an internally competitive and crucial area of economic activity that ought to be provided with a level playing field. Some form of government action was necessary to ensure the continued viability of agriculture. These considerations, reinforced by strong industry and congressional pressure for government support in the face of European intransigence, resulted in executive branch policies favorable to the agriculture sector. Given the consensus among domestic interest groups and the government institutions in favor of retaliation, the risk of trade war was much enhanced.

The dynamics of domestic politics in the EC enlargement case provides a good illustration of this broad pattern characterizing U.S.–EC agricultural trade conflicts. In EC enlargement, America's sanction threats designed to eliminate trade restrictions in the Spanish and Portuguese markets obtained the support of both U.S. exporters seeking to gain a greater share of the EC market and importers hurt by subsidized European agricultural exports in the United States, in addition to the backing of Reagan administration officials, who felt that some form of government intervention was needed to prevent U.S. agriculture from withering away in the face of unfair EC competition. The following section will describe in detail the positions adopted by the various actors involved in the enlargement dispute to reveal how the complex interplay of political forces shaped the U.S. response.

U.S. Farm Interests and EC Enlargement

An important reason why the trade dispute over enlargement evolved into an open trade war was the almost uniform policy preferences of U.S. farm groups. As the case study by John Odell suggests, the enlargement case unified major elements of the U.S. farm lobby. U.S. corn (maize) farmers were a major group that would be negatively affected by the restrictions the enlargement treaty placed on U.S. exports. But other groups targeted by EC retaliation, such as producers of feed grain, barley, and grain sorghum, also had strong grievances about the perceived unfair European agricultural policies and so had little incentive to oppose the sanction threats.[3] Broad sectors of American agriculture long have complained about the EC's protectionist agricultural policies that undercut American producers' ability to compete in the world market. At a time when U.S. farm exports and income were undergoing a steady decline, EC's import restrictions inevitably stirred American farmers into action.

American farmers of feed grains had a particularly strong stake in the dispute. Since the Spanish and Portuguese feed grains markets were one of the most important for U.S. exports, American feed grains farmers were loathe to seeing the protective walls that EC enlargement would erect in the Iberian market. While the Spanish and Portuguese markets absorbed 15 percent of U.S. exports in 1982, that number had declined to 8 percent by 1985. The additional loss in sales that EC enlargement would incur to the United States, estimated at $640 million per year in Spain and another $55 million in Portugal, was perceived as particularly damaging, as they merely added to the existing problems of deteriorating farm exports and income. In the mid-1980s, the U.S. farm sector was already mired in a crisis induced by declining export demands and the appreciation of the dollar, which in effect raised the price of U.S. exports vis-à-vis other major agricultural suppliers. For instance, in 1981–84, real farm income in the United States dropped to only half of the level in 1971.[4] A series of farm closures and widespread unemployment accentuated the appeal of calls for government support. Naturally, the EC's unfair trade practices, as embodied in the CAP, received the brunt of the blame for the problems plaguing the U.S. agriculture sector.

During the enlargement dispute, American farm interests accused the EC of supporting an inefficient farm sector through the use of variable import levies, thus displacing competitive world-market suppliers from both the European and third-country markets. They asserted that CAP policies were not only inefficient but also undermined the accepted norms of the international trading system. U.S. farm groups also denounced the EC practice of using export subsidies to dispose of its agricultural surpluses onto the world market, which in their view was the chief culprit behind the loss of U.S. export market shares. As one of the U.S. farm groups with a major stake in the enlargement dispute, feed grains producers had insisted on full compensation. They remained unconvinced of the argument that the lower Spanish and Portuguese industrial barriers would compensate for the higher agricultural duties and refused to accept any settlement that failed to offer full compensation to U.S. farmers, stressing that they were the ones with their "dollars on the line."[5]

Other U.S. farm groups such as producers of corn, barley, and sorghum, which similarly felt victimized by unfair EC competition, also supported efforts to expand U.S. market shares in the Iberian states. American corn farmers, for example, relied primarily on the domestic market and, thus, did not have the extensive investments in foreign markets that would expose them to the risks of EC counterretaliation. Between 1982 and 1985, even before the additional barriers associated with the Spanish and Portuguese entry came into place, U.S. corn exports to the EC had already dropped from 14.2 million tons to 6 million tons.[6] As a result, corn producers, far from constraining the retaliatory strategy, pushed for a tough negotiation position.

Thus, major U.S. farm interests, including producers of corn, feed grains, barley, and grain sorghum, had forged a unified position, forming a trade policy coordinating committee to protest the enlargement treaty. These groups urged the Reagan administration to take forceful action to press the EC to provide full compensation for U.S. farmers and to reduce agricultural export subsidies that dampened U.S. exports in third markets. U.S. producers insisted on the elimination of EC export subsidies because it was in this area that they felt most alarmed by EC's unfair trade practices. Yet this demand was also more sweeping and more difficult to meet than simply reducing the Spanish and Portuguese quotas to pre-accession levels.

The farm lobby obtained strong backing from legislators, who in April 1986 passed a resolution urging the president to retaliate. Representatives of the U.S. farm lobby visited European capitals in the summer to communicate directly with EC farm leaders and government officials about the United States' determination for a positive outcome. In the fall, farm groups launched an even more aggressive campaign for trade relief, explicitly making their endorsement of a GATT agreement on agricultural trade in the Uruguay Round contingent on the satisfactory settlement of the enlargement dispute.[7] At the end of the year the Feed Grains Council directly warned American negotiators:

> Our membership has clearly indicated that the feedgrains sector is willing to face the possible consequence of EC counter-retaliation. What they are not willing to face is anything less than full compensation for the Spanish market, or a lack of resolve by our government if such compensation cannot be achieved. . . . The time has come to draw the line and take a strong stand against the unfair trading practices of the European Community. Any further delay in the settlement of this dispute is totally unacceptable.[8]

Importantly, almost no interest group took any visible measures that could have undercut the effectiveness of the feed grain and corn growers. Importing interests, as well as a number of groups that could be hurt by possible EC counterretaliation, voiced their concerns about the sanction threats but did not push their case as forcefully as the corn and feed grain producers. A number of interest groups targeted by EC counterretaliation faced trade restrictions in Europe themselves and were willing to go along with the tough approach demanded by the corn and feed grain producers. In the words of one U.S. negotiator in reaction to the level of political activism of U.S. groups that would potentially lose from EC counterretaliation,

> Sure, we had heard from them [the groups targeted by EC]. We got a few letters saying they were concerned about it, but they were not beating our door down. It was not heavy-duty political pressure. The corn gluten feed people [targeted by Brussels] have their own zero [duty] binding in the EC. They know that if they want us to go to bat for them, they have to play along sometimes when we're working for somebody else. We did hear a lot from the import interests—representing the French products, Belgian endive, and so forth.[9]

In other words, political pressure exerted by groups that could suffer from possible EC counterretaliation was almost negligible. Neither was there much opposition from those whose imports might be cut off by potential EC retaliation, although these interests did raise some concerns. In short, since so many U.S. agricultural groups faced EC competition, both import-competing and export-seeking interests could expect to win from trade retaliation and, hence, both backed threats to open European agricultural markets. Virtually negligible domestic resistance allowed the feed grains and corn producers to exercise considerable political influence, intensifying the pressure on the Reagan administration to pursue a more aggressive approach in negotiations with the EC.

Reactions in Washington

U.S. farm groups' calls for trade sanctions received a sympathetic hearing in Washington. Indeed, the Reagan administration itself had become concerned about the impact of EC export subsidies on U.S. agriculture, one of the most important American exports. As the world's agricultural superpowers, both the United States and the EC had adopted policies privileging the agricultural sector. In providing European farmers with export subsidies and other restrictive import policies, the EC's CAP played a particularly important role in sustaining the steady growth of European agricultural exports. By compensating EC farmers for the difference between the higher internal EC price and the lower world market price, the CAP helped European farmers export their agricultural surpluses to the world market, in the process transforming the EC from a net food importer to the world's largest exporter of beef, sugar, poultry, and dairy products.[10]

But such substantial gains to European agriculture also came at the expense of American farmers. As the EC moved from a net importer to a self-sufficient exporter of a variety of agricultural commodities, the United States lost the ability to export to the EC a number of products for which it used to be a major supplier, as America's share of world trade steadily declined. Moreover, U.S. agricultural exports to the EC plummeted from $9.8 billion in 1980 to $6.7 billion in 1984; overall U.S. agricultural exports declined from $48 billion in 1981 to $26 billion in 1986.[11] In addition, the EC's aggressive trading posture induced a visible drop in America's share of world trade.

In an environment of steadily deteriorating farm exports, the executive branch had been subjected to enormous pressure from Congress, the media, and various domestic constituencies to provide trade relief. The U.S. Congress, in particular, agitated for reform of domestic support policies to combat the effects of the CAP, a policy that was alleged to be directly responsible for the plight of U.S. agriculture. Even before the dispute over EC enlargement took place, Congress had passed, and sent to the president for approval, highly protectionist bills targeted at Europe. Given the EC's competitive assault on world markets, there was a strong sentiment among legislators that the United States could no longer condone the EC's unfair trade practices that limited imports, drove down prices, encouraged overproduction, and displaced U.S. products.[12]

The EC's attempt to use the accession of Spain and Portugal to further restrict U.S. exports of corn, sorghum, and oilseeds logically became to many congressional members an excellent example of the distortions caused by unfair foreign trade practices. In the context of steadily rising U.S. trade deficits, the potential loss of another $1 billion in trade that EC enlargement would incur irritated many congressional members. Thus, despite many legislators' professed willingness to support the political integration of Spain and Portugal into the EC, there eventually emerged a congressional consensus that EC policies had created such excessive trade distortions that they could be corrected only through trade retaliation. As a manifestation of congressional determination, a group of twenty-one senators, including Senate

Majority Leader Robert Dole, submitted a letter to President Reagan calling on him to retaliate against the EC by withdrawing equivalent tariff concessions.

As Congress increasingly moved into the fray, the Reagan administration hardened both its rhetoric and policy stance. Indeed, beginning in the early 1980s, the executive branch adopted an increasingly mercantilist approach to counter the protectionist policies of its leading competitor in agricultural trade. Government support and retaliatory strategy, where necessary, were justified by the objective of maintaining the share of the world agricultural market going to one of the United States' internally competitive sectors. After the enlargement treaty took effect, the Reagan administration, with a view of protecting long-term U.S. agricultural interests, raised several objections to the treaty's provisions. Above all, Washington considered the 15 percent Portuguese quota reserved for EC countries to be clearly illegal under the terms of the GATT. It also strongly objected to the Spanish restrictions that raised the Spanish tariffs on imports of corn and sorghum from below 20 percent to over 100 percent, thus nullifying a prior bilateral agreement. American negotiators insisted that, in view of the substantial damage that the enlargement treaty imposed on American producers, the United States was entitled under the GATT's international rules to full compensation. Second, Washington was irritated by the fact that the Europeans resorted to the action without prior consultation with the United States. The Americans complained that they did not receive advance notice about the consequences of entirely new tariff structures for the two Iberian states and, therefore, were caught by surprise by the EC move.

Third, American officials raised their concerns about the substantial economic costs of EC enlargement, pointing out that the Spanish tariffs alone would cut American exports of maize and sorghum animal feed by roughly $500 million a year. At a time when Washington was increasingly occupied with its loss of world market share in agriculture and with its $170 billion trade deficit, including nearly $30 billion with Western Europe, many administration officials felt that the United States could no longer countenance half a billion dollars in trade losses in the name of preserving a harmonious alliance relationship.[13] Moreover, since one of the products involved was soybeans—the largest U.S. farm export to Europe, with annual sales of more than $4 billion—there was also a strong reluctance on the part of administration officials to surrender soybean export markets. Finally, the Reagan administration emphasized that, contrary to the EC's claims, the U.S.

loss in agricultural trade would outweigh the potential benefits of lower industrial tariffs in the EC and of the further integration of the two Iberian states into the Western alliance.[14]

Thus, as negotiations in late 1985 and early 1986 bogged down, the White House began to run out of patience. U.S. Commerce Secretary Malcolm Baldrige began to refer to an exceedingly difficult situation in which trade disputes would take precedence over issues of geopolitical relationship. Later in 1986, in a meeting with farm group leaders, Baldrige reassured them that the administration would not "sit by" and watch the farm sector continue its downward slide.[15] Similarly, USTR Clayton Yeutter reassured farm groups that the United States could not accept the accession agreement without adequate compensation. The rhetoric of senior administration officials sent an unmistakable signal that the Reagan team, having staved off protectionist pressures in the past, was no longer in a position to compromise on trade issues. Thus, in contrast to many trade disputes with the EC in which Congress usually played the leading role, the White House initiated the move for retaliation. Moreover, unlike past trade conflicts such as the Mediterranean citrus fruit case, the White House invoked the threat of retaliation at a fairly early stage in the dispute. These unusual moves reflected a clear shift of U.S. policy preferences away from adjudication to a more coercive strategy. The executive's increasingly tough stance made a trade war with the Europeans all the more likely.

The Negotiations

In early 1986, when the enlargement treaty took effect, American negotiators immediately demanded adequate compensation. When initial informal discussions led by USTR Clayton Yeutter and Secretary of Agriculture Richard Lyng failed to produce any change, the Reagan administration announced on March 31 that the United States would retaliate against the Portuguese quotas on oilseeds and grains by May 1 and the higher tariffs in Spain by July 1, unless the new restrictions were removed. The total amount of trade affected by the threatened sanctions amounted to about $1 billion, the estimated value that enlargement cost the U.S. farm sector.

In announcing the decision, U.S. negotiators took care to pick items that would inflict the most harm on politically well-organized EC groups. Almost half of the retaliation was directed at French exports (including white wine, brandy, cheese, and chocolates), with the rest of the sanctions targeted at exports from Germany, Italy, the Netherlands, and Britain. Notably, unlike U.S.–China trade disputes where the U.S. retaliation list was composed primarily of items no longer manufactured in America (such as bicycles, toys, shoes, and consumer electronics), U.S. sanctions against the EC deliberately targeted a wide range of products for which American importers could find ready American-made substitutes, thereby neutralizing resistance from U.S. importers. American negotiators backed up the retaliatory decision with tough rhetoric. President Reagan justified the retaliation as a means of preventing U.S. farmers from "once again" having to "pay the price for the European Community's enlargement." Secretary of Agriculture Richard Lyng stated that the retaliatory measures were designed to "bring the EC to the negotiating table as soon as possible."[16] Washington's retaliatory move was unprecedented and fully revealed the U.S. resolve because, in contrast to past negotiations, it took place early in the dispute, without several rounds of negotiations.

However, since the interests of the politically powerful European farm groups were diametrically opposed to those of their American counterparts, Washington's heavy-handed pressure was unable to make any substantial inroads in modifying EC policies. Indeed, the CAP enjoyed considerable support from European agricultural interests because it contributed significantly to the EC's ability to maintain its status as one of the important players in world agriculture trade[17] and to creating and maintaining a sense of cohesion among EC member states. CAP was particularly important to countries such as France, which viewed an enlarged and protected market as a guarantee to the viability of its large agriculture sector. Due to the unwavering support of European farmers with considerable political clout in European national capitals, the CAP had become one of the most entrenched policies of the EC. Consequently, any challenge to the CAP almost certainly would provoke a strong response from European farm interests. This helps to explain why, in the early stages of the enlargement dispute, the EC remained largely unmoved by American demands, insisting that the United States should not be given special agricultural compensation.

Determined to defend what it viewed as its legitimate trade interests, the EC on April 9 responded to the U.S. sanction threats with vows to counterretaliate, carefully selecting the products on the sanction list to target politically powerful U.S. groups, including producers of corn gluten feed, wheat, and rice. Since these products figured prominently in U.S. exports, the counterthreats were considered to be the equivalent of "using a nuclear weapon in a trade war."[18] During subsequent

Democracy and Trade Conflicts   207

negotiations in the spring, the two sides came up with various compromise proposals but could not narrow their differences. At this point, it was clear that neither was bluffing and that both were actively preparing for the trade war that seemed likely to follow.

While discussions were still under way, the U.S. government announced decisions to impose nonbinding quotas on a range of Portuguese products to retaliate against the Portuguese restrictions on soybeans and soybean oil. The imposition of quotas not only indicated the Reagan administration's resolve to attack the EC's continued assault on world markets but also reflected the political clout and influence of U.S. soybean producers. The American Soybean Association had long been actively involved in trade disputes with the EC because of the importance of the European market to the U.S. soybean industry. In the 1960s, the U.S. government had made as a precondition for its recognition of the CAP the European guarantee not to impose any tariffs on soybeans or corn gluten feed. This tacit agreement proved crucial to expanding American soybean exports to the EC. As EC enlargement seriously challenged the soybean zero-duty binding system, it nearly ensured that the soybean producers would launch an aggressive lobbying campaign against the new restrictions. The absence of opposition from other domestic groups, as described earlier, bolstered the soybean producers' chance of success in this case.

Since the retaliation against the Portuguese quotas still left the Spanish issue unresolved, Washington continued negotiations with the EC regarding Spanish restrictions throughout the year. On July 2, 1986, the two sides reached a temporary agreement whereby the EC promised to increase its imports of feed grains for six months in exchange for a U.S. guarantee to suspend the retaliatory tariffs until December 31, 1986. In essence, the agreement amounted to a concession on the part of the EC to temporarily provide the United States with some compensation and to increase EC purchases of U.S. grain, measures that the EC would not have taken in the absence of U.S. pressure. It addressed some of the most immediate concerns of the United States, thus providing the two parties with more time for negotiation and bargaining.

This interim agreement, while welcomed by both American and European negotiators, drew sharp criticism from farm interests on both sides of the Atlantic. The U.S. Feed Grains Council, for example, was critical of the amount of compensation provided in the agreement, which was less than half of the losses feed grain producers claimed they had suffered from Spanish accession. The council decried the agreement as "a bitter pill to swallow," stating that "any agreement that does not fully compensate the producers of corn and sorghum who have lost access to the markets of Spain and Portugal will be unacceptable to the U.S. Feed Grains Council and our members."[19] Then, toward the end of the year, as the negotiation deadline approached, the Feed Grains Council again urged American negotiators to stand firm, explicitly expressing their willingness to face the effects of EC counter-retaliation.

U.S. and EC negotiation positions remained far apart throughout the year. By November it was clear that the EC did not increase its imports of feed grains to the amount specified in the interim agreement. There was also evidence that the EC deliberately manipulated its import levy system in a way that continued to disadvantage U.S. exports. Given the lack of progress, the Reagan administration threatened to impose 200 percent retaliatory duties on $400 million of European agricultural exports by January 30, 1987, unless an agreement could be reached by then. Even at this point, the negotiations remained deadlocked. Washington clearly stated that it would carry through with the retaliation if no agreement were in sight. But, at the same time, U.S. negotiators were prepared to soften the severity of their blow: Washington reduced the total amount of compensation it demanded in the previous rounds of negotiations; it also contemplated the possibility of some form of industrial compensation.

The United States and the EC continued negotiations right up to the deadline and finally reached a settlement on January 29, 1987. Brussels agreed to substantially increase its imports of corn and sorghum from third countries in the next four years, with two-thirds of these purchases guaranteed to go to American producers. Moreover, it guaranteed zero-duty binding for American soybean products and corn gluten feed exports in Spain and Portugal, eliminated the 15 percent restrictions on the Portuguese import market for grain, and offered to reduce import duties on a variety of industrial products. The removal of restrictions on the Portuguese grain import market was particularly important to American producers, as it promised to substantially increase U.S. sales of cereal in the Portuguese market. Total EC agricultural and industrial concessions were estimated at $400 million. While the EC eventually conceded on the Spanish issue, both the Portuguese quotas on oilseeds and the U.S. retaliatory measure had remained in effect. It was not until 1991, when Portugal rescinded the oilseed quotas, that the United States removed the restrictions on Portuguese imports.

The Effect of American Politics on European Perceptions

The analysis just presented suggests that diametrically opposed domestic interests on both sides of the Atlantic was the main reason for the intense U.S.–EC trade confrontation over EC enlargement. Since American farmers faced across-the-board competition from the Europeans, EC enlargement united a broad spectrum of U.S. farm interests into aggressive lobbying campaigns. Not only did U.S. producers of corn, feed grains, and soybeans who were directly affected by the newly erected restrictions protest the enlargement treaty, but also even those targeted by EC counterretaliation such as producers of corn gluten feed, barley, and grain sorghum supported the sanction threats, as they would benefit from the restrictions on these European imports if the sanctions had to be carried out. Furthermore, the dispute against the EC was supported by Reagan administration officials, who felt that the new restrictions accompanying Spanish and Portuguese accession represented another episode in the history of unfair EC competition in the agricultural sector. U.S. retaliation in the Portuguese case resulted from, and reflected, these intense domestic pressures, which made the risk of trade war quite high.

Relative unity on the side of the United States helped to signal to the Europeans the strong U.S. resolve to obtain a positive outcome. At the same time it increased the risks of trade war, unified domestic support forced Brussels to back down from its original negotiation position. As Odell's first-hand account of the enlargement dispute reveals, by the end of 1986, EC member countries had unmistakably felt the highly orchestrated pressure from the United States. Indeed, in view of Washington's retaliatory measures against the EC in the past, the relevant EC officials all took the U.S. threat seriously and no one considered the U.S. move a mere bluff. An EC commission official reportedly stated, "I think everyone was pretty much convinced they would do it."[20] A French official concluded from his visit to Washington that "it was very clear that a very powerful lobby was working the agencies on this issue" this time around, as all the American officials with whom he had spoken, including even those at the Commerce Department, were of one mind with regard to Spanish accession. These reactions in Washington formed a sharp contrast with his past negotiation experience, where different agencies in Washington often came up with different views over a single issue.[21] Given the perception that some compromise would be inevitable, European negotiators began to show a greater willingness to reach a settlement. One European negotiator offered his explanation as to why the EC agreed to an interim agreement in July 1986:

> From the U.S. side, the EC was beginning to give up on its principle that we did not owe any compensation. For the European side, once we realized that there was a risk of a major trade war and possible strains on cohesion in the Community—our tendencies were far from unanimous—we saw that probably we would not have successfully resisted a trade war. It was decided that it would be better to drop something on the table, something limited, that would not prejudge our position later, but would allow time for people to realize that such a thing was a possibility.[22]

Thus, all the signals from Washington suggested that all relevant actors in the United States were resolved to obtain some concessions from the EC. These signals were filtered through EC internal politics and helped to induce the desired compromises from Brussels, although it did take Washington tremendous effort, including the imposition of retaliatory measures, to get Brussels to modify its policy.

U.S.–Canada Timber Trade Dispute

As the largest and most resilient trade dispute between the United States and Canada, the softwood lumber dispute spanned more than fifteen years, costing industry and government officials on both sides of the border considerable time and financial resources. The dispute began in 1982 when the U.S. Coalition for Fair Lumber Imports (CFLI) submitted a petition to the International Trade Administration of the Commerce Department calling for the imposition of CVDs on imports of softwood lumber supplied by Canada to compensate for the loss of employment resulting from the high level of Canadian stumpage price, or the price at which Canadian authorities sold the rights to remove trees from public forests to private lumber producers.[23] The U.S. Commerce Department conducted an investigation into these complaints but found no evidence of systematic government support that would justify levying CVDs. In 1984, the ITA in its ruling turned down the U.S. industry's request for protection on the grounds that Canadian stumpage programs were freely "available within Canada on similar terms regardless of the industry or enterprise of the recipient" and that there was "no evidence of governmental targeting regarding stumpage."[24]

The ITA's negative determination temporarily resolved the issue but did not prevent U.S. timber producers from mounting another major challenge to Canada's forest industry policies two years later. In 1985, in a prelude to the second softwood dispute, U.S. cedar shakes and shingles producers, confronted with growing import competition from Canada and declining supplies and rising costs of raw materials, requested and received government support to restrict Canadian exports of shakes and shingles. When the Reagan administration announced the imposition of ad valorem duties of 35 percent on wooden shakes and shingles supplied by Canada in June 1986, it immediately invited Canadian retaliation against such American products as computers, semiconductors, and books.[25] The U.S. sanctions remained in place until 1991. Although the shakes and shingles industry was relatively minor in both economies,[26] this confrontation heralded a more serious trade battle that would emerge between the United States and its largest trading partner later in the year.

Shortly after the settlement of the shakes and shingles dispute, the CFLI, with strong backing from congressional representatives, for a second time petitioned the ITC for trade relief on the grounds that the rates at which Canadian timber was sold in the United States constituted an explicit subsidy that would be countervailable under U.S. trade law. They further referred to a number of specific Canadian government programs and legislations as evidence of such subsidies. When the ITA and the Commerce Department determinations affirmed the existence of government subsidization, the Reagan administration imposed a 15 percent countervailing tariff on softwood (construction) lumber imports from Canada,[27] prompting the Canadians to retaliate with a 70 percent countervailing GATT duty on corn imported from the United States.[28] Canadian negotiators eventually reached an agreement with the United States to place a 15 percent export tax on softwood lumber exports to the United States, but the corn retaliation remained in effect.

The magnitude of this second round of the softwood lumber dispute was unprecedented when one takes into consideration the size of the import sector and the impact of the retaliatory duties on domestic prices. As Joseph Kalt points out, the U.S. lumber tariff represented the largest countervailing/antidumping action undertaken by the United States within the framework of the GATT. In addition, the

Canadian corn retaliation was not only the first CVD ever imposed on the United States by its trading partner but also one of the few CVDs Canada had ever implemented against any nation.[29] Moreover, the lumber trade war entailed considerable costs for both sides, given the importance of the softwood lumber industry to both economies. Total annual sales of softwood lumber in the United States and Canada amounted to about $10 billion and $5 billion, respectively. In particular, since Canada exported about $3 billion in softwood lumber to the United States each year, capturing nearly 30 percent of the U.S. market, a 5–15 percent duty could translate into hundreds of millions of dollars in lost sales each year.[30]

The U.S.–Canada timber trade rift reemerged in the 1990s. In 1991, when the Canadian government unilaterally eliminated the 15 percent export tax on the grounds that a series of stumpage pricing reforms had removed the subsidies to domestic producers, the ITA immediately self-initiated an investigation into Canadian stumpage policies. Based on its final determination that the Canadian stumpage policies constituted implicit subsidies, the ITA in 1992 imposed a CVD of 6.51 percent on lumber imports supplied by several Canadian provinces. The binational panel established according to the new free-trade agreement between the United States and Canada subsequently reviewed the case and requested the ITA to reconsider its determination. The ITA in its remand found additional evidence of subsidization by British Columbia and increased the CVD to 11.54 percent.[31] In 1993, the binational panel turned down the ITA's determination on the grounds that there was no convincing evidence that Canadian stumpage and export controls were "specific" or distorted. The ITA appealed this challenge to its authority without success. The binational panel eventually overruled the ITA's decision, allowing Canadian producers an important victory in this third round of the dispute.

Table 7.1 summarizes the militant history of U.S.–Canada timber trade conflicts. As we will see from the following discussions, the durability of the U.S.–Canada softwood lumber dispute can be explained by a combination of relentless lobbying by the softwood lumber industry and sustained congressional pressure on the executive to deter Canada's aggressive pricing policies. The softwood lumber industry, as a unified, orchestrated group, went out of the way to persuade congressional representatives and administration officials of the existence of Canadian subsidies. The regional concentration of the industry further enhanced the lobbying power of lumber producers, permitting them to apply tremendous pressure on their congressional delegates and, through them, on the executive branch of the U.S. government to garner sufficient support for the countervail.

Moreover, the softwood lumber producers' petition won the support of various segments of the U.S. forest products industry, including producers of plywood, fir, and shakes and shingles. Because Canadian producers had been capturing a growing share of the U.S. forest products market, these U.S. forest industries favored the sanction threats against Canada. Lumber users are a major group that had reason to object to the threats. However, these opposing interests did not have as great a stake in the outcome as did the lumber-producing interests. Their geographical dispersion and inadequate representation in individual constituencies further diminished their political influence on government action. Meanwhile, faced with the possibility of drastic action by Congress that would contradict and challenge the president's policy, the executive branch found it necessary to act in order to preserve a measure of control over future trade policy. Although the Commerce Department and the ITA under it were sympathetic to industry demands, the Reagan administration seemed unwilling to fuel congressional support for more restrictive trade legislation or to frustrate a domestic industry with allies on Capitol Hill. As in the enlargement

TABLE 7.1.   U.S.–Canada Timber Trade Disputes

Case	U.S. Charges	Commerce Department Finding	CVD Imposed	Result
Phase I	Canada's below-market stumpage rates constitute countervailable subsidies	Canadian stumpage subsidy is not specific	None	No further action
Phase II (1986)	Canada's below-market stumpage rates constitute countervailable subsidies	Canadian stumpage subsidy is both specific and distorting	14.5% ad valorem	Canada retaliates against U.S. corn exports; eventually agrees to replace U.S. CVD with 15% export tax.
Phase III (1992–94)	Canada's below-market stumpage rates and log export controls are countervailable under U.S. trade law	Both Canadian stumpage subsidy and export controls are specific and distorting	11.54% ad valorem	Commerce Department finding overruled by binational panel

Source: Kalt, *Political Economy.*

dispute, unity among domestic interest groups and government institutions heightened the risks of escalating the dispute.

Industry Coalition and the Countervail Petition

The U.S. timber industry started the campaign for trade relief in the early 1980s in light of deteriorating industry conditions. Starting in the early 1980s, the timber industry had experienced a steady erosion of comparative advantage due to shrinking sizes, declining productivity and quality of timber, and rising production costs of the extractive and processing sectors in the United States.[32] The success of timber producers in obtaining a favorable Commerce Department determination in the second and third phases of the timber trade rift can be attributed not only to the regional concentration of the industry and its effective lobbying effort but also to the absence of organized domestic opposition. The following analysis will focus on the second phase of the U.S.–Canada timber trade conflict, when both sides implemented trade sanctions, to illustrate the dynamics of interest group involvement.

In the 1986 U.S.–Canada lumber trade dispute, the CFLI, the main industry pressure group, launched the CVD action and orchestrated a highly effective lobbying campaign in Washington. The CFLI, which represented major softwood producer and forest products associations and was responsible for 70 percent of softwood lumber production in the United States, united both softwood lumber producers in the Northwest and those in the southern mountain states. In its 1986 petition to the ITA requesting administrative assistance, the CFLI presented a wide array of evidence supporting the contention that Canadian stumpage policy conferred a subsidy.

The CFLI pointed out that several indicators of industry performance fully revealed the extent of the distress faced by the U.S. lumber industry and sought to attribute the plight of the U.S. timber industry to unfair competition policies adopted by the Canadian government. First, the CFLI argued that the penetration of Canadian imports in the U.S. market had deepened steadily since the late 1970s. Between 1983 and 1985 the share of Canadian imports in the total U.S. consumption of softwood lumber had increased from 27.6 percent to 31.6 percent.[33] Second, profitability and productivity of the lumber industry had experienced a sharp decline over the last decade. Since the late 1970s, the growth rate of total productivity of the U.S. lumber industry had dropped by 2.63 percentage points per year. This distinctive lag in productivity growth would have sharply reduced the competitiveness of the lumber industry in the services of capital and labor in national markets.[34] Third, not only did sawmill capacity in the United States decline steadily, but real U.S. lumber prices remained stagnant despite some improvement in demand. The CFLI took these indicators as unmistakable evidence that "something is not right" with the workings of the free market, asserting that Canadian stumpage policy was directly responsible for the lackluster performance of the U.S. lumber industry.[35]

The CFLI emphasized that the U.S. stumpage price consistently outstripped the Canadian stumpage price (see figure 7.1). It charged that Canadian stumpage fees, unlike those in the United States, were not derived through a competitive bidding process and hence failed to reflect their full market values. The result was that Canadian prices were only a small fraction of U.S. prices. According to the CFLI, this huge gap gave Canadian producers such a crucial edge in the U.S. market that by 1984 Canadian softwood lumber imports had captured nearly one-third of the U.S. market.

The lumber producers defended their case by arguing that they were presenting new information regarding Canadian timber policies. They asserted that there had been a marked shift in the use of timber in Canada toward lumber production since 1983. In particular, government intervention at the provincial level channeled the bulk of timber resources into lumber production, much to the benefit of Canadian lumber producers. The CFLI contended that Canadian stumpage policy, by subsidizing Canadian loggers, indirectly subsidized the lumber industry. The CFLI petition cited a number of other Canadian programs and regulations—such as preferential tax treatment, loan guarantee programs, and public reforestation programs—as additional evidence of the implicit subsidies provided by the Canadian government.[36] To back up its argument, the petition further referred to a 1986 report produced by the ITA, which concluded that Canadian lumber producers were benefiting from an unfair advantage.[37]

The CFLI structured its petition around this factual evidence to meet the criteria of "specificity" and "preferentiality" required by ITA for CVD action. The CFLI also sought to develop the concept of a "primary beneficiary" of a certain government program to bolster its assertion that Canadian lumber practices provided benefits to a specific group or industry. Drawing on lessons from its past failed countervail initiatives, the CFLI devoted considerable attention to gathering necessary legal expertise and advice. For example, in 1985 the CFLI hired the law office of Dewey-Ballantine as its legal and political advisor to help reverse the ITA's earlier decision.[38]

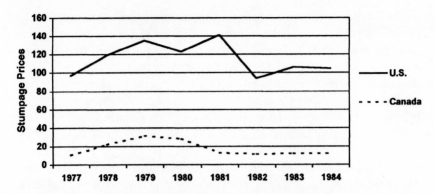

FIGURE 7.1.   U.S. and Canadian stumpage prices, 1977–84 (in U.S.$ per 1,000 board feet [mbf]). (Data from U.S. International Trade Commission, *Conditions Relating to the Importation of Softwood Lumber into the United States,* 1985.)

However, it was in the U.S. Congress that the CFLI spent most of its energy cultivating political support. The industry's unique geographical distribution enhanced its ability to take advantage of U.S. trade law to obtain import protection. As a resource extracting and processing industry, the forest products industry in the United States is an important element of the economic base of the Pacific Northwest and of certain states in the South. Many communities within these regions depend on lumber products as a main source of income and went through a difficult period adjusting to the decline of one of the most important pillars of the regional economy. As a result, these timber interests brought a considerable amount of political pressure to bear on congressional representatives, especially in the Senate, where they had strong representation. In view of the economic importance of the timber industry to the Pacific Northwest and to the South, senators and congressmen from these regions responded to the petition positively, vigorously advocating trade protection on behalf of the timber industry. By 1986, the timber industry had established such a solid friendship with Congress and a number of relevant administrative agencies that the Reagan administration found it difficult to ignore the demands of the timber industry and, in the end, was compelled to retaliate against softwood lumber imports from Canada, the largest U.S. trading partner and one of its closest allies.

As in the EC enlargement case, the absence of any organized, effective opposing domestic interests guaranteed the success of the softwood lumber producers' petition. Various segments of the U.S. forest products industry applauded the threats against Canadian softwood lumber products because Canadian producers' growing incursions into the U.S. market directly threatened competitiveness and employment in their own industries. For example, the American Plywood Association for several years had lobbied for a change in U.S. trade law to raise the tariffs on Canadian plywood imports. The association argued that, without effective government protection, U.S. producers would continue to trail in the market place behind less efficient Canadian mills.[39] U.S. producers of Douglas fir and white fir, two of the primary commodities that were being displaced in the U.S. markets by Canadian lumber exports, also called on the government to take measures to halt the Canadian forest industry's growing penetration of the U.S. market.

Shake and shingle manufacturers, another major component of the forest products industry that was confronted with a deteriorating market share, supported the sanction threats as well. For example, between the late 1970s and early 1980s, U.S. production of western red cedar shake had declined steadily so that total U.S. production in 1984 was only one-sixth of the 1977 level. The decline of U.S. production was accompanied by a perceptible increase in the Canadian share of the U.S. market, which rose from 21.3 percent in 1975 to an alarming 79 percent in 1984.[40] The U.S. Shake and Shingle Association attributed this growing import penetration to Canadian government subsidies that allowed Canadian producers to consistently undercut U.S. mill prices. The association urged the U.S. government to take actions to ensure the survival of the shake and shingle industry. Furthermore, the industry's successful Section 201 petition earlier in the year reflected the industry's determination to deter Canada's aggressive pricing strategies. When the softwood lumber producers filed their countervail petition, the shake and shingle industry expressed its support for the action.

Lumber users, the group with the most reason to oppose trade sanctions, did not strongly lobby against the protection sought by lumber producers. The National Association of Home Builders (NAHB), which represented construction contractors, estimated that a 15 percent duty on Canadian lumber would have only a marginal effect on the price of housing in the United States.[41] Because trade between the United States and Canada was competitive, and because housing was a large U.S. industry with surplus capacity, the import duty would be unlikely to induce sharp price hikes. Because they could afford a small increase in lumber prices, the NAHB did not make a visible effort to oppose the lumber producers' trade initiative. Although a small number of lumber dealers, home builders, unions, and railroad and port organizations had organized themselves into an ad hoc body, the Coalition to Stop Unfair Wood Tariffs, to defeat both the countervail petition and the proposed restrictive congressional legislation, they had minimal influence on government action both because of the lack of strong political incentive and because of the geographical dispersion of its membership.[42] The absence of effective domestic opposition increased both the attractiveness and the persuasiveness of the softwood lumber producers' countervail petition before the ITA.

Process and Rationale of the ITA Decision

U.S. lumber producers were highly successful in enlisting the support of individual congressmen and senators. Although these legislators were a minority in Congress, they were able to make substantial inroads in congressional debates. Meanwhile, to preempt a forceful and serious congressional challenge to the executive influence over trade policy, the Reagan administration responded favorably to industry pleas with full protection. Although the Commerce Department was supposedly more sympathetic to the perspective of business groups, the desire to avoid provoking Congress into adopting more restrictive trade legislation reinforced the appeal of policy proposals for trade relief. In particular, the ITA, despite its proclaimed political neutrality as a quasi-judicial body, turned out to be amenable to industry and congressional pressure. In addition, considerations for the viability of U.S. forest industries made the executive office more receptive to industry and congressional demands. The broad consensus that was eventually forged between the executive and legislative branches, reinforced by strong, unified industry pressure, resulted in a highly confrontational approach in the U.S. lumber trade dispute with Canada.

As mentioned earlier, U.S. lumber interests worked assiduously to impress upon congressional members the merit of their case and to lobby for a change in U.S. trade law in order to ensure the countervailability of subsidized natural resources. The softwood lumber issue appealed to many congressional representatives as a clear case of unfair foreign competition that placed U.S. producers at a disadvantage in international markets. Congress also was concerned about the economic viability of single-industry resource producers and, to some extent, about certain large regional economies. Many congressional members had linked the steadily rising Canadian share of the U.S. timber market to stagnant employment and investment levels at home. They alleged that the increasing ability of Canadian producers to penetrate the U.S. market did not reflect the two countries' comparative advantages in terms of the quality of natural resources and their costs of production. Rather, it resulted from government pricing policies that subsidized resource producers.[43] Thus, in view of the threat posed by unfair Canadian competition, Congress entered the debate on the side of the softwood lumber industry.

Congressmen and senators from timber-producing states in the South, Pacific Northwest, and mountain states played a crucial role in publicizing the plight of the industry and in extracting concessions from the administration. Their representation in certain important congressional committees, particularly those in charge of international trade policy, created a highly visible platform for the lumber industry. For example, Senator Robert Packwood of Oregon was chairman of the Senate Finance Committee and a member of the Subcommittee on International Trade. Senator Packwood was reportedly "compelled to oppose [U.S.–Canada free-trade] negotiations if no solution (to the Softwood Lumber dispute) appears."[44] Senator Russell Long of Louisiana was the ranking minority member. In addition, Representative Sam Gibbons of Florida was chairman of the Subcommittee on Trade of the House Ways and Means Committee.[45] Representative Don Bonker of Washington and Senator Max Baucus of Montana voluntarily stepped into the debate on behalf of lumber producers and soon became strong advocates on Capitol Hill.[46]

This emerging congressional coalition, at the urging of the CFLI, exerted tremendous pressure on the ITA to reverse its earlier ruling. Several legislative proposals were introduced to address the alleged unfair trade practices. Some of them aimed to place strict limits on Canadian softwood lumber exports to the United States; others sought to broaden the definition of subsidy so that there would be no doubt that Canadian provincial governments had subsidized their lumber industry.[47]

At the same time as the softwood lumber dispute unfolded, U.S. negotiators were seeking fast-track approval in Congress for the upcoming free-trade talks with Canada. Members of Congress quickly moved to make approval of a Canada-U.S. free-trade agreement contingent upon satisfactory resolution of the softwood lumber dispute. In other words, an important part of the congressional strategy was to forge a link between acceptance of trade liberalization and a specific case of administered protection.[48] Congress was positioned to do so because it would have been difficult for senators to justify free trade with Canada when Canadian import penetration was increasingly threatening a domestic industry that served as an important pillar of the economic base of certain regions.[49] To signal congressional determination to settle the dispute, a majority of senators sent a letter to President Reagan in late 1985 insisting that they would not proceed with the Canada-U.S. free-trade negotiations before the lumber dispute was resolved to their satisfaction. In February 1986, Senator Baucus, with the support of fifteen senators, warned Canada to reduce softwood lumber exports or to be prepared to face the consequences. Furthermore, half of the members of the Senate Finance Committee wrote to USTR Clayton Yeutter emphasizing their "concern about Canadian softwood lumber imports":

> Any free trade agreement must be built on a foundation of mutually advantageous trade practices. Therefore, we believe the administration should seek an early resolution of the softwood lumber trade issues. This would facilitate Finance Committee consideration of any Administrative proposals relating to the negotiation of a free trade agreement with Canada.[50]

Yeutter responded that the administration already had taken measures to address the issue and also had persuaded the Canadians to come to the negotiation table. Dissatisfied with Yeutter's response, a group of senators, led by Senator Baucus, again brought up the issue on the Senate floor in February 1986. Baucus reiterated the congressional position:

> They [Canadians] cannot have it both ways. If they expect the United States to enter a free trade agreement, they must engage in free trade. . . . I am optimistic about the benefits a free trade agreement might bring, but I cannot support such an agreement, so long as subsidized Canadian lumber makes a mockery of free trade.[51]

In April 1986, in an ultimatum to the Reagan administration, the Senate Finance Committee explicitly stated that it would deny fast-track approval of the Canada-U.S. free-trade talks unless the softwood lumber dispute could be addressed to industry satisfaction.

Besides its active effort to link the softwood lumber dispute to broader issues in U.S. trade policy, the U.S. Congress also tried to broaden the definition of "subsidy" to ensure the countervailability of Canadian softwood lumber practices. Even prior to the lumber dispute, Congress tried to seek a redefinition of "subsidy." In 1984, Congress amended the Tariff Act of 1930 to include provisions that would have made certain "upstream" or "input" products countervailable.[52] This broadening of the legal definition increased the chances of success of the softwood countervail appeal because it assured that subsidized log production also constituted a countervailable subsidy to the lumber industry.

In the face of enormous congressional pressure, the Reagan administration veered decisively toward a trade policy favoring the forest industry. With future control of the Senate at stake, the administration could no longer shield Canada, one of its closest allies, from charges of violating free-trade principles. At a 1985 "timber summit" sponsored by the CFLI, Commerce Secretary Malcolm Baldrige came under intense pressure from the CFLI and its congressional representatives to provide trade relief. At this point Baldrige still emphasized that the administration would adhere to the position adopted by ITA in 1983.[53] By the spring of 1986, however, growing congressional support for the lumber industry had fundamentally altered the administration's calculus.

For fear that lack of progress on the softwood issue would fuel protectionist sentiment in Congress, the United States managed to persuade Canada to resume negotiations in early 1986. At the same time, the administration undertook a series of initiatives to placate forest industry officials and their representatives in Congress. In his statements before the Senate Finance Committee, USTR Clayton Yeutter indicated a growing willingness to accept congressional proposals. Commerce and USTR officials also held meetings with industry leaders and senators from lumber-producing states, assuring them of the administration's willingness to resolve the dispute.[54] The executive department wanted to prevent Congress from derailing the talks with Canada over the Free Trade Agreement or from enacting more stringent, congressionally mandated legislation.

The changing mood of the administration was reflected in a discussion between President Reagan and advocates of the lumber issue in the Senate Finance Committee on the eve of congressional vote, where President Reagan finally succumbed to industry and congressional pressure. In a public letter to Senator Packwood, President Reagan promised for the first time to resolve the softwood lumber dispute before reaching a bilateral free-trade agreement with Canada. Reagan's political concessions signaled the evaporation of executive support that previously had protected Canadian softwood lumber from domestic protectionist pressure.

Furthermore, the Commerce Department, in which the ITA was

located, was not insulated from political pressure from Congress. Indeed, Congress's threat to pass legislation targeted specifically at foreign, "underpriced," raw material imports to resource processors had posed genuine concerns to the Commerce Department. In the event such legislative proposals became law, the United States would be seen to have violated its obligations under the GATT, thus inviting retaliatory legislation by its trading partners. Such congressional action could have made billions of dollars of U.S. agricultural and primary manufactured exports easy targets of foreign retaliatory duties, leaving the Commerce Department with the problem of how to deal with increasingly contentious trade disputes with major trading partners. Thus, the choice facing the Commerce Department was clear: either to achieve a satisfactory outcome in the softwood lumber dispute or to provoke a forceful legislative response that could affect other trade areas. The latter scenario was by no means appealing to the Commerce Department. Consequently, the Commerce Department decided to reverse its earlier ruling and to grant the softwood lumber industry a favorable determination.

Thus, when the ITA announced its determination on October 16, 1986, the result was hardly surprising. The ITA ruled that Canadian provincial stumpage programs conferred a subsidy on Canadian softwood lumber producers. Moreover, the ITA finding confirmed the CFLI's contention that Canadian subsidies were countervailable because they were targeted at specific lumber producers and caused distortions in the domestic lumber market. Given these findings and pursuant to U.S. trade law, the ITA imposed a 15 percent tariff on lumber imported from four Canadian provinces. Although the 15 percent figure was lower than the 25 percent duty sought by the lumber industry, U.S. lumber interests nevertheless emerged as the principal victors and beneficiaries in this dispute, as the ITA decision effectively barred a significant portion of Canadian softwood lumber exports from entering the United States. The imposition of sanctions thus, by and large, satisfied a domestic industry that had put forth the most compelling political demands.

Canadian Reactions

Just as lumber producers were politically active in the United States, their Canadian counterparts were influential in the making of Canadian public policy. Indeed, the lumber industry occupied an important place in the Canadian economy and was even dominant in several regions of the country. At the time of the second lumber dispute in the mid-1980s, softwood lumber production amounted to $5 billion a year; the softwood lumber industry was larger in size than the aggregate of metals, agriculture, fisheries, and autos. Lumber contributed roughly 4 percent of Canadian gross national product (GNP) and Canadian exports to the United States. Canadian imports supplied roughly 30 percent of the U.S. market and accounted for more than 99 percent of foreign lumber imported into the United States.[55]

Given the importance of the softwood lumber industry in the Canadian economy, it was not surprising that the Canadians responded so forcefully to Washington's trade restrictions. Canadian sawmills and the Canadian government had consistently organized active opposition to CVD actions against Canadian lumber. While provincial forestry ministries and, to a lesser extent, the federal government of Canada led and financed participation in legal proceedings, Canadian sawmill producers played the key supporting role, supplying the necessary information and testimony to assist in efforts to defend what were perceived as Canada's legitimate interests. Since Canadian mills clearly stood to lose from U.S. import restrictions, their stakes in influencing the role and forcefulness of the various Canadian government agents were indeed substantial. The Canadian Forest Industry Council, a coalition of forest industry enterprises in which the Forest Industries of British Columbia played a leading part, employed legal counsel in the United States, made submissions to the ITC, and actively opposed the countervail actions before the ITA.

Ever since the failure of the first countervail initiative, the Canadian forest industry learned that U.S. lumber producers were able to successfully elicit congressional support and that, to counter such strong protectionist pressure, it was necessary for them to adopt a "political" strategy focused on the U.S. Congress and to develop necessary legal expertise to help bolster the case of forest products producers in British Columbia. The second countervail appeal, in particular, convinced Canadian lumber producers that the adjudication process was politically influenced and that there was substantial support within the United States for CFLI's countervail appeal. As Apsey and Thomas reported on the reactions of Canadian forest producers, "We failed to appreciate that the case has taken on such significance in U.S. politics that the normal handling of a trade case would be put aside. We did not know that the professionalism and independence of judgment that had resulted in the earlier determination in Canada's favor had dissipated under intense political pressure."[56] The industry subsequently devoted most of its effort to influencing the decisions of the U.S. Congress.

The Canadian forest industry was not the only actor opposing U.S. CVD actions. Since U.S. CVD actions against Canadian stumpage and log export policies were perceived as frontal assaults on Canadian sovereignty in the area of natural resource policy, the fight against U.S. trade restrictions also gained the sympathy of the Canadian public as a whole. Such broad public support bolstered the government's active resistance to the CVD duties and heightened the risks of confrontation on the Canadian side as well.

Thus, in September 1986, Canadian federal, provincial, and forest industry representatives concerned with the countervail action conducted meetings to arrive at a common strategy of opposition. In early October, a week prior to the announcement of the U.S. lumber decision, Canada's minister for international trade called U.S. producers' lobbying for tariff protection "unjustified harassment . . . meddling around in our natural-resource pricing" and explicitly warned retaliation.[57] On November 7, with support from liberals and conservatives in Parliament, the Canadian government imposed a 67 percent CVD on U.S. corn exports to Canada, a duty that remained in place until 1987. The swift, highly visible, and vociferous retaliatory response of the Canadian government in Lumber II, the second episode of the softwood lumber dispute, reflected a strong domestic sentiment against aggressive U.S. trade action.

In this case, both the British Columbia industry and the federal government, operating on the assumption that they ought to have prevailed in a fight against the United States, would have preferred to fight this through the U.S. adjudication process were it not for intervention by British Columbia's new premier, Bill Vander Zalm, who considered an export tax a possible solution to British Columbia's revenue problem. The new premier, who was looking for new sources of revenue, apparently determined that if some form of duty had to be imposed on lumber it would benefit Canadian authorities to collect the tariff revenues to enrich British Columbia's coffer than to let this income go to the United States. Thus, two months later, soon before the 15 percent U.S. duty was scheduled to become permanent, U.S. and Canadian negotiators reached an agreement on December 31 that implemented a 15 percent Canadian export duty in exchange for the U.S. lumber industry dropping its countervail action. According to a key CFLI official, had it not been for the actions of the British Columbia government, the memorandum of understanding would never have come into place.[58] Since the Canadian lumber industry had experienced considerable distress, reflected in increasing numbers of layoffs and decreasing revenue, it was entirely possible that the Canadian lumber producers would have insisted on a hard-line position had it not been for Bill Vander Zalm's intervention. That the third episode of the lumber dispute would take place only a few years later reveals the intense pressure for trade conflict from Canadian lumber producers.

Conclusion

In both the EC enlargement case and the U.S.–Canada timber trade conflict, the United States escalated the disputes to trade wars because of the absence of major domestic opposition to sanction threats. In the EC enlargement case, both export-seeking and import-competing interests supported an aggressive negotiation strategy because both competed with EC agricultural products and would win whether the threat was carried out or not. Hence, the enlargement case united both producers seeking to remove the restrictions in the Iberian market and import-competing interests targeted by EC counterretaliation. Similarly, in the timber trade conflict, U.S. softwood lumber producers did not encounter domestic resistance. Since many U.S. forest product groups were alarmed by the growing Canadian penetration of the U.S. market and in the past had pushed for restrictions on Canadian products, they simply had no reason to object to the retaliatory measures. Moreover, import users did not oppose the threats, as they easily could substitute reduced imports with domestic products at comparable qualities without paying substantially higher prices, an option that import users in a complementary trade situation simply did not have. Table 7.2 presents a summary of the impact and position of the key actors involved in the EC enlargement and the U.S.–Canadian softwood lumber disputes.

This unity among U.S. domestic interest groups was reinforced by the executive branch's willingness to level the playing field for U.S. industries that it viewed as fundamentally competitive but suffering from unfair barriers and subsidies. With regard to EC enlargement, the executive was sufficiently concerned about declining farm exports and the deleterious effects of protectionist EC agricultural policies to initiate trade retaliation. It viewed the new EC trade restrictions as reflecting another conspicuous attempt by the EC to block U.S. products from the European market. In the dispute with Canada, the timber

TABLE 7.2. Profiles of Main Actors Involved in U.S.–EC Enlargement and U.S.–Canada Softwood Lumber Disputes

	Companies and Associations	Position	Impact
U.S.–EC: EC Enlargement			
Directly Affected Exporters	Feed Grains Council (representing feed grains producers)	Demanded full compensation to American farmers caused by increased Spanish and Portuguese tariffs associated with EC enlargement.	Instrumental in pushing for trade sanctions.
Exporters Not Directly Affected	Other agricultural groups such as producers of corn, barley, and grain sorghum	Have long complained about the EC's protectionist trade policy; came out in favor of trade sanctions.	Increased the pressure for proactive trade policy.
Import-Competing Interests	Producers of corn (maize), barley, and grain sorghum	Supported efforts to expand U.S. market shares in the Iberian states, as they similarly felt victimized by unfair EC competition.	Supported sanction threats; strengthened the impact of feed grain producers.
Import-Using Interests	—	—	—
U.S.–Canada: Lumber			
Directly Affected Exporters	—	—	—
Exporters Not Directly Affected	—	—	—
Import-Competing Interests	U.S. Coalition for Fair Lumber Imports; softwood lumber producers; producers of plywood, fir, shake, and shingle; American Plywood Association; U.S. Shake & Shingle Association	Claimed that Canadian stumpage and export control policies caused considerable harm to U.S. producers and remained countervailable under U.S. trade law.	Was major actor pushing for trade sanctions.
Import-Using Interests	National Association of Home Builders	Because there is a large domestic industry with surplus capacity, users did not face any price hike and therefore did not oppose the sanction threat.	Unlike in U.S.–China cases, did not oppose sanction threats.

industry, which had traditionally enjoyed a home market advantage, was able to exert sufficient political pressure on executive action. Both in 1986 and in 1991, the lumber industry, with the help of Congress, solidified its friendship with relevant administrative agencies and gained their full support in obtaining protection from Canadian imports. By 1991, this friendship was so strong that it led the Commerce Department to take the unusual step of initiating a Section 301 petition. Such sympathetic hearings from administrative agencies increased the chances of successful industry petition.

This pattern of unified domestic support contrasts with the highly divisive domestic politics in U.S.–China trade disputes. Because of competitive trade relations between the United States and its European and Canadian trading partners, there were very few import-using groups, as in the U.S.–China cases, that sought to undermine the sanction threats. Instead, import-competing interests entered the policy debate in favor of trade retaliation. Trade structures affected domestic politics in these two sets of cases in different ways, increasing the likelihood of trade wars in the U.S.–EC and U.S.–Canadian cases while reducing the chances of escalation in trade disputes between the United States and China. The discussions in this chapter have focused on the internal political dynamics in the sender of threats, without discussing how trade structure impinges on the political processes in the EC and Canada. This question will be taken up in the next chapter, which briefly examines the political dynamics in target countries with varying degrees of trade competitiveness with the United States to show how trade structure shapes political coalitions in the target in a way that reinforces patterns of trade war and threat effectiveness described so far in this book.

The conclusion that countries with competitive trade relations (such as U.S. trade relations with Canada or the EU) face heightened risks of trade war is particularly salient in view of the belief that international institutions presumably serve to ameliorate trade conflicts for such states. For example, many trade conflicts between the United States and Europe are undertaken within the framework of the WTO, whereas U.S.–Canada trade conflicts are increasingly placed within the orbit of the Free Trade Agreement/North American Free Trade Agreement (NAFTA). Scholars in the neoliberal institutional tradition have argued that institutions may enhance the prospects for international cooperation by altering the transaction costs faced by the states, lengthening their time horizons, creating issue linkages, producing iterated games, and reducing the incentives to cheat by increasing the transparency of information.[59] If institutions do help to reduce states' incentives for defection by helping to routinize conflicts between member states and by preventing escalation into wider trade wars, then the reality that trade wars do frequently take place between competitive trade partners only serves to highlight the intense domestic pressure generated by trade complementarity. For example, in the most recent trade spats between the United States and the EU over bananas and beef hormone, the two sides barely avoided a tit-for-tat retaliation, even given the presence of international institutions, suggesting that the asymmetrical domestic interests generated by competitive trade structure may produce highly contentious trade conflicts that preclude institutional solutions.

Moreover, the specific designs of certain international institutional arrangements may not be particularly conducive to insulating domestic pressure for trade relief. Some international institutions may have actually heightened, rather than lessened, protectionist pressure. The third episode of the softwood lumber dispute (Lumber III) provides an example in support of this argument. Judith Goldstein, for example, argues that the establishment of binational panels under FTA/NAFTA was intended by Congress to insulate itself from protectionist pressures by transferring some of its authority to the FTA.[60] Benjamin Cashore argues to the contrary that protectionist pressure at the congressional level actually increased after the third softwood countervail attempt, even though agency discretion appeared to have been reduced during Lumber III. He finds that rather than shielding congressional members from powerful domestic interests, as Goldstein's argument would predict, the binational panel helped to formalize the procedures employed by the Commerce Department to affirm the existence of a subsidy in Lumber III, thereby reducing the possibility of a finding in favor of a foreign competitor in the future and increasing congressional activism on the countervail file. In other words, the establishment of a binational panel actually strengthened the U.S. domestic industry's ability to threaten or to use countervail actions to secure increased relief, in the process reducing the likelihood that future NAFTA binational panels would remand ITA and ITC decisions.[61] Therefore, even though international institutions do play an important role in helping to constrain trade conflicts among countries such as the United States, the EU, and Canada from spilling over into wider trade wars, they do not always prevent trade wars both due to the asymmetric interest structure between the parties and because of specific features of institutional design.

CHAPTER 8

Conclusion

The previous chapters have examined in detail the conditions under which the United States would find the use of coercive trade negotiation strategies to be effective in securing concessions from the target country and the coalitional politics in the sender of threats that enhances the risks of aggressive escalation to trade war. Both the quantitative analyses and the detailed case studies suggest that competitive versus complementary trade structure shapes patterns of interest group alignment and institutional support in the sender of threats in sharply contrasting ways. These different dynamics at the domestic level in turn lead to substantial variations in the effectiveness of American threats and in the possibility of trade retaliation.

In the following pages, I piece together evidence gleaned from various parts of this book to present a profile of the major groups involved in each of the case studies, their position, and their influence on the resultant pattern of negotiations. As I have demonstrated throughout the case study chapters, the views of export-seeking interests (including both exporters with direct stakes in the negotiations and those who are not directly involved in the dispute and yet would be indirectly affected if trade sanctions were imposed against the target), import-competing groups, and import users differ substantially under different trade structures, affecting both the ability of American negotiators to elicit a positive response from the target country and the possibility of escalation to trade war. Because evidence about interest group involvement is scattered throughout the case study chapters, the section that follows will more systematically synthesize my previous analyses to highlight the differences in the positions of the key actors involved in the policy process and their impact on the policy outcome.

While the preceding analyses confirm my theoretical expectations regarding the centrality of trade structure, they also raise several questions that are not adequately addressed by my initial hypotheses. For instance, the research has found that non-directly involved exporters can be important players in the anti-sanctions coalition, further buttressing import users' opposition to threats to cut off imports from the target. In a similar vein, cases aimed at greater market access and those intended primarily to bar foreign exports from the home market seem to exhibit somewhat different patterns of interest group mobilization, as the latter seem to elicit greater domestic support for retaliatory measures. These factors are not incorporated into my initial hypotheses but nevertheless are important for understanding the pattern of domestic support for aggressive negotiation tactics. I therefore discuss the relevance of these additional findings for trade negotiations.

After addressing these additional findings, I then proceed to raise several questions encountered during this research that merit further investigation. Two questions that seem particularly worthy of future research relate to the domestic politics of the target country and the impact of the strengthened dispute settlement mechanism of the WTO on America's unilateral pursuit of unilateral market-opening policies. First, since trade disputes involve the dynamic interaction of both parties, how domestic politics in the target country shapes the government's response to sanction threats is a key theoretical question that warrants further exploration. Examination of the domestic politics of the target may yield insights that lend further support to the propositions advanced in this book. I therefore address the need for undertaking careful research of the political economy of the target state and offer some tentative hypotheses about how trade structure influences domestic politics in the target in a way that reinforces the two empirical patterns analyzed in previous chapters.

Second, since the findings of this research are supported primarily with evidence from the 1975–95 period, before the introduction of the new dispute settlement procedures of the WTO, one may wonder to what extent my key hypothesis about trade competitiveness versus complementarity can accommodate these recent changes in the context of American trade policy. To address these concerns, I discuss the relevance of this study for recent U.S. trade actions. Referring in particular to U.S. trade policy toward China, I suggest possible avenues through which American negotiators may better achieve their policy objectives.

In the final section, I place this research within the context of the relevant literature on international relations and revisit the theoretical questions that motivate this research, focusing in particular on the contributions of this study to the two-level game approach and its potential for improving our understanding of the different strands of the democratic peace theory. I conclude by discussing the implications of my study for the execution and design of American trade policy, emphasizing in particular the ramifications of my findings about the important role of domestic politics for the United States' pursuit of aggressive negotiation tactics in trade policy.

Toward a Systematic Analysis of Domestic Politics

Earlier scholarship on two-level game theory has emphasized the nexus between domestic and international politics. This book contributes to the research program on two-level games by engaging in a systematic investigation of the domestic sources of international behavior and by developing a more complete characterization of the domestic game. Consistent with my initial hypothesis, trade structure affects both the pattern of domestic interest group alignment and the degree of institutional divisions in the sender of threats, with important consequences for the probability of trade war and the level of threat effectiveness. Specifically, a more competitive trade structure produces greater unity in favor of aggressive negotiation tactics, leading to the adoption of tough bargaining strategies by policymakers. Domestic unity not only enhances the credibility of U.S. threats in the eyes of the target country but also increases the risk of aggressive escalation to trade war. Conversely, a complementary trade structure aggravates divisions in domestic support for trade sanctions, resulting in reduced threat credibility and lower risks of trade war.

In each of the cases analyzed in the previous chapters, four major groups of actors have played decisive roles in influencing negotiation outcomes. Specifically, these groups are (1) exporters seeking to improve the access of their specific products to the target market. This group of actors has often turned out to be among the most vocal advocates of sanction threats; (2) firms exporting other goods to the target. The position of these groups depends on the specific negotiation context. They either support sanctions if they expect that sanction threats against a particular product would have spillover effects that could help to improve their own sales to the target (as in most U.S.–Japan trade negotiation cases), or they oppose sanctions if they expect that sanction threats would invite foreign retaliation, reducing exports of their products to the target (as in U.S.–China cases); (3) firms competing with products made in the target country. These import-competing interests tend to be another major force supporting sanction threats, as they could benefit from the increased prices at which foreign producers have to market their products in the home country; (4) firms that import and use goods from the target. Since sanctions often threaten to either increase the costs or to interrupt the flow of their supplies, the degree to which these importers and users support sanction threats depends on the magnitude of the price increase, shaped in large part by the availability of alternative sources of supply inside the United States. Under competitive trade, these import-using groups ought to be less inclined to resist sanctions because they could obtain the same products from other domestic suppliers at comparable prices.

For example, if we compare U.S.–China trade disputes with U.S.–Japan or U.S.–Europe cases, we can see that in the former set of cases there are few, if any, firms that compete with imports from the target. In the MFN and textile trade disputes, textile producers did mount an attack on textile imports from China. However, they seemed to be unable to compete in the policy process with a fairly large constituency of firms that export to and import from China. Even exporters whose products were not targeted by trade sanctions opposed sanction threats out of fear that sanctions would provoke Chinese retaliation against their own products, thus threatening to reduce American access to the potentially lucrative Chinese market. Such highly polarized positions held by domestic interest groups lessened the credibility of sanction threats and at the same time minimized the chances for dispute escalation.

The dynamics of U.S. negotiations with Japan and Europe contrasts sharply with the pattern just described. The extent to which both export-seeking and import-competing firms share the same pro-sanction policy preferences distinguishes these negotiations from U.S.–China cases. Since trade between the United States and these trading partners is highly competitive, there is a large constituency in the United States competing with European and Japanese imports. This import-competing constituency has virtually no incentive to resist sanction threats because it could benefit from the restrictions placed on foreign imports in the event that sanctions were carried out. With such solid support from both export-seeking and import-competing firms, both the credibility of the U.S. negotiation position and the chances for aggressive dispute escalation are greatly enhanced.

To be sure, as with complementary trade, competitive trade creates its own winners and losers. In particular, competitive trade could generate opposition from downstream firms and from consumers whose welfare may be negatively affected by the increased prices induced by the new trade barriers. For example, in the U.S.–Japan semiconductor trade conflict, sanction threats met with resistance from semiconductor users, who objected to the increased chip prices. Similarly, in the U.S.–Canada trade dispute over softwood lumber, lumber users and homebuilders raised concerns about increases in lumber prices. However, while competitive trade structure generated domestic opposition as well, these opposing interests were far less organized and coherent as a political force than under complementary trade. When trade is competitive, a large import-competing industry with surplus capacity typically exists in the country issuing the threat. As a result, the price hikes generated by trade sanctions are not nearly as steep as if trade were complementary, nor do they affect as large a segment of U.S. business interests as in the latter case. This explains why import users have exhibited a far lower level of political organization and activism in U.S.–Japan trade negotiations than in U.S.–China cases. In short, the case studies suggest that trade structure is an important factor explaining the pattern of trade war and threat effectiveness. The distributional consequences of competitive versus complementary trade relations matter for international negotiation outcomes.

Qualifications

An important caveat follows from the analysis just described. My case studies reveal that, in addition to the influence of trade structure on my two dependent variables, it also makes a difference whether threats are used to expand overseas export markets or are employed primarily to reduce foreign imports into the home market. Compared to cases related to exports, issues concerning foreign imports on the whole seem to have generated stronger domestic pressure in support of trade retaliation. The U.S.–Canada negotiations over softwood lumber and the U.S.–China trade row over textiles are both examples of disputes in which aggressive trade negotiation strategies have been employed to prevent import penetration. In these cases, sanction threats did not engender exporters' active participation because threats did not directly impinge on exporters' interests except when they faced the likelihood of retaliation. Exporters' inactivity in these situations allowed highly protectionist import-competing interests to define the issue and to exert considerable influence throughout the dispute to obtain trade relief. This partly explains why, although the United States was able to peacefully settle those disputes with the Chinese where threats were carried out to open the Chinese market (e.g., IPR, market access, and MFN), it had greater difficulty achieving cooperation in the textile dispute, which primarily concerned imports. Thus, the cases remind us that the nature of the trade dispute, in addition to the structure of trade between two states, seems to be another important variable that needs to be taken into consideration to understand the dynamics of foreign trade policy.

Furthermore, in discussing trade relations between complementary trading partners, my original hypothesis focuses primarily on the role of exporters seeking improved market access to the target country and that of import users in the sender of threats, leaving out considerations of the influence of exporters who had no direct stakes in the dispute but who could nevertheless suffer from the possible effects of counterretaliation from the target. Yet in the process of tracing the activities of various domestic groups in the policy-making process, the case studies have exposed the active role of these non–directly involved exporters in opposing sanction threats. The coalition between these export-oriented industries and import users has provided an important counterbalance to the forces pushing for trade sanctions. Exporters' participation in the anti-sanctions coalition reinforced the divisions in American politics, both reducing the coherence of the American negotiation position and allowing complementary trading partners to capitalize on these internal strains in the sender of threats to their own advantage. For example, aware of both American importers' and retailers' reliance on labor-intensive products made in China and of the attraction of the Chinese market to American exporters, trade negotiators of complementary trading states such as China have frequently stated that they had nothing to lose in the event of a trade war, as the American exporting industry would have to forego valuable business opportunities in such an event.

Since the extent to which non–directly involved exporters will mobilize against threats of trade sanctions depends to a considerable extent on the scale of the target market, one may argue that it is possible that sanction threats will be particularly ineffective in gaining concessions in large developing country markets such as China or India but may not be as fruitless in other developing countries with smaller domestic markets such as Thailand or Indonesia. This is a reasonable conjecture. Future studies could more closely examine trade negotiations between the United States and its complementary trading partners with smaller domestic markets to see whether the size of the target market makes any substantive difference. However, since my argument about threat effectiveness relates primarily to the role of import-competing versus import-using interests under different trade structures, it may be argued that, as long as there exists an active import lobby in the sender of threats, one would expect the sender of threats to experience difficulties establishing its credibility vis-à-vis the target, the size of the target market notwithstanding. While an active lobby by those exporters indirectly implicated in the dispute could further enhance the powers of the import users and hence the anti-sanctions coalition, it is not the only plausible explanation for the variations in threat effectiveness and the probability of trade war.

Finally, this study defines trade structure at the level of dyadic interactions without identifying industries or sectors with an active import lobby. This is justifiable, as sanction threats are often targeted at groups outside of the sector with protectionist practices and can thus bring additional actors from other industries into the picture. It is possible, though, to extend this analysis to identify industry-specific characteristics that impact on negotiation outcomes. For example, the reason why the United States and Canada have not fought more trade wars may be that the trade overlaps between the two countries involve predominantly automobile trade in which the same three companies (i.e., GM, Ford, and Chrysler) supply the bulk of U.S. and Canadian output. In addition, this trade has long been governed by a bilateral free-trade agreement in automobiles. Specific industry-level characteristics, such as the existence of intrafirm trade, could be taken into consideration in future research to address the question of why trade wars are more likely to take place in one sector than another.

Questions for Future Research

This book raises several issues that merit further research. First, although the logic of my argument ought to be applicable to bilateral trade disputes involving different country dyads over a longer time span, the empirical analysis of trade negotiations in this study is confined to trade disputes between the United States and its top twenty-five trading partners between 1980 and 1995, largely because of the difficulty of obtaining standard trade structure data for dyads of which the United States is not a part. But if the argument developed previously is valid, then it will be possible to test my argument against a larger sample of dyads over a longer period of time, including those disputes initiated by countries other than the United States. Such a comprehensive empirical investigation, by varying the power asymmetry between the parties involved in the disputes, will allow us to capture better the complexity of international trade bargaining to determine that the empirical patterns established here are not a unique feature of American trade policy or of trade negotiations between great powers.

Second, although the United States has a greater tendency to be involved in trade wars with its competitive trade partners, not all trade conflicts between such pairs have ended up in a trade war. For example, although the United States has threatened economic sanctions against Japan for its unfair trade practices numerous times and has on a few occasions imposed trade sanctions against Japan, none of the trade conflicts between the two countries has flared up into a tit-for-tat trade war. This raises the question of why states with a competitive trade structure are willing to risk trade war in some industries but not in others. As mentioned earlier, inquiring into industry-specific characteristics may generate useful answers to these questions.[1]

Third, it may be interesting to compare domestic politics in the sender of threats with the domestic political economy of the receiver of threats. Since domestic politics in the target represents the flip side of the coin, an examination of how competitive versus complementary trade structure affects the coalitional patterns in the targets may yield additional insights that complement the story on the side of the sender and thus provide additional support for my overall argument. Such an analysis may also allow us to see, for example, why, given the greater pressure that competitive trade exerts on import-competing groups in the target to resist concessions, some competitive trading partners are simultaneously more likely to offer concessions *and* more likely to get into trade wars with the United States. In the following section, I present some tentative hypotheses about how trade structure influences domestic politics in the targets in a way that complements my hypotheses about the connection between trade structure and the sender of threats, hypotheses that can form the basis for future research.

Trade Structure and the Political Economy of the Target States: Preliminary Hypotheses

The anecdotal evidence on domestic politics in the receiver of threats uncovered during this research suggests that trade structure reverberates in the target in a way that reinforces the causal logic developed in this book. When the United States threatens to restrict trade with its partner country because the latter fails to address its unfair trade practices, sanction threats typically create a schism between industries whose protectionist trade practices constitute the source of the trade dispute and those whose exports to the United States would be jeopardized if sanctions were actually carried out. Thus, the degree to which export-oriented interests could overcome resistance from the former group of players for resisting concessions crucially determines the extent to which the target country will concede to the sender's demands.

When trade is complementary, exporters in target countries are less likely to be able to successfully resist forces opposed to concessions than are their counterparts in countries with a complementary trade relationship with the United States. This is because, under complementary trade, protectionist trade practices targeted by U.S. trade actions often involve industries that enjoy strong protection from the state. These industries, many of which are import-substituting ones, will tend to draw on their ties with the state, which has an interest in economic development, to fight against exporters' push for moderation. The strong connections between the state and the import-substituting industries may help to explain why complementary trading partners can simultaneously be less concessionary and more likely to be willing to endure the cost of a trade war.

For example, in U.S.–China negotiations over IPR, Beijing did not meet all U.S. demands on the IPR issue in part because it was confident that the United States, due to its conflicting domestic interests, would not go so far as to actually carry out the threats. But another important reason why Beijing was unable to honor its promises was that many local authorities have come to see pirating as a profitable rather than illegal activity, especially in a context of almost feverish squabbling for wealth among local governments in the 1990s, and consequently have scuttled those provisions of the agreements that called for strict enforcement of existing rules and regulations. That free riding on Western technology could expedite China's drive for economic catch-up made pirating activities less problematic from the point of view of local administrators. As a result, even though some exporters in China, particularly those located in the most dynamic coastal areas of China, had voiced their concerns about the impact of retaliation, it would have been very difficult to break the ties between the pirate entrepreneurs and the state.

As USTR reports pointed out, most pirating activities were taking place in the southern provinces of China, where free-market activities first flourished following the country's opening up to the outside world. In the fledgling free-market atmosphere in these provinces, many local governments have come to view pirating industries as lucrative businesses that could bring significant economic benefits to their localities. Furthermore, many foreign reports have linked pirate entrepreneurs with officials within both the central and provincial governments. Some news reports pointed out that Chinese military and civilian government agencies and some influential Communist Party officials were involved with at least a few of the twenty-nine factories singled out by the USTR for producing pirated CDs. Some of these officials were even the so-called princelings, or offspring of key party and government officials, who were able to draw on a closely knitted web of political connections to refuse to obey the agreements the central governments entered into with foreign countries.[2]

Consequently, Chinese negotiators have frequently defended themselves in trade negotiations by arguing that they were trying their best to reform China's IPR laws but had little control over enforcement, the responsibility for which resides primarily with provincial governments. However, since the criteria for judging the effectiveness of trade pressure include both the extent to which an agreement is signed and the degree to which the signed agreement is implemented to U.S. satisfaction, the close ties between pirate entrepreneurs and officials at the level of both the central and local governments, which account for why the Chinese have repeatedly exacerbated difficulties on the enforcement front, would have made it difficult to offer a positive evaluation of the effectiveness of U.S. pressure.

The U.S.–China textile dispute provides another example of how the connection between the state and the industry influences the dynamics of the negotiations. When the United States threatened to scale back China's textile quotas for its illegal transshipment of textile products in the 1980s, the Chinese government, which has placed the textile industry at the forefront of the country's drive for export-oriented growth, retaliated against the U.S. quota restrictions by targeting U.S. agricultural exports to China. However, when the United States scaled back Chinese textile quotas in the 1990s, the Chinese government threatened retaliatory moves but did not follow through with its threats, instead urging the U.S. government to remove the quota restrictions. No direct evidence on the rationale of the Chinese action is now available. It is possible that, as the Chinese began to place more emphasis on the more balanced development of various industrial sectors and on the need to switch from an economy characterized by labor-intensive manufacturing to one led by technology, the incentive for confrontation in the textile dispute was much reduced. Future research could generate more evidence to corroborate this claim.

Similarly, in the informatics dispute between the United States and Brazil documented by Odell and others, the Brazilian government refused to make concessions, even when faced with countervailing pressure from exporters who would lose from the imposition of sanctions. Primarily, this refusal reflected the fact that the informatics program the United States chose to attack formed the basis for an emerging autonomous computer industry and, as a result, enjoyed substantial support from all major actors in the Brazilian policy establishment. Not surprisingly, the U.S. campaign against the informatics law has been considered as a frontal assault on Brazil's national sovereignty in the area of advanced technology and has encountered fierce resistance by the relevant actors in Brazil.[3]

Politics in target countries with competitive trade ties with the United States presents a different story. Just as a competitive trade relationship solidifies domestic support for coercive action in the United States, it also leads the import-competing groups in the target countries to fiercely resist making concessions that will erode the amount of rents that such groups can accrue through protectionist policies. Indeed, highly asymmetrical interests between import-competing groups on both sides of the dispute often generate highly contentious pressures leading to tit-for-tat retaliation, especially in the early stages of the dispute, when exporters may not have sufficiently mobilized against import-competing groups' resistance to concessions. Since a primary means through which the import-competing interests in America's competitive trading partners can avoid concessions is by issuing threats of counterretaliation, competitive trading partners are in fact more likely to get into a trade war with the United States.

However, it is important to bear in mind that, in such cases, exporters who stand to suffer from the imposition of sanctions would push for moderation. Indeed, in the absence of strong ties between the state and import-competing interests, exporters are sometimes able to resist pressure from the latter for standing fast to foreign pressure, although they may fail to dampen pressure for escalation when the interests of the import-competing groups on both sides of the dispute are so incompatible as to preclude any resolution of the dispute. Therefore, it is possible that the United States may obtain, on average, more concessions from its competitive trading partners and may engage in more trade wars with these countries (in those cases where concessions are not made). Moreover, the United States may also be able to extract concessions from its competitive trading partners following unilateral trade retaliation or a trade war, as the recent U.S.–EU banana trade dispute illustrates. Indeed, in many trade wars between countries with competitive trade relations, it is not unusual to observe a high degree of tension at the initial stages of the dispute leading to tit-for-tat retaliation, followed by concessions from the target countries in the aftermath of actual retaliation.

For example, in the U.S.–EC enlargement dispute discussed in chapter 7, it was only after the retaliation episodes, when the policy process had brought in a greater number of actors, notably exporters with greater stakes in an agreement, that voices for moderation prevailed in the EC, thus gradually allowing some concessions to be made. At the outset of the dispute, European agricultural interests whose income had undergone a steady decline in the mid-1980s, in particular French producers of maize who competed with American exports in the Spanish maize market, strenuously resisted concessions. For example, after EC negotiators, out of fear of creating an open break among EC member states, concluded an interim agreement with the United States in July 1986, they soon encountered a barrage of criticism from European farm interests. The French Association of Maize Producers (AGPM) and a number of other French farm groups staged vocal demonstrations in Paris on July 4. In the quintessential French style, they dumped two tons of maize onto the streets in protest. Calling the settlement a "veritable Munich,"[4] they contended that it was unfair for French farmers alone to pay for the costs of enlargement. The EC-wide farm lobby joined AGPM with its own demonstrations and denunciations.

But even though French agricultural interests continued to embrace a hard-line position, dissenting voices began to emerge at this time. European exporters who would suffer from U.S. retaliatory action, most notably cognac and gin producers, in addition to manufacturers of some industrial products, began to press for accommodation through indirect contact with government officials. French cognac producers' lobbying gained them assurances from the French government that no trade retaliation would take place.[5] At the same time, "The British, the gin people and so forth, were working frantically to try to head off U.S. retaliation."[6] Industrialists were apprehensive of a trade war as well. Indeed, even though they did not face retaliatory threats from the United States, automobile manufacturers such as Volkswagen and producers of whiskey turned out to be most concerned with the long-term repercussions of a large U.S.–EC trade war on both bilateral trade relations and on the world trading system. Another important objective of industrialists was to prevent French farmers from agreeing to take more industrial imports as substitutes for maize. Thus, exporters' desire to avoid trade sanctions eventually dampened the incentives for escalation, allowing the EC to gradually offer some concessions on the maize issue to prevent the further aggravation of U.S.–EC trade relations.

In short, the few examples cited here are illustrative of how trade structure could possibly influence both the distribution of gains and the possibility of agreement in international trade negotiations via its impact on domestic politics in the target of threats. My hypothesis about the influence of trade structure on domestic politics in the target countries is fully consistent with that developed for the sender of threats and may help to strengthen my argument about the centrality of domestic politics. But since this book focuses primarily on the sender of threats and since the domestic political economy of the target states merits further careful research, I have not provided an extensive treatment of politics in the target of sanction threats. Future research could systematically flesh out and empirically test these tentative hypotheses about how politics in the target shapes the negotiations and, in particular, how coalitional patterns and institutional arrangements in the target influence the decision-making process. Future study could also combine findings about the domestic political economy of both the sender and the target of threats to generate an interactive, more fine-tuned typology of the conditions that facilitate the effective use of threat tactics as well as those that influence the possibility of cooperation or conflict in international trade disputes.

From "Aggressive Unilateralism" to "Aggressive Multilateralism": The Impact of the Establishment of the World Trade Organization

Since much of the evidence for my central claims derives from cases settled prior to the establishment of the WTO, with its newly innovated dispute settlement mechanism, one may ask to what extent these recent changes in the institutional context of American trade policy may have altered the determinants of Washington's threat and actual use of retaliatory measures. Institutionalists have argued that international regimes may promote international cooperation by reducing states' fears of cheating, improving the transparency of information, lengthening the shadow of the future, and establishing linkages across issue areas.[7] A reasonable question to ask, therefore, is whether the establishment of the WTO and the concomitant changes it introduced in the dispute settlement mechanism have constrained the use of retaliatory strategies and reduced the risks of escalation to trade war.

The experience with the WTO so far only provides tentative answers to these questions. First, it seems that, even at a time when states seem to be increasingly resorting to a strategy of "aggressive multilateralism" by taking advantage of the innovations of the WTO dispute settlement procedures, the creation of the WTO has by no means sounded the death knell for unilateral market-opening tactics. While the new WTO dispute settlement procedure does affect the operation of the "aggressively unilateral" American trade policy under Section 301 by making it more difficult for the United States to retaliate in those cases in which the WTO has not ruled in favor of the United States, Washington has not abandoned aggressively unilateral trade policies. Indeed, the United States has continued to use unilateral market-opening strategies in conjunction with the aggressive persecution of trade disputes under both multilateral and bilateral forums. The pursuit of aggressively unilateral trade strategy under Section 301 has retained its utility as the U.S. domestic authority against practices of nonmember countries of the WTO (such as China, Russia, Taiwan, and Vietnam) and against foreign policies in areas not yet covered or comprehensively regulated by the WTO (such as competition rules, labor standards, and intellectual property protection). The frequency of Section 301 initiation is comparable to, and indeed even slightly higher than, that in the GATT era.[8] It is reasonable to expect that trade structure will continue to be an important determinant of the success of both bilateral and unilateral policy measures undertaken outside of the WTO framework or parallel with WTO decisions.

Second, it may be argued that, although the experience to date with the WTO seems to pose certain challenges to my previous analyses, it does not yet constitute disconfirming evidence. For instance, one may point to the substantial market access concessions that China offered to the United States during the negotiations leading up to the country's entry into the WTO as evidence of the success of a multilateral strategy in opening markets in complementary trading partners. However, although Beijing's willingness to offer market-access concessions during the WTO accession negotiations does offer a stark contrast with its reluctance to respond to American pressure during the period when the United States threatened unilateral trade sanctions, this change in Chinese behavior may at least in part be explained by the leadership's interest in using the opportunities provided by international integration to advance its domestic reform agenda.[9] Moreover, since the United States did not employ a coercive bargaining strategy by threatening to restrict Chinese exports to the United States, importers and retailers of Chinese products, who had in the past sought to block attempts by the administration to cut imports from China in order to punish that country's restrictive domestic practices, seem to have remained remarkably reticent in the policy process, broadly endorsing exporters' push for free trade. American importers of textile and apparel, represented by the U.S. Association of Importers of Textiles and Apparel, even welcomed the agreement, which among other things promised the elimination of textile and apparel quotas by the year 2005.[10] For these reasons, the significant market liberalization concessions that the United States obtained from China during the WTO negotiations do not refute my argument about how trade complementarity may undercut the effectiveness of the U.S. negotiation strategy. How the United States and China settle disputes under the WTO—in particular, the distributive dimension of these dispute settlements— may constitute the more interesting and direct test of the relevance of my argument to the post-GATT era.

Similarly, judgment about the effectiveness of Washington's negotiation strategy under the new dispute settlement procedures of the WTO may be premature. While the United States seems to have encountered a lot of difficulties in achieving its core objectives in some individual fights with its competitive trading partners (such as the one with Japan over auto parts), it should be noted that the application of unilateral market-opening pressure in the past has not produced uniformly positive results vis-à-vis America's competitive trading partners. Even in the pre-1995 period, a fair amount of variation existed in the degree to which the United States successfully pursued its objectives even in bargaining with a single nation. Thus, a more comprehensive assessment of whether trade structure is a significant determinant of U.S. trade strategy in light of the recent changes in the WTO dispute settlement mechanism can be made with the assistance of a larger sample of disputes settled under the world trade body.

Third, even within the framework of the WTO, where institutional rules and regulations may have exerted a significant impact on state behavior, it may be argued that trade structure determines the basic structure of domestic interests underlying the negotiations, some of which may not be entirely amenable to institutional solutions. For example, given the importance of trade structure and its domestic consequences, we may better understand the two U.S.–EU trade disputes over bananas and beef hormones that almost flared up into trade wars in 1999. Because of American and European farmers' competition for agricultural markets and because of the absence of any countervailing domestic forces, it is not surprising that these two trading partners had so much difficulty containing the escalation of these disputes, even with their close alliance relationship and the constraints of the WTO.

Indeed, while the WTO embodies and institutionalizes democratic norms of peaceful conflict resolution, its dispute settlement mechanisms nevertheless leave open the possibility of high-intensity trade conflict involving mutual retaliation. For example, Reinhardt and Busch have explained patterns of WTO dispute initiation and settlement outcome (i.e., whether the defendant has conceded to some or all of the complainants' demands for trade liberalization) in terms of the pressure for protection from domestic interest groups.[11] Rosendorff and Milner have explored how the institutionalization of uncertainty allows international institutions such as the GATT/WTO to foster sustained international cooperation. Specifically, they argue that, by incorporating escape clauses, the GATT/WTO permits countries confronted with intense, unexpected political pressure to shy away from their obligations on a short-term basis, in the process encouraging cooperation without increasing the risks of systemic breakdown.[12] In other words, even under the institutional framework of the GATT/WTO, states can find recourse to retaliatory measures under conditions of intense and highly asymmetric domestic political pressure. While offering the possibility of dispute settlement via adjudication, the WTO can still be an arena for conflict, allowing states with competitive trade structures to engage in trade wars under specified conditions.

Implications

Implications for Dependency Theory and for the Literature on the Trade-Conflict Nexus

When will the United States find the use of aggressive bargaining tactics most successful in opening foreign markets? Under what conditions will tit-for-tat trade retaliation most likely occur in international trade negotiations? With respect to the first question, this book posits that the United States is unlikely to obtain the same concessions from countries such as China, Brazil, and India as from countries such as Japan, the EU, and Canada. Because the first group of countries produces commodities that are no longer manufactured on a large scale in the United States, American sanction threats against these states almost always will encounter strong opposition from domestic interest groups and hence will be less credible and effective.

This finding about the bargaining power of America's complementary trading partners, many of which are third world countries engaged primarily in labor-intensive production, poses a challenge to the realist and dependency theories that are highly pessimistic about the possibility of less-developed countries negotiating favorable dispute settlement deals with their partners in the industrialized world. The realist theory views international bargaining outcomes mainly as reflecting the underlying power balances of the parties involved in the dispute. The dependency theory shares with the realist theory an emphasis on the distribution of capabilities in the international economic system, arguing that the organization of the world economy systematically puts at a disadvantage countries in the periphery of the world economic order by preventing them from making a leap from producers of raw materials and primary products to manufacturers of industrial products. Given such a subordinate position within the international division of labor, it is not surprising that many developing countries have found it difficult to resist the demands of the more powerful countries in the advanced industrialized world.

However, if the analysis in the preceding chapters has any validity, we can see that, as labor-intensive industries in industrialized countries experience a steady decline or are eventually phased out, industrialized countries have come to develop a significant degree of dependence on the supply of raw materials and other labor-intensive products manufactured in the developing world. As importers and retailers in developed countries join the fray against the sanctions strategy, the credibility and effectiveness of sanction threats are substantially reduced. Viewed from the perspective of the target state, the sender's dependence on their products is a bargaining chip that can be used effectively in negotiations with the sender of threats. In other words, trade complementarity provides developing countries with considerable leverage in international negotiations, frequently allowing them to stave off trade pressure from their powerful negotiation partner. As such, an important aspect of third world bargaining power that has not received adequate attention by the realist and dependency theories is revealed.

By extension, this finding may have implications for the literature on the relationship between economic interdependence and conflict. Among the various arguments it offers to explain why interdependence fosters peace, economic liberalism emphasizes that complex interdependence involving "mutual dependence" or "vulnerability" creates incentives for peace and cooperation among nations because interdependence increases the costs of disruption of commercial ties by military action.[13] It is assumed that by engaging in trade in goods in which they have a comparative advantage, states have incentives to avoid conflict that promises to jeopardize the gains they could otherwise reap from trade. In particular, trade in goods with few substitutes is likely to facilitate cooperation.[14] Realists challenge the liberal conception of interdependence as mutual and symmetrical interactions, asserting instead that interdependence entails elements of both dependence and independence and that power relations embedded in asymmetrical economic relations are highly consequential to the onset of international conflict.[15] It has been also argued that trade generates negative security externalities and causes nations to maximize their relative trade gains, thereby creating conflict.[16] In particular, when it comes to trade involving strategic goods, or goods for which a country has no ready domestic substitutes, states will be prone to conflict due to their desire to minimize their vulnerability.[17]

Existing empirical studies of the relationship between trade and conflict typically focus on aggregate trade levels and conceive of the state as a unitary actor, although some scholars have argued for the need to modify the unitary actor assumption to explore the possibility that trade in different types of goods may differently shape levels of conflict.[18] It may be further argued that, besides studying the effect of different types of goods on conflict behavior, one may also wish to examine the impact of different facets of economic interdependence, of which trade structure may be an example, to tease out those specific characteristics of interdependence that are more or less likely to restrain belligerent behavior.[19] The two-level game approach, with its emphasis on the interaction between domestic and international political forces, may prove useful to this endeavor. If it can be shown that certain types of trade are more likely to create a domestic coalition against trade disruptions, then we will have made an important theoretical advance in sorting out the relationship between interdependence and conflict.

Implications for the "Democratic Peace" Thesis

In addition to shedding light on the debated relationship between interdependence and trade, this research addresses the literature on democratic peace by examining democracies' proclivity to become involved in aggressive escalation in trade conflicts. As explained in chapter 1, while scholars of international security have rather extensively explored the relationship between regime type and the possibility of military wars, researchers are now only beginning to try to sort out the connection between regime type and the probability of trade conflicts. My empirical analysis takes up the latter question, suggesting that even though a cursory examination of the pattern of trade conflict might reveal a positive association between regime type and the likelihood of trade war, this pattern is really a statistical artifact generated by the competitive trade relations between many democratic pairs. In other words, a competitive trade structure and other factors pertaining to the specific trade relations (such as the volume of trade), rather than democratic institutions, are the more proximate causes of trade wars. Because of the way in which competitive trade relations between many democratic dyads shape their domestic politics, democracies seem to experience more intense trade confrontation leading to heightened risks of tit-for-tat retaliation than do mixed pairs. In underscoring the importance of competitive versus complementary trade structure, this project reveals an important countervailing force in trade disputes and challenges the assumption, as espoused by recent writings on democracy and trade, that institutional features of democracies such as greater voter control or the need for legislative ratification facilitate democratic cooperation on trade issues. Indeed, my quantitative analysis of trade conflicts involving the United States reveals that regime type has no significant bearing on the probability of trade war in either a positive or a negative direction. The case studies bear out this finding, suggesting that, even though democratic norms of peaceful conflict resolution and the existence of multiple veto points via mechanisms such as "separation of powers" seem to act as a brake on the tendency for aggressive escalation in trade disputes, other aspects of democracy, in particular democracies' susceptibility to producer interests, frequently make democracies more prone to trade conflict. These countervailing pressures inherent in a democratic polity thus render the association between regime type and patterns of trade dispute escalation anything but a foregone conclusion.

Besides addressing the growing body of literature on democracy and trade conflicts,[20] this research provides us with a basis for evaluating the different strands of theories developed to explain the democratic peace in security. As explained in chapter 1, proponents of both the normative and the structure-based explanations for the democratic peace have grounded their respective arguments in empirical studies of military wars. The pattern of democratic peace that both have found in security affairs consequently leaves open the question as to what is the real causal mechanism for democracies' less belligerent behavior in international conflicts. The preceding analysis, by showing that democracies are not necessarily more "pacific" in trade disputes despite their superior signaling capacities and structural advantages, points at the norms-based argument as the more direct explanation for the pattern of democratic peace in security affairs.

Summarized briefly, the "audience cost" rendition of the democratic peace theory stresses how the information transmission properties of democratic institutions strengthen democracies' ability to send credible signals about their true intentions. In this view, threats of war made by a democracy better convey the state's actual willingness to fight because of the high domestic audience costs involved. The other side, knowing that its opponent means business and fearing the costs of war, will be more likely to refrain from further escalatory steps that will bring the two parties to war. In other words, from the point of view of the signaling literature, democratic institutions provide the key mechanism for the peaceful resolution of international conflicts and this mechanism ought to apply to both trade *and* security issues.

Yet, the finding that democratic regimes have found it difficult to take advantage of their superior signaling capacities to arrive at negotiated settlements challenges the institutional argument. Instead, the alternative causal mechanism proposed by this study, the structure of trade, produces such significant domestic repercussions that it overwhelms democratic institutions' capacity of information provision and conflict aversion, in spite of the fact that many democracies are superior information providers and that many of them are members of trade organizations such as the GATT/WTO, which place them in a better position to avail of the judicial dispute resolution proceedings of international trade institutions to reach negotiated solutions.

To put it another way, this book reveals that, at least as far as trade is concerned, the informational properties of democratic institutions have failed to prevent democracies from escalating trade disputes to the level of a "war." Given the assumption that security and trade issues share the same underlying strategic structure, as explicated by

Fearon,[21] this finding casts doubt on the ability of democratic institutions to dampen the incentives for democratic pairs to escalate their conflicts, leaving the other pillar of the democratic peace theory, the norms-based explanation, as the more plausible explanation of the pattern of democratic peace that many analysts have observed in security affairs. This result reinforces the importance of democratic norms as a powerful constraint on the use of force among democracies, suggesting that liberal norms such as "live and let live" and the principle of peaceful settlement of conflicts may have served as the more powerful restraint on belligerent behavior among democracies. If this is the case, then the message this study conveys to American policymakers is that the construction of international peace depends not simply on the introduction of democratic institutions but on the development of attitudinal traits and behavioral norms that buttress the institutional structures of democratic polities. Thus, in their attempt to prevent violence in many conflict zones in the Third World, policymakers not only should devote their attention to instituting democratic regimes in many formerly authoritarian states but should also take care to promote democratic ideals, habits, and principles that not only would serve as a safeguard of budding democratic institutions but would also pave the way for peace among states.

Implications for Public Policy

The findings of this study may help us to understand the patterns of emerging trade conflicts between developing and advanced industrialized countries. For example, China's remarkable export growth not only has created opportunities for trade conflict with the United States but also has more recently begun to engender heated trade confrontation with other developed countries such as Japan. In early 2001, China and Japan became embroiled in a trade dispute when Japan moved to impose import tariffs on three agricultural products from China to protect domestic farmers from cheap Chinese imports. In addition, as the surge in Chinese imports has increasingly prompted calls for safeguards, antidumping measures, and other import restrictions in Japan, there have already emerged voices for settling the dispute with China without resorting to retaliatory measures. The rationale behind such calls for moderation is that trade restrictions would impose an enormous burden on both Japanese consumers and the Japanese industry. In particular, it would prevent Japan from capitalizing on the trade complementarity between the two economies to build an international division of labor that would allow Japan to achieve industrial upgrading as well as other related economic objectives of the structural reform program that currently constitutes one of the government's key policy planks.[22] Thus, since reports about trade frictions between rapidly growing economies and advanced industrialized states such as the emerging U.S.–China trade conflicts will likely appear with greater frequency in newspaper headlines, the conclusions of this book ought to offer lessons for industrialized country governments in dealing with such trade disputes as well as a potentially useful framework for analyzing and predicting the patterns of these new issues in international trade relations.

Furthermore, my argument about how trade competitiveness versus complementarity affects the degree to which the United States is successful in extracting concessions has important implications for Washington's pursuit of unilateral market-opening strategies. In particular, given the difficulties the United States faces in garnering domestic support for aggressive bargaining tactics in dealing with complementary trading partners such as China, it seems that American negotiators may want to be more selective about the kinds of threats they make vis-à-vis such countries and to avoid making demands that lack domestic support. In cases where threats would have to be invoked, it is essential that American negotiators be aware of dissenting voices at home and effectively address these internal differences in order to present a more unified negotiation position vis-à-vis their foreign counterparts.

Offering side payments to the main domestic groups that would have been adversely affected by the sanctions and that are therefore opposed to the sanctions strategy may help to ameliorate the difficulties faced by American negotiators in marshaling support for threat tactics. By promising to address import users' demands in other issue areas or to provide government support in helping import users to adjust to the possible disruption of trade with the target, American negotiators may be able to convert formerly staunch opponents to the trade sanction strategy to their potential allies. Toward this objective, American negotiators may want to involve the relevant actors in close consultations in the early stages of the dispute. In particular, they may want to work closely with industry groups that may have the most reason to be upset about the pressure tactics in an attempt to come up with feasible plans for addressing the latter's concerns. This proposition is consistent with Putnam's argument that chief negotiators ought to seek to maximize the cost-effectiveness of their own threats and demands by paying close attention to the domestic repercussions of their initiatives.[23] It also requires chief negotiators to expend more time and energy to identify and to work with industry groups at home to minimize domestic opposition and to forge a broad coalition behind the sanctions strategy.

Replacing "unilaterally aggressive" negotiation tactics with bilateral talks targeted more specifically at the issues of interest to the United States without making specific threats may provide another partial solution to the credibility problem. While it may be difficult for American negotiators to give up making threats, the futility of unilateral market-opening measures against complementary trading partners that I have documented throughout this book suggests that the United States may indeed have a better chance of achieving its objectives by opting for persuasion and other diplomatic routes of dispute settlement.

Alternatively, U.S. negotiators may want to more firmly embrace the multilateral negotiation strategy, bargaining hard for American interests under the aegis of such organizations as the WTO or APEC. Even though the structure of domestic interests still influences the perception of the target state and even though evidence on the efficacy of the WTO in settling trade disputes is still inconclusive, hopefully the United States will be better able to achieve its policy objectives by adding international opprobrium to the alleged unfair trade practices and by taking advantage of the judicial route to dispute settlement. Moreover, since both the United States and the target countries may be required to adjust their policies in such cases, the possibility that the target country will make concessions in one issue area in exchange for U.S. concessions in another area will be enhanced, thereby alleviating the difficulties the United States would have faced in establishing credibility had it chosen to pursue the dispute unilaterally.

While these recommendations do not guarantee success, they nevertheless point at potentially fruitful courses of actions for the United States. If the findings of this research are of any validity, then an important message it conveys to practitioners is that one should not only "know thy enemies" but also be aware of those impediments to effective policy implementation that can be found at home. As an ancient Chinese military strategist, Sun Zi, once said: "If you know the enemy and know yourself, you need not fear the result of a hundred battles. . . . If you know neither the enemy nor yourself, you will succumb in every battle."[24]

Notes

CHAPTER 1

1. U.S. Department of Commerce, International Trade Administration, *U.S. Foreign Trade Highlights.*

2. Figure 3.1 depicts the relationship between the level of asymmetrical export dependence and the degree of responsiveness to American pressure of several major U.S. trading partners. Level of asymmetrical export dependence is measured by comparing a given target country's exports to the United States as a percentage of its GNP to U.S. exports to that target state as a percentage of U.S. GNP. The responsiveness index is based on the average of each of the target's concession scores under Section 301, as provided by Bayard and Elliott, *Reciprocity and Retaliation;* and Elliott and Richardson, "Determinants and Effectiveness."

3. Bayard and Elliott's study on the effectiveness of Section 301 in opening overseas markets provides data illustrating the variations in the effectiveness of American pressure across countries. See Bayard and Elliot, *Reciprocity and Retaliation,* 355–67; see also figure 3.1.

4. Chan, "Mirror, Mirror on the Wall"; Maoz and Russett, "Normative and Structural Causes"; Russett, *Grasping the Democratic Peace;* Ray, *Democracy and International Conflict;* and Oneal and Russett, "Classical Liberals Were Right."

5. Among the studies that examined the relationship between regime type and trade policy are Milner and Rosendorff, "Domestic Politics and International Trade Negotiations"; Mansfield, Milner, and Rosendorff, "Why Democracies Cooperate More"; Reinhardt, "Aggressive Multilateralism"; Sherman, "Democracy and Trade Conflict"; and Busch, "Democracy, Consultation."

6. Fearon, "Domestic Political Audiences."

7. See, for example, Milner, *Interests, Institutions, and Information;* Milner and Rosendorff, "Domestic Politics and International Trade Negotiations"; and Mansfield, Milner, and Rosendorff, "Free to Trade?"

8. See, for example, Zartman, *Politics of Trade Negotiations;* Odell, "Latin American Trade Negotiations"; Odell, "Outcome of International Trade Conflicts."

254 Notes to Pages 6–12

9. I refer to cases involving the EU by its present name except when the case under consideration took place in an earlier period when the European Economic Community or the European Community was in place.

10. Bayard and Elliott, *Reciprocity and Retaliation*, 355–68; Elliott and Richardson, "Determinants and Effectiveness," 221–25. Successful cases are defined in a way that includes both the conclusion of an agreement and the actual achievement of American negotiating objectives when the agreement was implemented.

11. Various studies have shown how the effectiveness of U.S. economic coercion varies in ways that do not correspond with the underlying power balances. In his study of the Brazilian informatics and EC enlargement cases, for example, Odell finds that the United States was more successful in winning concessions from Europe than from Brazil, although in theory Brazil should be less able to resist U.S. demands. Similarly, the study by Bayard and Elliott on the effectiveness of Super 301 investigations against Japan, Brazil, and India between 1989 and 1990 has shown that, while the Japanese gave in to most American demands, India completely refused to yield to U.S. pressure. The relative power positions of these two countries obviously cannot explain this outcome. Odell, "International Threats and Internal Politics"; Bayard and Elliot, *Reciprocity and Retaliation*, 101–70.

12. Bayard and Elliott, *Reciprocity and Retaliation*, 368.

13. Maoz and Russett, "Normative and Structural Causes"; Russett, *Grasping the Democratic Peace*; Ray, *Democracy and International Conflict*.

14. See, for example, Maoz and Russett, "Normative and Structural Causes"; Owen, "How Liberalism Produces Democratic Peace"; Weart, "Peace among Democratic and Oligarchic Republics."

15. Russett, *Grasping the Democratic Peace*, 31.

16. Ibid., 30–38; Doyle, "Liberalism and World Politics."

17. Russett, *Grasping the Democratic Peace*, 38–40. Some other scholars have made similar structural arguments. See, for example, Lake, "Powerful Pacifists"; and Schweller, "Domestic Structure and Preventive War."

18. Bueno de Mesquita and Lalman, *War and Reason*, chap. 5.

19. Fearon, "Domestic Political Audiences." The argument is explained in more detail in chapter 2.

20. Schultz, "Domestic Opposition and Signaling."

21. Fearon, "Bargaining, Enforcement, and International Cooperation," 276.

22. Ibid.

23. Verdier, *Democracy and International Trade*, 293–94.

24. Dixon and Moon, "Political Similarity," 10–11.

25. Mansfield, Milner, and Rosendorff, "Free to Trade"; Mansfield, Milner, and Rosendorff, "Why Democracies Cooperate More."

26. Leeds, "Domestic Political Institutions."

27. Dixon, "Democracy and the Management of Conflict"; Dixon,

"Democracy and the Peaceful Settlement"; Raymond, "Democracies, Disputes."

28. Verdier, "Democratic Convergence and Free Trade."

29. Reinhardt, "Aggressive Multilateralism."

30. Sherman, "Targeting Democracies"; Sherman, "Democracy and Trade Conflict."

31. Remmer, "Does Democracy Promote Interstate Cooperation?"; Bliss and Russett, "Democratic Trading Partners"; Morrow, Siverson, and Tabares, "The Political Determinants of International Trade"; Mansfield and Bronson, "Political Economy of Major-Power Trade Flows"; Busch, "Democracy, Consultation."

32. Mansfield, Milner, and Rosendorff, "Free to Trade"; Mansfield, Milner, and Rosendorff, "Why Democracies Cooperate More"; Milner and Kubota, "Why the Rush to Free Trade?"

33. Conybeare, *Trade Wars.*

34. Ibid., 5.

35. Ibid., 1–6.

36. The structure of trade will be defined in more detail in chapter 2.

37. George and McKeown, "Case Studies and Theories," 35. See also the discussion by King, Keohane, and Verba, *Designing Social Inquiry,* 225–28.

38. George and McKeown, "Case Studies and Theories," 41.

39. King, Keohane, and Verba, *Designing Social Inquiry,* 137.

40. According to Bayard and Elliott, in *Reciprocity and Retaliation,* American negotiators were largely successful in achieving their negotiation objectives in the satellite case, partially successful in the supercomputer and wood products cases, and nominally successful in the semiconductor trade conflict.

41. Reinhardt, *Posturing Parliaments.*

42. See, for example, Wallerstein, *Modern World-System;* Cardoso and Falleto, *Dependency and Development;* Furtado, *Development and Underdevelopment.*

43. For comprehensive reviews of the large body of literature on trade and military conflict, see, for example, Reuveny, "Trade and Conflict Debate"; McMillan, "Interdependence and Conflict."

CHAPTER 2

1. Hirschman, *National Power and the Structure of Foreign Trade;* Baldwin, "Interdependence and Power."

2. Gilpin, *Political Economy of International Relations;* Lake, *Power, Protection, and Free Trade;* Grieco, *Cooperation among Nations;* Krasner, *Structural Conflict.*

3. Keohane and Nye, *Power and Interdependence.*

4. Zartman, *Politics of Trade Negotiations.*

5. Habeeb, *Power and Tactics in International Negotiation.*

6. Wriggins, "Up for Auction."

7. Odell, "Latin American Trade Negotiations"; Odell, "Outcome of International Trade Conflicts."

8. Odell, "International Threats and Internal Politics," 238–41.

9. Bayard and Elliott, *Reciprocity and Retaliation;* Duchesne, "International Bilateral Trade."

10. Meunier, "Europe Divided but United."

11. "Trade Peace: Deja Vu Again," *Economist* 334, no. 7904 (March 4, 1995): 86.

12. Drezner, *Sanctions Paradox.*

13. An interview with USTR officials involved in U.S. negotiations with East Asian countries confirmed this view.

14. Prestowitz, *Trading Places.*

15. Odell, "Latin American Trade Negotiations"; Odell, "Outcomes of International Trade Conflicts"; Habeeb, *Power and Tactics in International Negotiation,* 21–22.

16. Schelling, *Strategy of Conflict;* Evans, Jacobson, and Putnam, *Double-Edged Diplomacy.*

17. Scholars such as Howard Raiffa, James Sebenius, and David Lax provide detailed case studies to show how these tactics can help to enhance threat credibility by expanding the perceived zone of possible agreement of the parties involved. See, for example, Sebenius, *Negotiating the Law of the Sea;* Lax and Sebenius, *Manager as Negotiator;* Raiffa, *The Art and Science of Negotiation.*

18. Schoppa, *Bargaining with Japan,* 27.

19. Yoffie, *Power and Protectionism.*

20. Habeeb, *Power and Tactics in International Negotiations.*

21. Bayard and Elliott, *Reciprocity and Retaliation,* 86.

22. Ibid., 80.

23. Ibid., 81.

24. Schelling, *Strategy of Conflict;* Schelling, *Arms and Influence;* Snyder and Diesing, *Conflict among Nations.*

25. See chapter 3 for a more detailed discussion of the relationship between bilateral economic interdependence and threat effectiveness.

26. Note that some traditional bargaining theories do have an implicit domestic component. For example, Thomas Schelling emphasizes many of the same domestic constraints stressed by two-level game theorists. The two-level game approach discussed later differs from traditional bargaining theories in its more explicit focus on the connection between domestic politics and international behavior.

27. Examples of works that focus on the international systemic sources of state behavior include the following: Waltz, *Theory of International Politics;*

Keohane, *After Hegemony;* Gowa, *Allies, Adversaries, and International Trade;* and Grieco, *Cooperation among Nations.*

28. Putnam, "Diplomacy and Domestic Politics"; Moravcsik, "Introduction."

29. See the cases in Evans, Jacobson, and Putnam, *Double-Edged Diplomacy,* especially Odell, "International Threats and Internal Politics"; Krauss, "U.S.-Japan Negotiations." See also Lehman and McCoy, "Dynamics of the Two-Level Bargaining Game"; Knopf, "Beyond Two-Level Games"; Mayer, "Managing Domestic Differences"; Schoppa, "Two-Level Games and Bargaining Outcomes."

30. Bueno de Mesquita and Lalman, *War and Reason.*

31. Lohmann and O'Halloran, "Divided Government and U.S. Trade Policy"; O'Halloran, *Politics, Process, and American Trade Policy.*

32. Schoppa, *Bargaining with Japan,* 28–32.

33. Mertha, "Pirates, Politics, and Trade Policy."

34. Goldstein, *Ideas, Interests, and American Trade Policy.*

35. DeSombre, *Domestic Sources of International Environmental Policy.*

36. Martin, *Democratic Commitments.*

37. Odell, "International Threats and Internal Politics," 234.

38. Moravcsik, "Introduction," 33.

39. Some authors have proposed more rigorous and formal treatment of the domestic game. See, for example, Iida, "Analytic Uncertainty and International Cooperation"; Iida, "When and How Do Domestic Constraints Matter?"; Tsebelis, *Nested Games;* Mo, "Logic of Two-Level Games"; Mo, "Domestic Institutions and International Bargaining"; Mayer, "Managing Domestic Differences"; Pahre, "Endogenous Domestic Institutions."

40. Milner, *Interests, Institutions, and Information,* 37–43.

41. Note that Milner treats "divided government" as a continuous variable measuring the degree of disagreement between Congress and the president. Her conception differs from the most common definition of "divided government" in the trade policy literature, which refers to situations when different parties control the executive and legislature branches. Recent studies have debated the effect of divided government in the partisan sense on trade policy but have yet to reach definitive conclusions as to whether different party control of the two branches increases interbranch disagreements on trade issues. See Lohmann and O'Halloran, "Divided Government and U.S. Trade Policy"; Hammond and Prins, "Impact of Domestic Institutions on International Negotiations"; Karol, "Divided Government and U.S. Trade Policy"; and Pahre, "Divided Government and International Cooperation." The rest of this study follows Milner's treatment of the term and conceives of divided government as the degree of policy disagreement between the two government institutions.

42. Milner, *Interests, Institutions, and Information,* 234–40.

43. An exception to this general tendency is Eric Reinhardt's work on the determinants of trade dispute settlement under the GATT, which examines in detail how structural features of the political institutions (such as legislative organization, party structure, electoral rules, and elections) of both parties involved in the dispute can affect both the distribution efficiency and the possibility of cooperation of GATT negotiations. See Reinhardt, "Posturing Parliaments."

44. Conybeare, *Trade Wars,* 47–48.

45. Ibid., 47.

46. The relevance of trade structure has been explored in other contexts. For example, studies of trading bloc formation have found that countries with similar economic structures make it easier for the two governments involved to satisfy their respective national lobbies, thus reducing the political costs associated with regionalism. See, for example, Hyclak, "Introduction"; and Melo, Panagariya, and Rodrik, "New Regionalism." For an empirical test of the argument, see Li and Jo, "Trading-Bloc Formation and Influence of Politics."

47. Krauss, "U.S.-Japan Negotiations," 278; Woodall, *Japan under Construction.*

48. Odell, "International Threats and Internal Politics," 241–43.

49. Krauss and Reich, "Ideology, Interests, and the American Executive," 861–65. Note that here the word "competitive" means something very different from the way it was used earlier in this chapter. Whereas earlier the word "competitive" refers to the degree to which two countries engage in the production and export of a similar range of commodities, here it means that a given U.S. industry enjoys a home market advantage, or a competitive edge over foreign producers.

50. Krauss and Reich, "Ideology, Interests, and the American Executive," 861–65.

51. Numerous studies of American foreign trade policy have shown that Congress is likely to be more protectionist than the president. Since congressmen seek reelection, they are primarily responsible to their own local constituents. Designing policies that benefit these constituents helps to increase their chances of reelection. The executive, in contrast, is charged with overseeing the general performance of the economy and is therefore less likely to be driven by special interests to provide protectionist policies that are inefficient. The importance of constituent demands in the formation of legislators' preferences explains why legislators are more protectionist than the executive. Mayhew, *Congress;* Lohmann and O'Halloran, "Divided Government and U.S. Trade Policy"; Baldwin, *Political Economy.*

52. Chapter 3 will provide evidence showing that the vast majority of democracies do have fairly competitive trade relations.

CHAPTER 3

1. This study looks primarily at trade conflicts initiated by the United States under both the GATT/WTO framework and Section 301 of the Omnibus Trade and Competitiveness Act of 1988. I had to limit my analysis to U.S.–initiated disputes due to the lack of comprehensive data on trade structure. Further study could test the argument developed in the previous chapter against a larger sample of dyads that includes cases initiated by countries other than the United States.

2. Bayard and Elliott, *Reciprocity and Retaliation*, 29.

3. Stern, "U.S.-Japan Trade Policy and FDI Issues."

4. Ibid.

5. Trade and Related Agreements Database (TARA), compiled by the Trade Compliance Center, U.S. Department of Commerce, <http://www.mac.doc.gov/TCC/DATA/index.html>.

6. Ibid.

7. Hoekman and Kostecki, *Political Economy*, 77–78.

8. Reinhardt, "Aggressive Multilateralism."

9. See Bayard and Elliott, *Reciprocity and Retaliation*, 59–64, 355–69; Elliott and Richardson, "Determinants and Effectiveness," 221–25.

10. We can also evaluate the two cases discussed later involving China not covered by Section 301 negotiations—MFN and textiles—according to the criteria specified by Bayard and Elliott. The MFN case can be considered a failure since U.S. policy of threatening to revoke China's MFN status produced virtually no tangible changes in Chinese policies in the areas of trade, human rights, and weapons proliferation. The textile case can be classified as a partial success since even though a bilateral textile agreement was reached the Chinese side frequently evaded the quota restrictions by transshipping textile exports through third countries. If we add these two cases, China's level of responsiveness to American pressure remains the same as that evaluated by Bayard and Elliott in *Reciprocity and Retaliation*.

11. For example, an interview with a former government official involved in negotiations with both China and Japan offers a rather different view of U.S. negotiation outcomes. According to the interviewee, the United States has been able to get the Chinese to alter their policies to a greater extent than the Japanese.

12. Bayard and Elliott, *Reciprocity and Retaliation*, 68.

13. Tyson, *Who's Bashing Whom?* 106–13; Bergsten and Noland, *Reconcilable Differences?* 127–40.

14. Bayard and Elliott, *Reciprocity and Retaliation*, 118.

15. Ibid.

16. Ibid., 445–48.

17. Schoppa, *Bargaining with Japan*, 267–70.

18. Export figures are obtained from the IMF, *Direction of Trade Statistics Yearbook;* and Department of Commerce, International Trade Administration, *U.S. Foreign Trade Highlights,* various years. GDP figures, which are in nominal dollars, are based on the World Bank's *World Tables.*

19. In Bayard and Elliott's statistical analysis, nineteen cases were excluded from the total of ninety-one investigations initiated between 1975 and June 1994. Fifteen of these cases were dropped because they did not involve any negotiations. For a list of these excluded cases, see Bayard and Elliott, *Reciprocity and Retaliation,* 59. I update the remaining four cases excluded from Bayard and Elliott's study with Elliott and Richardson's data from "Determinants and Effectiveness."

20. Of the fifteen observations included in Elliott and Richardson's updated database in "Determinants and Effectiveness," I exclude the so-called p-list of Section 301 petitions filed but not formally investigated by the USTR and a case involving Taiwanese footwear (case no. 301–38) for which no clear evaluation of U.S. negotiation success is available. The six cases I take from Elliott and Richardson's modified sample include EU meatpacking (301–83), Chinese market access (301–88), Taiwanese intellectual property protection (301–89), Brazilian intellectual property protection (301–91), Japanese auto parts (301–93), and Canadian country music cable television (301–98). The fifteen countries included in the estimation sample are Guatemala, Canada, the EU, Taiwan, Japan, the USSR, Argentina, South Korea, Brazil, India, Norway, Spain, Portugal, Thailand, and China.

21. Data for the size of the U.S. bilateral trade balance are drawn from the Department of Commerce, International Trade Administration, *U.S. Foreign Trade Highlights;* and IMF, *Direction of Trade Statistics Yearbook.*

22. Many studies consider the U.S. ability to harm the target country an important component of bargaining power and a significant determinant of Section 301 success rates. See, for example, McMillan, "Strategic Bargaining and Section 301," 207; Noland, "Chasing Phantoms," 381–82.

23. A GATT panel ruling of noncompliance can shore up U.S. credibility by enhancing the perceived legitimacy of American threat. According to Ryan, *Playing by the Rules,* trade officials in East Asia often regarded GATT as the key because "it may determine win or lose for the U.S. If U.S. has a strong GATT case, the case will go differently. The U.S. can use GATT as a very effective tool" (43).

24. Bayard and Elliott, *Reciprocity and Retaliation,* 85; Elliott and Richardson, "Determinants and Effectiveness," 228–29.

25. Of all the countries targeted under Section 301, only three—the EU (in various disputes between 1982 and 1991), Canada (1986, 1991, and 1993), and China (in the textile dispute in 1983)—have ever counterretaliated against the United States in past disputes. Bayard and Elliott, *Reciprocity and Retaliation,* coded all disputes with countries with a record of counterretaliation as 1.

However, since it seems reasonable that the United States would only be concerned about counterretaliation from a specific trading partner after it took place, I only coded those disputes that occurred after the counterretaliation episode as 1. It turns out that this modification to Bayard and Elliott's original coding method did not affect the interpretation of the relationship between COUNTER and SUCCESS.

26. It is also possible to measure trade competitiveness by looking at the number of overlaps between the top twenty sectors in which the United States produces goods and services and the top twenty products the United States imports from a particular country in a given year. This procedure is not followed here because of the incomplete coverage of the industrial production data and the difficulties of converting industrial production data into trade data.

27. Specifically, the country with the most competitive relationship with the United States in a given year is assigned a number of 10. The competitiveness index for other U.S. trading partners in that year is adjusted accordingly.

28. Bayard and Elliott, *Reciprocity and Retaliation,* 84.

29. In my data set, the number of cases varies both cross-sectionally (i.e., thirteen cases for Japan and four for India) and in the time dimension (x cases in 1975 and y cases in 1995), thus creating the problem of "uneven" panel data. I used STATA to estimate probit models for such cross-sectional time-series data sets where data for some of the time periods are missing. This method is robust to the problem of unbalanced data. For an overview of cross-sectional time-series (panel) data techniques and a discussion of why one does not need to have balanced cases to generate appropriate results, see Greene, *Econometric Analysis,* chap. 16; and Baltagi, *Econometric Analysis of Panel Data.* See STATA manual version 6.0 for the practical issues.

30. Snyder, "Security Dilemma in Alliance Politics"; Huth, *Extended Deterrence;* Fearon, "Signaling Foreign Policy Interests."

31. Bayard and Elliott, in *Reciprocity and Retaliation,* did find a positive and statistically significant relationship between TBAL and SUCCESS. This discrepancy in test results may be due to different sample composition.

32. For arguments about why democracies may be more or less likely to settle trade disputes cooperatively, see Dixon, "Democracy and the Management of Conflict"; Dixon, "Democracy and the Peaceful Settlement"; Raymond, "Democracies, Disputes"; Bliss and Russett, "Democratic Trading Partners"; Verdier, "Democratic Convergence and Free Trade"; Leeds, "Domestic Political Institutions"; Reinhardt, "Aggressive Multilateralism"; Mansfield, Milner, and Rosendorff, "Free to Trade"; and Sherman, "Democracy and Trade Conflict." The widely used Polity III data developed by Jaggers and Gurr, in *Polity III,* are used to measure the regime type (REGIME) of each of the target countries. By subtracting the target country's autocratic

index from its democratic index, I arrive at a continuous variable ranging from –10 for a highly autocratic state to +10 for a highly democratic one.

33. See Drezner, *Sanctions Paradox* and "Outside the Box."

34. The coding of this variable follows the scheme developed by Hufbauer, Schott, and Elliott, in their study of the effectiveness of economic sanctions, *Economic Sanctions Reconsidered*. It is coded as 1 if the relationship between the United States and the target is antagonistic, 2 if the relationship is neutral, and 3 if the relationship is cordial.

35. In this test, REGIME, GDPCAPITA, and ALIGNMENT turned out to be individually insignificant. The significance of the trade competitiveness variable (COMPET) dropped to the .10 level with a one-tailed test as the standard error substantially increased with the addition of the two nonsignificant variables. A likelihood ratio test suggests that REGIME, GDPCAPITA, and ALIGNMENT do not significantly contribute to the overall fit of the model. In fact, the log likelihood of the restricted model is 33.35 and the log likelihood of the unrestricted model is 33.16. The log likelihood ratio is only .38, which is far from any conventional level of significance. Consequently, I accept the restricted model, given the sample size and the additional loss of degrees of freedom, without improved fit, associated with the unrestricted model. In addition, restricting the parsimonious model even further by omitting COMPET results in a significant loss of fit, indicating that COMPET does significantly contribute to the overall fit of the model. These test results are available by request.

36. Maoz and Abdolali, "Regime Type and International Conflict"; Dixon, "Democracy and the Peaceful Settlement"; Levy, "Domestic Politics and War"; Bremer, "Dangerous Dyads."

37. Lardy, *China in the World Economy,* 83–84

38. Bayard and Elliott, *Reciprocity and Retaliation,* 460–61.

39. The twenty-five U.S. trading partners are Canada, Japan, Mexico, China, the EU, Taiwan, South Korea, Singapore, Malaysia, Brazil, Hong Kong, Venezuela, Thailand, the Philippines, Saudi Arabia, Switzerland, Australia, Indonesia, Israel, India, Argentina, Columbia, Dominican Republic, Russia, and Nigeria.

40. The literature on democracy and democratization includes fairly similar criteria. Huntington, in *The Third Wave,* for example, considers a democratic system to be one in which "the most powerful collective decision makers are selected through fair, honest, and periodic elections in which candidates freely compete for votes and in which virtually all the adult population is eligible to vote" (7). See also Dahl, *Polyarchy.* These criteria have also been used in various studies of the relationship between regime type and international security conflicts. See, for example, Russett, *Grasping the Democratic Peace;* Farber and Gowa, "Polities and Peace"; Mansfield and Snyder, "Democratization and the Danger of War."

41. Jaggers and Gurr, *Polity III.*

42. For example, the data have been used by Russett, *Grasping the Democratic Peace;* Mansfield and Snyder, "Democratization and the Danger of War"; Farber and Gowa, "Polities and Peace"; and Oneal and Russett, "Classical Liberals Were Right."

43. Alternatively, the REGIME index can be treated as a dichotomous variable if we recode the original REGIME score greater than 10 as 1 and those smaller than 10 as 0. Statistical tests using the dichotomous variable yield essentially the same results. Since the EU is not rated in Jaggers and Gurr's data set from *Polity III,* the EU's democracy score is derived by averaging all member countries' democracy scores in a given year. Some scholars have argued that the EU suffers from a "democratic deficit" due to the lack of democratic control of the national and European parliaments over the decision-making process in the European Council and the EU Council of Ministers, as well as the secrecy and technocracy in the EU policy-making process. Such a "democratic deficit" should cause the level of democracy in the EU to be lower than the average of all EU member states. To take into account this possibility, I recoded EU's democracy score from the average of its member states, 10, to 9 and then reran the models using the recoded democracy score for the EU. Test results show that this procedure changes neither the sign nor the significance of the results reported later using the average democracy score of EC members. Consequently, I only report results of statistical analyses using the average EC democracy level. For the "democratic deficit" argument, see Featherstone, "Jean Monnet and the 'Democratic Deficit,'"; Scharpf, "Economic Integration"; and Schmidt, "European Integration and Democracy."

44. Data for 1980–81 are based on IMF, *Direction of Trade Statistics Yearbook.*

45. Gowa and Mansfield, "Power Politics and International Trade"; Mansfield and Bronson, "Political Economy of Major-Power Trade Flows." This assumption has encountered increasing criticism in recent years though. For opposing arguments and empirical evidence, see Morrow, Siverson, and Tabares, "Political Determinants of International Trade"; and Bliss and Russett, "Democratic Trading Partners."

46. I considered controlling for country-specific effects by creating a dummy variable for each of the countries that have most frequently been singled out as the target of aggressive U.S. trade actions (such as Japan and Europe). The expectation is that there should be more trade wars with countries that have received the most attention of U.S. trade negotiators. But since the total number of cases involving each of these countries is fairly small compared to the sample size, I did not include country-specific dummy variables as controls. In future research, I plan to test my hypotheses against a larger sample including a greater number of countries over a longer time span to ascertain if certain countries are more likely to have trade wars with the United States.

CHAPTER 4

1. For example, as part of the WTO agreement, China committed over a span of five years to reduce tariffs and eliminate quantitative restrictions on both industrial and agricultural products. It also agreed to open a broad range of services, including telecommunications, insurance, banking, securities, and professional services, to foreign service providers. These concessions, unprecedented in their scope, offered the prospect of greatly expanded market access to China for a wide array of U.S. industries and sectors.

2. Lampton, "Ending the MFN Battle," 7.

3. Yuan, "Sanctions, Domestic Politics," 110–12.

4. For a more detailed discussion of the origin of the congressional debate over China's MFN status, see U.S. House Committee on Ways and Means, *Disapproval of Extension of Most-Favored-Nation Treatment,* 1–2.

5. Dumbaugh, "Making of China Policy," 17–18.

6. For instance, the bill introduced by Senate Majority Leader George Mitchell in 1991 (S 1367) and another legislative proposal introduced in 1992 (HR 5318) threatened to cut off China's MFN status unless it could be shown that the Chinese government had stopped arrests of prodemocracy activists, ceased the export of products made with prison labor, provided U.S. exporters nondiscriminatory access to the Chinese market, and ended unreasonable and discriminatory unfair trade practices against the United States.

7. For example, the American trade deficit with China swelled from $6.2 billion in 1989 to $18.2 billion in 1992. Trade barriers limiting opportunities for the sale of American goods and services remained formidable. Also, concerns grew that China was using convict labor to produce goods that subsequently were exported to the United States. On human rights, the Chinese had released a handful of political prisoners. But for human rights activists, these measures were purely symbolic. Moreover, the basic human rights situation had not improved substantially. At the same time, although China had agreed to abide by the guidelines and parameters of the Missile Technology Control Regime (MTCR), which bars the transfer of medium- and long-range missiles, there were a number of reports showing that Beijing continued to sell M-11 missiles to Pakistan. "U.S. Faces Dilemma in Setting China Policy," *Washington Post,* March 9, 1993, A28.

8. "Press Conference of the President," Office of the Press Secretary, White House, May 26, 1994.

9. Since the mid-1980s, the growth of China's exports to the United States has taken place primarily in labor-intensive industries in which China has been able to take advantage of its abundant labor force and low wage level to build strong comparative advantages. The bulk of Chinese exports to the United States was in the following labor-intensive sectors: miscellaneous manufactured articles such as toys, games, footwear, clothing and apparel, baby carriages, watches, and instruments; manufactured materials including textile

manufactured materials, fabrics, machine tools, and paper products; and mineral fuels. In contrast, a large portion of U.S. exports to China has concentrated on technology-intensive products such as machinery and equipment, especially aircraft and parts, industrial machinery, civil engineering plant and equipment, automatic data-processing machines and machine tools. For example, between 1986 and 1990, China was able to increase its exports of toys, games, sporting goods, and baby carriages from roughly $370 million to $2.2 billion, footwear from $76 million to $1.5 billion, and more than double the value of its exports of suitcases, textiles, and apparel to the United States. Department of Commerce, International Trade Administration, *U.S. Foreign Trade Highlights,* various years; see also Rondinelli, "Resolving U.S.-China Trade Conflicts," 66.

10. Sutter, *U.S. Policy toward China,* 56–57.

11. U.S. House. *United States-People's Republic of China Trade Relations.*

12. U.S. Department of Commerce, International Trade Administration, *U.S. Foreign Trade Highlights,* 1991.

13. "Sentiment Grows in Congress to Reject MFN for China," *Congressional Quarterly Weekly Report* 49, no. 17 (April 27, 1991): 1044.

14. Mann, *About Face,* 275–76.

15. "Will China Remain a Most-Favored Dictatorship?" *Business Week,* July 29, 1991, 38.

16. Mann, "U.S. Firms Lobby for China Trade Benefits."

17. Gargan, "Gauging the Consequences of Spurning China."

18. Mann, *About Face.*

19. U.S. House Committee on Ways and Means, *Disapproval of Extension of Most-Favored-Nation Treatment,* 208.

20. Keatley, "U.S. Firms Worry."

21. "China Fever Strikes Again," *Business Week,* March 29, 1993, 46.

22. Ibid., 47.

23. Ibid.

24. "The Case for China's MFN Status," *China Business Review* 19, no. 4 (July–August 1992): 14–16.

25. Sutter, *U.S. Policy toward China,* 57–58.

26. Ibid., 56.

27. Schoenberger, "Question of Conscience."

28. Business Coalition for U.S.-China Trade, "Business Leaders Urge U.S."

29. Kaslow, "President Urges Renewal."

30. Locin, "Trade Chief Hints."

31. Walter, "Firms Unshaken by U.S. Terms for China."

32. Behr, "U.S. Businesses Waged Year-long Lobbying Effort."

33. For a more detailed discussion of the weaknesses of the coalition opposing China's MFN status, see Sutter, *U.S. Policy toward China,* 54–56.

34. Sutter, "American Policy toward Beijing," 3.

35. Ibid.

36. See, for example, Bush's speech at Yale University on May 15, 1991. "Bush Seeks to Renew China Trade Status," *Washington Post,* May 16, 1991, A1.

37. For example, during the first six months of 1991, American officials on several occasions met with senior Chinese officials to discuss human rights. In April, to convey to the Chinese authorities U.S. dissatisfaction, President Bush met with the Dalai Lama in the White House. On April 26, several weeks before Congress would make the decision on MFN status, USTR Carla Hills cited China for inadequate protection of IPR and named it one of three "priority foreign countries" under the Special 301 provisions of the 1988 Trade Act. Also, a delegation led by assistant USTR Joseph Massey visited Beijing in June to discuss a wide range of trade problems with senior officials in Beijing. Hendry, "Limited Protection."

38. "The Case for China's MFN Status," *China Business Review* 19, no. 4 (July–August 1992): 14.

39. As the president stated clearly in his Yale address, "China can—easily can—affect the stability of the Asian Pacific region and therefore affect the entire world's peace and prosperity. The Chinese play a central role in working to resolve the conflict in Cambodia, to relax tensions on the Korean peninsula. China has a voice now in multinational organizations and its votes in the United Nations Security Council against Iraq's brutal aggression helped us forge the broad coalition that brought us victory in the gulf." "Bush Says China MFN Status Will Be Catalyst for Change," *Congressional Quarterly Weekly Report* 49, no. 22 (June 1, 1991): 1459.

40. By the end of 1992, Beijing had done little to lower its trade barriers to foreign businesses. It blocked inspection of factories that allegedly used prison labor to make export goods. Moreover, Chinese authorities had released only a limited number of Tiananmen prisoners. Chinese premier Li Peng directly told President Bush in a meeting in New York in January 1992 that human rights concerns were being used as an excuse by outsiders to meddle in China's internal affairs. Moffet, "Bush, Congress Clash on China."

41. Lampton, "America's China Policy," 599.

42. Tyler, "Beijing Says It Could Live Well."

43. Walsh, "Clinton Indicts Bush's World Leadership."

44. The executive order established seven human rights-conditioning factors: halting exports of goods produced by prison labor, allowing freedom of emigration, observing the Universal Declaration of Human Rights, protecting Tibet's distinctive culture, treating prisoners humanely, permitting international radio and television broadcasts in China, and releasing and accounting for prisoners held for the nonviolent expression of political and religious beliefs.

45. Lampton, "America's China Policy," 610.

46. Greenberger, "Restraint of Trade."

47. Lampton, "America's China Policy," 616.

48. Ibid.

49. Dunne, "Beijing and the Business of Human Rights."

50. Greenberger and Frisby, "Clinton's Renewal of Trade Status."

51. Ibid.; Greenberger, "Restraint of Trade."

52. Friedman, "Clinton Votes for Business."

53. Sutter, *U.S. Policy toward China*, 50.

54. Lampton, "America's China Policy," 613.

55. *Financial Times,* March 17, 1994, 7.

56. Jones, "Chinese Officials Say MFN Status Benefits"; Bansberg, "China Steps up Campaign."

57. Bansberg, "China Steps up Campaign."

58. *South China Morning Post,* April 15, 1994, 9.

59. Greenberger, "Restraint of Trade."

60. Jen, "Background to China's 'Four Nots' Policy"; Lu, "New 'Eight-Character Principle.'"

61. Tyler, "Beijing Says It Could Live Well." As Jiang Zemin commented on his meeting with Clinton in Seattle in 1993, the two sides "were of the same opinion that a long-term view should be taken of the development of Chinese-U.S. relations, looking toward the 21st century." In "Jiang on Sino-U.S. Relations," Xinhua News Service, September 1994.

62. Mann, *About Face,* 296.

63. Tefft, "China Sends Huge Trade Vanguard," 9.

64. Sun, "China Detains Dissident."

65. Warren Christopher, "China's MFN Status: Summary of the Report and Recommendations of Secretary of State Warren Christopher," released by the Department of State, May 26, 1994.

66. Comment by a Chinese foreign relations analyst in Beijing in May 1994. See Lampton, "America's China Policy," 613.

67. Yuan, "Sanctions, Domestic Politics," 110.

68. Bayard and Elliott, *Reciprocity and Retaliation,* 461.

69. Goldstein, "Brawling in the Ring."

70. *Washington Post,* October 10, 1992, A19.

71. "Nike, Adidas Fear Tariffs' Effect on Hong Kong; Top Shoemakers Warn U.S," *South China Morning Post,* August 5, 1992, 1.

72. Wu, "U.S.-China Tensions Frighten Importers."

73. "Nike, Adidas Fear Tariffs' Effect on Hong Kong; Top Shoemakers Warn U.S," *South China Morning Post,* August 5, 1992, 1.

74. Wu, "U.S.-China Tensions Frighten Importers."

75. "China, U.S. to Resume Trade Talks in Atmosphere Strained by Threats," *Journal of Commerce,* September 14, 1992, 3A.

76. "Nike, Adidas Fear Tariffs' Effect on Hong Kong; Top Shoemakers Warn U.S," *South China Morning Post,* August 5, 1992, 1.

77. Letter from President Bush to Senator Baucus, July 19, 1991, 3–10.

78. Mann, "U.S. China Averts Clash over Trade," A1.

79. Author's interview with a former MOFERT official, October 12, 2001.

80. Odell, "International Threats and Internal Politics."

81. Ibid., 239.

82. Between 1983 and 1987, the top five commodities the United States imported from Brazil, in the order of the volume traded, were coffee, petroleum products, footwear, fruits and nuts, and plates and sheets. Department of Commerce, International Trade Administration, *U.S. Foreign Trade Highlights,* 1987.

83. Graham, "Washington Angered by Extension."

84. Sparks, "Inter Trade."

85. Odell and Dibble, *Brazilian Informatics and the United States,* 14.

86. Odell, "International Threats and Internal Politics," 240.

87. "Brazil Acts to Defuse U.S. Software Row," *Financial Times,* November 27, 1987, 9.

88. "Will Keep Computer Import Limits—Brazil," *Los Angeles Times,* December 5, 1987, 2.

89. "Brazil to Reconsider Ban on U.S. Software," *Journal of Commerce,* November 6, 1987, 5A.

CHAPTER 5

1. For a detailed account of the relative development of the American and Japanese semiconductor industries and the difficulties that the ascendance of the Japanese semiconductor industry posed to American manufacturers, see Okimoto, Sugano, and Weinstein, *Competitive Edge;* Prestowitz, *Trading Places;* Borrus, *Competing for Control;* Borrus, Millstein, and Zysman, "Trade and Development in the Semiconductor Industry."

2. O'Shea, "U.S.-Japan Semiconductor Problem," 61.

3. Ibid., 61–62.

4. For example, the SIA's lobbying effort led to the passage of a 1984 law providing intellectual property protection to chip manufacturers in the United States and a 1985 agreement between the United States and Japan eliminating tariffs on semiconductor imports in the United States. See Yoffie, "How an Industry Builds Political Advantage"; and Nanto and McLoughlin, *Japanese and U.S. Industrial Associations.*

5. Ryan, *Playing by the Rules,* 99.

6. Quoted in Irwin, "Trade Politics and the Semiconductor Industry," 39.

7. Ryan, *Playing by the Rules,* 97.

8. Wolff, "Petition of the Semiconductor Industry Association," 1–4.

9. Tyson, *Who's Bashing Whom?* 108.

10. Prestowitz, *Trading Places,* 57.

11. Irwin, "Trade Politics and the Semiconductor Industry," 43–44.

12. Krauss, "U.S.-Japan Negotiations."

13. Kehoe, "U.S. Savours Electronics Showdown."

14. Yoffie, "How an Industry Builds Political Advantage," 86.

15. Krauss, "U.S.-Japan Negotiations," 269.

16. In her analysis of the ideational sources of trade policy, Judith Goldstein argues that ideas provide decision makers with strategies or road maps that serve to maximize their interests. While material interests provide a good basis for understanding the positions of various groups and coalitions, policy ideas, often embedded and encased in institutions, help to mold policy choices. Thus, the ascendance of the "strategic trade" argument provided a justification for addressing unfair trade within the context of a liberal trade regime. Goldstein, *Ideas, Interests, and American Trade Policy*, 176–80.

17. O'Shea, "U.S.-Japan Semiconductor Problem," 67.

18. Ibid., 72.

19. As Prestowitz pointed out, "Because Japan is both friend and ally, and because the problem with Japan arose from a set of interrelated policies carried out over many years rather than from a specific trade action, there was great reluctance in Washington, particularly at the Department of State and the National Security Council, to brand Japan an unfair trader." Prestowitz, *Trading Places*, 160.

20. O'Shea, "U.S.-Japan Semiconductor Problem," 72.

21. This is essentially the strategic trade argument espoused by the trade agencies.

22. Irwin, "Trade Politics and the Semiconductor Industry," 41.

23. Ryan, *Playing by the Rules*, 103–4.

24. Prestowitz, *Trading Places*, 59–60.

25. Ibid., 59.

26. Tanaka et al., "Reply of the Electronics Industries Association of Japan," cited in Ryan, *Playing by the Rules*, 104.

27. Krauss, "U.S.-Japan Negotiations," 267–68.

28. For example, at a meeting in Tokyo on May 28, Yeutter directly told Minister of International Trade and Industry Michio Watanabe of Japan that the United States would like a Japanese government pledge to establish an effective cost-price monitoring system to prevent dumping and to substantially increase the U.S. share of the Japanese market to a 20 percent target within five years. Then in late June, a deputy USTR announced that the United States would retaliate with economic sanctions if a settlement agreement could not soon be reached. The move was unusual in that it signaled that the United States would no longer be willing, as it had been in the entire postwar period, to tolerate unfair Japanese trade practices in order to maintain a friendly overall bilateral relationship. In doing so, the American side indicated to Japan the seriousness it attached to the matter as well as its resolve to find an equitable settlement.

29. With regard to dumping, Japan agreed to assign each of its chip pro-

ducers a foreign market value based on the firm's manufacturing costs to measure the extent of dumping. In addition, MITI agreed to monitor the costs and prices of semiconductor exports to both the United States and to third markets and to provide firm-specific manufacturing data to the Commerce Department to determine whether dumping had actually occurred. It also agreed to engage in consultations with the United States and to take appropriate action if American negotiators could present evidence that dumping was taking place. In return for Japan's pledge, the United States agreed to suspend the dumping investigations on EPROMS and DRAMS.

30. "Arrangement between the Government of Japan and the Government of the United States of America Concerning Trade in Semiconductor Products," September 2, 1986.

31. According to the side letter, "The Government of Japan recognizes the U.S. semiconductor industry's expectation that semiconductor sales in Japan of foreign capital-affiliated companies will grow to at least slightly above 20 percent of the Japanese market in five years" and that the Japanese government "considers that this can be realized and welcomes its realization." Letter to Ambassador Clayton Yeutter from Ambassador Matsunaga, quoted in Wolff, "Identification of Japan's Failure to Abide by the Semiconductor Agreement," 8.

32. Bergsten and Noland, *Reconcilable Differences?* 132; Tyson, *Who's Bashing Whom?* 109.

33. Krauss, "U.S.-Japan Negotiations," 187, 270.

34. Prestowitz, *Trading Places,* 64–65.

35. Ibid., 67.

36. Farnsworth, "End Believed Near for U.S. Sanctions," A1.

37. *Far Eastern Economic Review,* September 25, 1986.

38. *Wall Street Journal,* February 27, 1987, 44.

39. *New York Times,* March 27, 1987, 1; *New York Times,* March 28, 1987, 1; *Wall Street Journal,* March 30, 1987, 1.

40. Yoffie and Coleman, "Semiconductor Industry Association," 1–2; Keopp, "Fighting the Trade Tilt," 50.

41. Tyson, *Who's Bashing Whom?* 106.

42. In the 1991 agreement, Japan committed itself to achieving the goal of a 20 percent market share by encouraging the development of long-term buyer-supplier relationships in return for Washington's promise to remove the remaining sanctions against Japanese producers for violating the provisions of the 1986 accord. Japanese producers further agreed to facilitate antidumping investigations by providing data on cost and price to the American side. The agreement also contained provisions that would facilitate American firms' efforts to deter aggressive pricing strategies by Japanese companies.

43. Specifically, Japan agreed to give advance public notification of public procurement, publish specific performance criteria on the bids, and establish

specific procedures for making complaints and protests. Tyson, *Who's Bashing Whom?* 77–78.

44. U.S. House Office of Technology Assessment, *Competing Economies,* 25–28.

45. One report estimated that by the late 1980s American firms' share of the Japanese public sector supercomputer market, including Japan's universities, was a meager 6 percent. Between 1987 and 1989, Japanese public institutions purchased fifty-one supercomputers, but only five were obtained from foreign suppliers. Japanese companies such as Fujitsu continued their dominance of the Japanese supercomputer market. Herbst, "A More Open Market for Supercomputers,"123.

46. According to Cray Research, while it accounted for approximately 63 percent of the world market, 84 percent of the American market, and 81 percent of the European market, its share of the Japanese market was only 15 percent.Tyson, *Who's Bashing Whom?* 78.

47. Schatz, "Who's Winning the Supercomputer Race?" 18.

48. U.S. House Committee on Government Operations, *Is the Administration Giving away the U.S. Supercomputer Industry?* 125.

49. Bergsten and Noland, *Reconcilable Differences?* 145; see also Tyson, *Who's Bashing Whom?* 77.

50. LaRussa, "AEA Lauds U.S. Move on Trade."

51. U.S. Senate Committee on Finance, *Super 301,* 1–3.

52. U.S. House Committee on Ways and Means, *USTR Identification of Priority Practices and Countries.*

53. Silk, "Japan Tops Sanction 'Hit List,'" 9A.

54. See Mastanduno, "Setting Market Access Priorities."

55. Bayard and Elliott, *Reciprocity and Retaliation,* 101–2.

56. See Pear, "Far-off Silver Lining."

57. Ibid.

58. According to the 1989 *National Trade Estimate Report,* "U.S. suppliers found themselves excluded from serious consideration in Japanese government procurements due to technical specifications favoring incumbent Japanese suppliers. Extraordinarily low Japanese government supercomputer budgets effectively require massive discounts of up to 80 percent off list price." U.S. Trade Representative, *National Trade Estimate Report,* 1989, 103.

59. *International Trade Reporter,* July 1989; U.S. House Office of Technology Assessment, *Competing Economies,* 276.

60. Specifically, the 1990 agreement mandated that performance requirements be based on real rather than peak-performance data; it required that the machine had to be delivered by the announced delivery date in order to prevent Japanese companies from bidding for a product that did not yet exist (i.e., "paper machines"); it responded to American complaints by setting more transparent and nondiscriminatory criteria for evaluating bids; and, finally, the agreement limited price discounting by outlawing bids that violated

Japan's antitrust regulations and established a Procurement Review Board to consider complaints of violations of the accord's provisions.

61. Bayard and Elliott, *Reciprocity and Retaliation,* 119.

62. Ibid., 112.

63. See the evaluation of the 1990 supercomputer agreement by Bayard and Elliott, *Reciprocity and Retaliation,* 119–20; and Tyson, *Who's Bashing Whom?* 79.

64. U.S. Senate Committee on Commerce, *Japanese Space Industry—An American Challenge,* testimony of J. Michael Farren, Undersecretary for International Trade, U.S. Department of Commerce, before the Senate Commerce Subcommittee on Foreign Commerce and Tourism, October 4, 1989, 14.

65. Wray, "Japanese Space Enterprise," 469.

66. The plan by Japan's telecommunications giant NTT to buy Hughes's satellite technology in 1983 reportedly "sent shock waves through Washington," leading American decision makers to direct more attention to the trade effects of Japanese public procurement policies. See Prestowitz's discussion of the incident, in *Trading Places,* 122–24.

67. Importantly, Tokyo allowed private companies to purchase foreign satellites and to compete with NTT in the provision of satellite communication services. It also approved the establishment of two joint ventures.

68. See, for example, U.S. Senate Committee on Commerce, *Japanese Space Industry—An American Challenge,* testimony of J. Michael Farren.

69. Mastanduno, "Do Relative Gains Matter?" 98–99. See also Wray, "Japanese Space Enterprise," 470.

70. Mastanduno, "Do Relative Gains Matter?" 100.

71. U.S. Senate Committee on Commerce, *Japanese Space Industry—An American Challenge,* testimony of S. Lynn Williams and J. Michael Farren; see also Wray, "Japanese Space Enterprise," 470.

72. U.S. Senate Committee on Commerce, *Japanese Space Industry—An American Challenge,* testimony of J. Michael Farren, 14.

73. U.S. Senate Committee on Commerce, *Japanese Space Industry—An American Challenge,* testimony of S. Lynn Williams, 7.

74. The State Department and the Council of Economic Advisors voiced their concerns that designating Japan could harm the bilateral political relationship and incite a trade war with Japan. See Powell, Thomas, and Martin, "Japan Makes the Hit List."

75. Mastanduno, "Do Relative Gains Matter?" 97.

76. U.S. House Committee on Ways and Means, *USTR Identification of Priority Practices and Countries,* 33–37.

77. Ibid., 41–56.

78. Ibid., 59.

79. Ibid., 100–101, 105–10.

80. Japan Economic Institute, *JEI Report,* no. 16B, April 20, 1990, 12.

81. Wray, "Japanese Space Enterprise," 473.

82. Ibid., 472.

83. U.S. communications satellite manufacturers held about 65 to 70 percent of the global market estimated at $1.2 billion to $1.4 billion annually in the early 1990s. See U.S. Department of Commerce, *U.S. Industry Output 1992*.

84. Hershey, "A Basic Pact with Japan," D1.

85. Bayard and Elliott, *Reciprocity and Retaliation,* 134.

86. According to wood products manufacturers, this was reflected in the disparity between Japan's share of world trade volume in logs, which ranged somewhere between 40 to 45 percent in the mid-1980s, and its share of world trade in processed wood products, which hovered at only 10 percent during the same period. ABARE, *Japanese Agricultural Policies,* 253.

87. U.S. Department of Commerce, *Japanese Solid Wood Products Market,* chap. 3.

88. U.S. House Committee on Finance, *Japanese Trade Barriers to Forest Products,* 14.

89. Ibid., 135–37.

90. U.S. Department of Commerce, *Japanese Solid Wood Products Market,* 135–54.

91. Ibid., 137–57.

92. *Journal of Commerce,* April 24, 1989, 5.

93. *Journal of Commerce,* December 1989, 1A.

94. National Forest Products Association, "Comments Concerning Japanese Restrictions Affecting Importation of Forest Products," July 18, 1989, on file in the USTR reading room.

95. U.S. House Committee on Finance, *Japanese Trade Barriers to Forest Products,* 11–16.

96. Ibid.

97. U.S. House Committee on Ways and Means, *USTR Identification of Priority Practices and Countries,* 39–40.

98. Ibid., 33–37.

99. U.S. Department of Commerce, *Japanese Solid Wood Products Market,* 142.

100. Bayard and Elliott, *Reciprocity and Retaliation,* 146–47.

101. U.S. Department of Commerce, *Japanese Solid Wood Products Market,* 143–44.

102. U.S. Senate Committee on Finance, *Super 301,* 29.

103. Yabunaka, *Taibei keizai kosho* (Economic negotiations with the United States), 136.

104. Interview with a Japanese official personally involved in the negotiations, September 9, 2001.

105. Cited in U.S. House Office of Technology Assessment, *Competing Economies,* 276.

106. Yabunaka, *Taibei keizai kosho* (Economic negotiations with the United States).

107. For further discussions of the strategic trade policy, see Krugman, *Strategic Policy;* Krugman, "Strategic Sectors and International Competition"; and Sandholtz et al., *Highest Stakes.*

CHAPTER 6

1. Interviews with China experts confirm this interpretation.
2. Ibid.
3. Sands and Lehr, "IPR Watchdogs."
4. Lachica, "Plan for Tariffs against China."
5. Belsie, "China Trade through Lens."
6. Ruzicka, "U.S.-China Tension Building over Piracy."
7. Ibid.
8. Belsie, "China Trade through Lens."
9. Ibid.
10. Ibid.
11. *Wall Street Journal,* February 1, 1995.
12. Ruzicka, "U.S.-China Tension Building over Piracy."
13. *Washington Post,* May 16, 1996, A21.
14. *Los Angeles Times,* May 15, 1996, A1.
15. *Strait Times,* May 15, 1996, 13.
16. Stevenson, "Tread Carefully with China."
17. Smith and Chen, "U.S. Business Concerned."
18. Robert S. Greenberger and Jeff Cole, "China Sanctions Put U.S. Firms in a Bind," *Wall Street Journal,* May 30, 1996.
19. Stevenson, "Tread Carefully with China."
20. Ibid., 5 (sect. 1).
21. Jayakar, "United States-China Copyright Dispute," 553–54.
22. Sanger and Erlanger, "United States Warns China."
23. Jehl, "Warning to China on Trade."
24. "Tariffs Won't Hurt, China Warns," *Toronto Star,* February 6, 1995, B2.
25. "China Defiant in Piracy Dispute with U.S.," *Financial Times,* February 15, 1996, 4.
26. "China Warns U.S. to Return to Trade Talks," *Toronto Star,* May 20, 1996, C6.
27. "China: U.S. Trade Deficit, Sino-U.S. Trade Wrangles, Are Washington's Fault," *Agence France Presse,* May 19, 1996.
28. According to Lardy, one year after the agreement came into existence, Chinese textile exports to the United States grew by nearly two-thirds. Lardy, *China in the World Economy,* 83.

29. Zhang, "Maoyi Baohu Zhuyi Dui Zhongmei Liangguo de Weihai," 113.

30. Ibid.

31. According to the Commerce Department, Chinese exports increased by 40 percent in 1980, 73 percent in 1981, and 23 percent in 1982. By 1982 China had become the fourth largest textile exporter to the U.S. market, supplying 10.5 percent of overall U.S. textile imports. The remarkable growth of Chinese exports took place at a time when the U.S. textile industry was suffering from a shrinking domestic market and rising industry unemployment. Department of Commerce, International Trade Administration, *U.S. Foreign Trade Highlights,* 1985.

32. *Washington Post,* November 21, 1982, 6A.

33. For example, President John F. Kennedy, by promoting the establishment of the Short-Term and Long-Term Arrangements Regarding Textiles (the STA and the LTA), and President Richard Nixon, by fostering the development of the Multifiber Agreement, had set precedents of offering policy concessions in exchange for political support. Hufbauer and Rosen, *Trade Policy for Troubled Industries;* Friman, *Patchwork Protectionism.*

34. Destler, *American Trade Politics.*

35. Destler and Odell, *Anti-Protection,* 89–93.

36. "A Spring Offensive," *Wall Street Journal,* March 29, 1983, 1.

37. *Washington Post,* July 13, 1983, 1F.

38. *Wall Street Journal,* September 7, 1983, 3.

39. *Journal of Commerce,* August 1, 1983, 5A.

40. Ryan, *Playing by the Rules,* 158–59.

41. Ibid., 159–61.

42. Madison, "Textile Talks Will Put Stance to Real Test," 883.

43. Under the executive order, the interagency Committee for the Implementation of Textile Agreements was authorized to engage in bilateral consultations with the Chinese government with regard to textiles and apparel products. CITA would be mandated to implement new restrictions if imports exceeded 20 percent of total U.S. production or if the annual growth rate of textile imports in specific product categories reached 30 percent. This new policy was not limited to China but covered imports from America's major textile suppliers as well. Ryan, *Playing by the Rules,* 163.

44. Lardy, *China in the World Economy,* 85.

45. "U.S. Cuts Imports of Chinese Textile By $1 Billion," *St. Petersburg Times,* January 7, 1994, 13A; "Ending the Textile Rift," *China Business Review* 21, no. 3 (May–June 1994): 9.

46. *Washington Post,* January 7, 1994, A8; John Davies, "U.S. Importers Fear Big Loss," 5A.

47. "U.S.-China Trade War Looms over Textiles," *Gazette,* January 8, 1994, C3.

48. Ibid.

49. Friedman, "U.S. Pares Imports of China's Fabrics."
50. Ibid.
51. Dunne, "Washington Speaks with One Voice," *Financial Times,* January 8, 1994, 3.
52. Green, "U.S. Textile Makers, Importers Clash."
53. Green, "Trade Office Braces for Lobbying Blitz."
54. Bangsberg, "China Warns of Retaliation," 3A.
55. English "Text" of Interview on U.S. Textile Issue. FBIS-CHI-96–195, October 6, 1996.

CHAPTER 7

1. For a more detailed account of these disputes, see, for example, Yannopoulos, *Customs Unions and Trade Conflicts;* and Paalberg, *Fixing Farm Trade.*
2. Bayard and Elliott, *Reciprocity and Retaliation,* 428–30.
3. Odell and Matzinger-Tchakerian, "European Community Enlargement," 136.
4. Gardner, "Political Economy of U.S. Export Subsidies," 295.
5. Farm groups contended that, since the enlargement treaty required the *elimination* of Spanish and Portuguese tariffs on manufactured goods imported from other E.C. countries, American industries would be placed at a distinctive disadvantage vis-à-vis their European competitors. Letter from U.S. Feed Grains Council to U.S. Department of Agriculture, June 20, 1986, cited in Odell and Matzinger-Tchakerian, "European Community Enlargement," 137.
6. Odell, "International Threats and Internal Politics," 241.
7. Odell and Matzinger-Tchakerian, "European Community Enlargement."
8. Letters to USTR, December 2, 1986, quoted in Odell, "International Threats and Internal Politics," 242.
9. See Odell, "International Threats and Internal Politics," 242.
10. Heavy subsidies allowed the EC to increase its share of the world export market for wheat and flour from 9.5 percent during the 1970s to 15.7 percent in 1984–85. EC agricultural subsidies in 1984 alone amounted to $5.2 billion. Strokes, "Trade Disputes Are Straining the Ties," 1985.
11. "Close U.S.-E.C. Links Sometimes Result in Trade Strains," *Europe* 271 (November 1987): 46.
12. Statement by Rep. Doug Berueter (R-NE), member of the House Foreign Affairs Subcommittee on International Economic Policy and Trade, 1986.
13. Yeutter, "Preserving the Atlantic Peace," 23.
14. Address by Commerce Secretary Malcolm Baldrige before the Ameri-

can Chamber of Commerce, "U.S.-E.C. Trade Dispute," *Department of State Bulletin* 86 (June 1986): 43.

15. Johnston, "U.S., Europe Achieve Truce."

16. Odell and Matzinger-Tchakerian, "European Community Enlargement," 144–45.

17. EC agricultural exports accounted for about one-fifth of world agriculture trade in 1985. IMF, *Direction of Trade Statistics Yearbook, 1986.*

18. Odell and Matzinger-Tchakerian, "European Community Enlargement," 145.

19. Ibid., 149.

20. Odell, "International Threats and Internal Politics," 243.

21. Ibid.

22. Ibid., 246.

23. Cashore, *Flights of the Phoenix,* 10–11.

24. U.S. Department of Commerce, International Trade Administration, *Preliminary Negative Countervailing Duty Determination,* 1.

25. Kalt, *Political Economy of Protectionism,* 1–2.

26. U.S. sales of shakes and shingles were $80 million a year, with Canada being a major supplier to the United States.

27. Specifically, U.S. importers were required to post bonds of up to 15 percent on shipments of softwood lumber from Canada.

28. Kalt, *The Political Economy of Protectionism,* 3.

29. Ibid., 340.

30. Ibid.

31. Kalt, "Precedent and Legal Argument in U.S. Trade Policy," 270–71.

32. Constantino and Percy, "Political Economy of Canada-U.S. Trade," 56.

33. See Percy and Yoder, *Softwood Lumber Dispute,* 23.

34. Bailey, "The Productivity Growth Slowdown by Industry," 437.

35. Coalition for Fair Lumber Imports, *Petition for the Imposition of Countervailing Duties.*

36. Kalt, *Political Economy of Protectionism,* 8–9.

37. Coalition for Fair Lumber Imports, *Petition for the Imposition of Countervailing Duties.*

38. Cashore, *Flights of the Phoenix,* 11.

39. Ibid.

40. Geoffrey Carliner's comments in Krueger, *Political Economy of American Trade Policy,* 289–90.

41. Ibid.

42. Fox, "Politics of Canada-U.S. Trade," 27.

43. Percy and Yoder, *Softwood Lumber Dispute,* 1.

44. Lewington, "Senators Warn Canada," B12.

45. Fox, "Politics of Canada-U.S. Trade," 27.

46. Bonker in the House and Baucus in the Senate sponsored the Wood

Products Trade Act of 1985, requesting that the president negotiate voluntary export restraints with Canada and impose a 10 percent ad valorem duty on softwood lumber imports from Canada in the absence of voluntary restraints. See Doran and Naftali, *U.S.-Canadian Softwood Lumber*, 9.

47. Vernon, Spar, and Tobin, *From Triangles and Revolving Doors*, 30; Cashore, *Flights of the Phoenix*, 12.

48. Cashore, *Flights of the Phoenix*, 12.

49. Hayter, "International Trade Relations"; Tougas, "Softwood Lumber from Canada," 156–57.

50. Letter from ten senators to Clayton Yeutter, October 1, 1985. Reproduced in Tobin, "U.S.-Canada Free Trade Negotiations."

51. Quoted in Vernon, Spar, and Tobin, *From Triangles and Revolving Doors*, 33.

52. Tougas, "Softwood Lumber from Canada," 144.

53. Doran and Naftali, *U.S.-Canadian Softwood Lumber*, 10.

54. Lewington, "U.S. Administration Courts Key Senators."

55. Kalt, *Political Economy of Protectionism*, 340.

56. Apsey and Thomas, *Lessons of the Softwood Lumber Dispute*.

57. Hepburn, "U.S. Imposes 15% Tariff," A1.

58. Cashore, *Flights of the Phoenix*, 16.

59. Keohane, *After Hegemony*.

60. Goldstein, "International Law and Domestic Institutions," 541–64.

61. Cashore, *Flights of the Phoenix*, 25–26.

CHAPTER 8

1. Marc Busch, for example, provides one interpretation of why states are willing to fight for their national champions in some high-technology industries but not in others. See Busch, *Trade Warriors*.

2. Soh, "To Earn Respect, China Must Respect Global Rules."

3. Odell, "International Threats and Internal Politics," 248–52.

4. *Le Monde,* July 6/July 7, 1986, 13.

5. Odell, "International Threats and Internal Politics," 247.

6. Ibid.

7. See, for example, Keohane, *After Hegemony*.

8. Between January 1995 and August 1999, the United States initiated a total of 25 Section 301 cases. This amounts to an average of 5.4 cases per year, compared to 4.75 cases per year in the period between 1975 and 1994.

9. Lardy, "Permanent Normal Trade Relations for China."

10. McCurry, "U.S., China Agree on WTO."

11. Reinhardt, "Aggressive Multilateralism"; Busch, "Democracy, Consultation."

12. Rosendorff and Milner, "Optimal Design of International Trade Institutions."

13. See, for example, Rosecrance, *Rise of the Trading State;* Stein, "Governments, Economic Interdependence"; Cain, "Capitalism, War, and Internationalism."

14. Polachek, "Conflict and Trade"; Gasiorowski and Polachek, "Conflict and Interdependence"; Hirschman, *National Power and the Structure of Foreign Trade.*

15. See, for example, Waltz, "Myth of National Interdependence," 214.

16. Gowa, *Allies, Adversaries, and International Trade;* Mastanduno, "Do Relative Gains Matter?"; Tyson, *Who's Bashing Whom?*

17. Gilpin, "Structural Constraints on Economic Leverage"; Borrus and Zysman, "Industrial Competitiveness"; Baldwin, *Economic Statecraft.*

18. See, for example, Reuveny, "Disaggregated Bilateral Trade and Conflict"; McMillan, "Interdependence and Conflict."

19. Recent studies have investigated the effect of financial and monetary integration on peace. See, for example, Gartzke, Li, and Boehmer, "Investing in the Peace."

20. Refer to chapter 1 for the debate over the relationship between regime type and democracies' involvement in trade disputes.

21. Fearon, "Bargaining, Enforcement, and International Cooperation."

22. Kwan, "Turning Trade Frictions into a Win-Win Game."

23. Putnam, "Diplomacy and Domestic Politics," 451.

24. Sun, *Art of War* (Sunzi Bing Fa), chap. 3.

Bibliography

Apsey, T. M., and J. C. Thomas. "Lessons of the Softwood Lumber Dispute: Politics, Protectionism, and the Panel Process." Manuscript, April 1997. Available at <http://www.acah.org/aspey.htm>.

Australian Bureau of Agricultural and Resource Economics (ABARE), ed. *Japanese Agricultural Policies: A Time of Change.* Policy Monograph no. 3. Canberra: Australian Government Publishing Service, 1988.

Bailey, Martin F. "The Productivity Growth Slowdown by Industry." *Brookings Papers on Economic Activity,* no. 2 (1982): 423–54.

Baldwin, David. "Interdependence and Power: A Conceptual Analysis." *International Organization* 34, no. 4 (Autumn 1980): 471–506.

———. *Economic Statecraft.* Princeton: Princeton University Press, 1985.

Baldwin, Robert E. *The Political Economy of U.S. Import Policy.* Cambridge, MA: MIT Press, 1985.

Baltagi, Badi H. *Econometric Analysis of Panel Data.* New York: John Wiley & Sons, 1995.

Bansberg, P. T. "China Steps up Campaign to Retain MFN Status." *Journal of Commerce,* April 9, 1991, 5A.

———. "China Warns of Retaliation if U.S. Cuts Textile Quotas." *Journal of Commerce,* June 19, 1995, 3A.

Bayard, Thomas O., and Kimberly Ann Elliott. *Reciprocity and Retaliation in U.S. Trade Policy.* Washington, DC: Institute for International Economics, 1994.

Behr, Peter. "U.S. Businesses Waged Year-long Lobbying Effort on China Trade." *Washington Post,* May 27, 1994, A28.

Belsie, Laurent. "China Trade through Lens of Local Mall." *Christian Science Monitor,* June 11, 1996, 4.

Bergsten, Fred C., and Marcus Noland. *Reconcilable Differences? United States-Japan Economic Conflict.* Washington, DC: Institute for International Economics, 1993.

Bhagwati, Jagdish. "Aggressive Unilateralism: An Overview." In Jagdish Bhagwati and Hugh T. Patrick, eds., *Aggressive Unilateralism: America's 301 Trade Policy and the World Trading System.* Ann Arbor: University of Michigan Press, 1990.

Bliss, Harry, and Bruce Russett. "Democratic Trading Partners: The Liberal

281

Connection, 1962–1989." *Journal of Politics* 60, no. 4 (November 1998): 1126–47.

Borrus, Michael. *Competing for Control: America's Stake in Microelectronics.* Cambridge, MA: Ballinger, 1988.

Borrus, Michael, James E. Millstein, and John Zysman. "Trade and Development in the Semiconductor Industry: Japanese Challenge and American Response." In John Zysman and Laura Tyson, eds., *American Industry in International Competition: Government Politics and Corporate Strategies.* Ithaca: Cornell University Press, 1983.

Borrus, Michael, and John Zysman. "Industrial Competitiveness and American National Security." In Wayne Sandholtz, Michael Borrus, John Zysman, Ken Conca, Jay Stowksy, Stephen Vogel, and Steve Weber, eds., *The Highest Stakes.* New York: Oxford University Press, 1992.

Bremer, Stuart. "Dangerous Dyads: Conditions Affecting the Likelihood of Interstate War, 1816–1965." *Journal of Conflict Resolution* 26 (June 1992): 309–41.

Bueno de Mesquita, Bruce, and David Lalman. *War and Reason.* New Haven: Yale University Press, 1992.

Busch, Marc L. *Trade Warriors: States, Firms, and Strategic Policy in High-Technology Competition.* New York: Cambridge University Press, 1999.

———. "Democracy, Consultation, and the Paneling of Disputes under GATT." *Journal of Conflict Resolution* 44, no. 4 (2000): 425–46.

Business Coalition for U.S.-China Trade. "Business Leaders Urge U.S. to De-link Trade Sanctions and Human Rights." Press release, May 6, 1994.

Cain, Peter. "Capitalism, War, and Internationalism in the Thought of Richard Cobden." *British Journal of International Studies* 5 (1979): 229–47.

Cardoso, Fernando Henrique, and Enzo Falleto. *Dependency and Development in Latin America.* Berkeley: University of California Press, 1979.

Cashore, Benjamin. *Flights of the Phoenix: Explaining the Durability of the Canada-U.S. Softwood Lumber Dispute.* Canadian-American Public Policy, no. 32. Orono, ME: Canadian-American Center, University of Maine, 1997.

Chan, Steve. "Mirror, Mirror on the Wall. . . . Are the Freer Countries More Pacific?" *Journal of Conflict Resolution* 28 (1984): 617–48.

Christopher, Warren. "China's MFN Status: Summary of the Report and Recommendations of Secretary of State Warren Christopher." Department of State Release, May 26, 1994.

Coalition for Fair Lumber Imports. *Petition for the Imposition of Countervailing Duties: Certain Softwood Lumber Products from Canada.* Case no. C-122–602. vol. 1. Dewey, Ballantine. Washington, DC: May 19, 1986.

Constantino, Luis, and Michael Percy. "The Political Economy of Canada-U.S. Trade in Forest Products." In Russell S. Uhler, ed., *Canada-United States Trade in Forest Products.* Vancouver: University of British Columbia Press, 1991.

Conybeare, John A. C. *Trade Wars: The Theory and Practice of International Commercial Rivalry.* New York: Columbia University Press, 1987.

Cox, Irving K. "The Politics of Canada-U.S. Trade in Forest Products." In Russell S. Uhler, ed., *Canada-United States Trade in Forest Products.* Vancouver: University of British Columbia Press, 1991.

Dahl, Robert. *Polyarchy: Participation and Opposition.* New Haven: Yale University Press, 1971.

Davies, John. "U.S. Importers Fear Big Loss From China-Textile Quota Cut." *Journal of Commerce,* January 12, 1994, 5A.

DeSombre, Elizabeth. *Domestic Sources of International Environmental Policy: Industry, Environmentalists, and U.S. Power.* Cambridge, MA: MIT Press, 2000.

Destler, I. M. *American Trade Politics.* 3d ed. Washington, DC: Institute for International Economics, 1995.

Destler, I. M., and John S. Odell. *Anti-Protection: Changing Forces in United States Trade Politics.* Washington, DC: Institute for International Economics, 1987.

Dixon, William J. "Democracy and the Management of International Conflict." *Journal of Conflict Resolution* 37 (March 1993): 42–68.

———. "Democracy and the Peaceful Settlement of International Conflict." *American Political Science Review* 88 (March 1994): 14–32.

Dixon, William J., and Bruce Moon. "Political Similarity and American Foreign Trade Patterns." *Political Research Quarterly* 46 (March 1993): 5–25.

Doran, Charles F., and Timothy J. Naftali. *U.S.-Canadian Softwood Lumber: Trade Dispute Negotiations.* Washington, DC: Pew Charitable Trusts, 1988.

Doyle, Michael W. "Liberalism and World Politics." *American Political Science Review* 80, no. 4 (December 1986): 1151–69.

Drezner, Daniel W. *The Sanctions Paradox: Economic Statecraft and International Relations.* New York: Cambridge University Press, 1999.

———. "Outside the Box: Explaining Sanctions in Pursuit of Foreign Economic Goals." *International Interactions* 26 (2001): 379–410.

Duchesne, Erick. "International Bilateral Trade and Investment Negotiations: Theory, Formal Model, and Empirical Evidences." Ph.D. diss., Michigan State University, 1997.

Dumbaugh, Kerry B. "The Making of China Policy since Tiananmen." *China Business Review* 19, no. 1 (January–February 1992): 16–19.

Dunne, Nancy. "Beijing and the Business of Human Rights." *Financial Times,* March 16, 1994.

———. "Washington Speaks with One Voice and Sends Mixed Messages." *Financial Times,* January 8, 1994, 3.

Elliott, Kimberly Ann, and J. David Richardson. "Determinants and Effectiveness of 'Aggressively Unilateral' U.S. Trade Actions." In Robert C.

Feenstra, ed., *The Effects of U.S. Trade Protection and Promotion Policies.* Chicago: University of Chicago Press, 1997.

Evans, Peter B., Harold K. Jacobson, and Robert D. Putnam, eds. *Double-Edged Diplomacy: International Bargaining and Domestic Politics.* Berkeley: University of California Press, 1993.

Farber, Henry S., and Joanne Gowa. "Polities and Peace." *International Security* 20 (1995): 123–46.

Farnsworth, Clyde H. "End Believed Near for U.S. Sanctions Imposed on Japan." *New York Times,* April 27, 1987, A1.

Fearon, James D. "Domestic Political Audiences and the Escalation of International Disputes." *American Political Science Review* 88, no. 3 (1994): 577–87.

———. "Signaling Foreign Policy Interests: Tying Hands versus Sinking Costs." *Journal of Conflict Resolution* 41, no. 1 (1997): 68–90.

———. "Bargaining, Enforcement, and International Cooperation." *International Organization* 52, no. 2 (1998): 269–305.

Featherstone, Kevin. "Jean Monnet and the 'Democratic Deficit' in the European Union." *Journal of Common Market Studies* 32, no. 2 (1994): 149–70.

Fox, Irving K. "The Politics of Canada-U.S. Trade in Forest Products." In Russell S. Uhler, ed., *Canada-United States Trade in Forest Products.* Vancouver: University of British Columbia Press, 1991.

Friedman, Thomas. "U.S. Pares Imports of China's Fabrics in a Punitive Move." *New York Times,* January 7, 1994, A1.

———. "Clinton Votes for Business." *New York Times,* May 27, 1994, A1.

Friman, H. Richard. *Patchwork Protectionism: Textile Trade Policy in the United States, Japan, and West Germany.* Ithaca: Cornell University Press, 1990.

Frost, Robert B., Jr. "Intellectual Property Rights Disputes in the 1990s between the People's Republic of China and the United States." *Tulane Journal of International and Comparative Law* 4, no. 1 (Winter 1995): 119–37.

Furtado, Celso. *Development and Underdevelopment.* Berkeley: University of California Press, 1964.

Gardner, Bruce L. "The Political Economy of U.S. Export Subsidies for Wheat." In Anne O. Krueger, ed., *The Political Economy of American Trade Policy.* Chicago: University of Chicago Press, 1996.

Gargan, Edward. "Gauging the Consequences of Spurning China." *New York Times,* March 21, 1994, D1.

Gartzke, Erik, Quan Li, and Charles Boehmer. "Investing in the Peace: Economic Interdependence and International Conflict." *International Organization* 55, no. 2 (2001): 391–438.

Gasiorowski, Mark, and Solomon Polachek. "Conflict and Interdependence: East-West Trade and Linkages in the Era of Détente." *Journal of Conflict Resolution* 26, no. 4 (1982): 709–29.

George, Alexander L., and Timothy McKeown. "Case Studies and Theories of Organizational Decision Making." *Advances in Information Processing in Organizations* 2 (1985): 21–58.

Gilpin, Robert. "Structural Constraints on Economic Leverage: Market-Type Systems." In Gordon H. McCormick and Richard E. Bissell, ed., *Strategic Dimensions of Economic Behavior.* New York: Praeger, 1984.

———. *The Political Economy of International Relations.* Princeton: Princeton University Press, 1987.

Goldstein, Carl. "Brawling in the Ring." *Far Eastern Economic Review,* September 24, 1992, 97.

Goldstein, Judith. *Ideas, Interests, and American Trade Policy.* Ithaca: Cornell University Press, 1993.

———. "International Law and Domestic Institutions: Reconciling North American 'Unfair' Trade Laws." *International Organization* 50, no. 4 (1996): 541–64.

Gowa, Joanne. *Allies, Adversaries, and International Trade.* Princeton: Princeton University Press, 1983.

Gowa, Joanne, and Edward D. Mansfield. "Power Politics and International Trade." *American Political Science Review* 87, no. 2 (1993): 408–20.

Graham, Bradley. "Washington Angered by the Extension of Protectionist Restrictions to Software." *Washington Post,* November 1, 1987, H10.

Green, Paula. "U.S. Textile Makers, Importers Clash over Chinese Products." *Journal of Commerce,* May 16, 1996, 2A.

———. "Trade Office Braces for Lobbying Blitz to Keep Products off China Sanctions List." *Journal of Commerce,* May 28, 1996, 1A.

Greenberger, Robert S. "Restraint of Trade: Cacophony of Voices Drowns Out Message from U.S. to China." *Wall Street Journal,* March 22, 1994, A1.

Greenberger, Robert S., and Jeff Cole. "China Sanctions Put U.S. Firms in a Bind." *Wall Street Journal,* May 30, 1996, A2.

Greenberger, Robert S., and Michael K. Frisby. "Clinton's Renewal of Trade Status for China Followed Cabinet Debates, Congress's Sea Change." *Wall Street Journal,* May 31, 1994, A18.

Greene, William H. *Econometric Analysis.* 2d ed. New York: Macmillan, 1993.

Grieco, Joseph. *Cooperation among Nations: Europe, America, and Non-Tariff Barriers to Trade.* Ithaca: Cornell University Press, 1990.

Haass, Richard N., ed. *Economic Sanctions and American Diplomacy.* New York: Council on Foreign Relations, 1998.

Habeeb, William Mark. *Power and Tactics in International Negotiation: How Weak Nations Bargain with Strong Nations.* Baltimore: Johns Hopkins University Press, 1988.

Hammond, Thomas H., and Brandon C. Prins. "The Impact of Domestic Institutions on International Negotiations: A Taxonomy of Results from a

Complete-Information Spatial Model." Paper presented at the annual meeting of the American Political Science Association, Atlanta, GA, 1999.

Hayter, Robert. "International Trade Relations and Regional Industrial Adjustment: The Implication of the 1982–86 Canadian-U.S. Softwood Lumber Dispute for British Columbia." *Environment and Planning A* 24 (January 1992): 153–70.

Hendry, Sandy. "Limited Protection." *Far Eastern Economic Review* 153, no. 29 (July 1991): 61–62.

Hepburn, Bob. "U.S. Imposes 15% Tariff on Canada's Lumber." *Toronto Star,* October 17, 1986, A1.

Herbst, Kris. "A More Open Market for Supercomputers." *Datamation* 36, no. 18 (September 15, 1990): 123–25.

Hershey, Robert D. "A Basic Pact with Japan." *New York Times,* April 4, 1990, D1.

Hirschman, Albert O. *National Power and the Structure of Foreign Trade.* Berkeley: University of California Press, 1945.

Hoekman, Bernard M., and Michael M. Kostecki. *The Political Economy of the World Trading System: The WTO and Beyond.* 2d ed. New York: Oxford University Press, 2001.

Hopmann, Terrence P. *The Negotiation Process and the Resolution of International Conflicts.* Columbia: University of South Carolina Press, 1996.

Hudec, Robert E. *Enforcing International Trade Law: The Evolution of the Modern GATT Legal System.* Salem, NH: Butterworth Legal Publishers, 1993.

Hufbauer, Gary Clyde, and Howard F. Rosen. *Trade Policy for Troubled Industries.* Washington, DC: Institute for International Economics, 1986.

Hufbauer, Gary Clyde, Jeffrey J. Schott, and Kimberly Ann Elliott. *Economic Sanctions Reconsidered: History and Current Policy.* 2d ed. Washington, DC: Institute for International Economics, 1990.

Huntington, Samuel. *The Third Wave: Democratization in the Late Twentieth Century.* Norman: University of Oklahoma Press, 1991.

Huth, Paul K. *Extended Deterrence and the Prevention of War.* New Haven: Yale University Press, 1988.

Hyclak, Thomas. "Introduction." In David Greenaway, Thomas Hyclak, and Robert J. Thornton, eds., *Economic Aspects of Regional Trading Arrangements.* New York: New York University Press, 1989.

Iida, Keisuke. "Analytic Uncertainty and International Cooperation: Theory and Application to International Economic Coordination." *International Studies Quarterly* 37 (1993): 431–57.

———. "When and How Do Domestic Constraints Matter?" *Journal of Conflict Resolution* 37, no. 3 (1993): 403–26.

International Monetary Fund (IMF). *Direction of Trade Statistics Yearbook.* Washington, DC: International Monetary Fund.

Irwin, Douglas A. "Trade Politics and the Semiconductor Industry." In Anne

O. Krueger, ed., *The Political Economy of American Trade Policy.* Chicago: University of Chicago Press, 1996.

Jaggers, Keith, and Ted Robert Gurr. *Polity III: Political Structures and Regime Change, 1800–1994.* Study no. 6695. Ann Arbor: Inter-University Consortium for Political and Social Research, 1996.

Japan Space Activities Commission, Long Range Vision Special Committee. *Long Range Vision for Japanese Space Development,* July 1983. Tokyo: Ad Hoc Committee on Long-Range Prospects, Space Activities Commission, Japan.

Jayakar, Krishna P. "The United States-China Copyright Dispute: A Two-Level Games Analysis." *Communication Law and Policy* 2 (1997): 527–61.

Jehl, Douglas. "Warning to China on Trade." *New York Times,* April 30, 1994, 39 (sect. 1).

Jen, Hui-wen. "Background to China's 'Four Nots' Policy toward the United States." Hong Kong *Hsin Bao,* September 17, 1993, in Foreign Broadcast Information Service, no.179, 1–3.

Johnston, Oswald. "U.S., Europe Achieve Truce in Spain Trade." *Los Angeles Times,* July 3, 1986, 1.

Jones, Brian. "Chinese Officials Say MFN Status Benefits Both China and the U.S." *Journal of Commerce,* April 30, 1993, 4A.

Kalt, Joseph P. *The Political Economy of Protectionism: Tariffs and Retaliation in the Timber Industry.* Cambridge, MA: Harvard University Energy and Environmental Policy Center, 1987.

———. "Precedent and Legal Argument in U.S. Trade Policy: Do They Matter to the Political Economy of the Lumber Dispute?" In Anne O. Krueger, ed., *The Political Economy of American Trade Policy.* Chicago: University of Chicago Press, 1996.

Karol, David. "Divided Government and U.S. Trade Policy: Much Ado about Nothing?" *International Organization* 54 (2000): 825–44.

Kaslow, Amy. "President Urges Renewal of China's Top Trade Status." *Christian Science Monitor,* May 28, 1993, 4.

Keatley, Robert. "U.S. Firms, Anticipating Huge Market, Worry China May Lose Its MFN Status." *Wall Street Journal,* May 7, 1993, B8.

Kehoe, Louise. "U.S. Savours Electronics Showdown." *Financial Times,* May 12, 1989, 6.

Keohane, Robert O. *After Hegemony.* Princeton: Princeton University Press, 1984.

Keohane, Robert O., and Joseph S. Nye. *Power and Interdependence.* Glenville, IL: Scott, Foresman, 1989.

King, Gary, Robert O. Keohane, and Sidney Verba. *Designing Social Inquiry: Scientific Inference in Quantitative Research.* Princeton: Princeton University Press, 1994.

King, Gary, and Langche Zeng. "Logistic Regression in Rare Events Data." *Political Analysis* 9, no. 2 (2001): 137–63.

Knopf, Jeffery W. "Beyond Two-Level Games: Domestic-International Inter-action in the Intermediate-Range Nuclear Forces Negotiations." *International Organization* 47, no. 4 (1993): 599–628.

Koepp, Stephen. "Fighting the Trade Tilt: The U.S. Fires Protective Tariffs at Japanese Electronic Products." *Time* 129 (April 6, 1987): 50–51.

Krasner, Stephen D. *Structural Conflict: The Third World against Global Liberalism.* Berkeley: University of California Press, 1985.

Krauss, Ellis S. "U.S.-Japan Negotiations on Construction and Semiconductors, 1985–1988: Building Friction and Relation-Chips." In Peter B. Evans, Harold K. Jacobson, and Robert D. Putnam, eds., *Double-Edged Diplomacy: International Bargaining and Domestic Politics.* Berkeley: University of California Press, 1993.

Krauss, Ellis S., and Simon Reich. "Ideology, Interests, and the American Executive: Toward a Theory of Foreign Competition and Manufacturing Trade Policy." *International Organization* 46 (1992): 857–97.

Krueger, Anne. *The Political Economy of American Trade Policy.* Chicago: University of Chicago Press, 1996.

Krugman, Paul R. "Strategic Sectors and International Competition." In Robert M. Stern, ed., *U.S. Trade Policies in a Changing World Economy,* 207–32. Cambridge, MA: MIT Press, 1987.

————, ed. *Strategic Policy and the New International Economics.* Cambridge, MA: MIT Press, 1986.

Kwan, Chi Hung. "Turning Trade Frictions between Japan and China into a Win-Win Game." Research Institute of Economy, Trade, and Industry (RIETI) Report, 2001. Available at <http://www.rieti.go.jp/column/2001/0003e.html>.

Lachica, Eduardo. "Plan for Tariffs against China Provokes Many U.S. Retailers to Protest Strongly." *Wall Street Journal,* January 30, 1995, B6E.

Lake, David A. *Power, Protection, and Free Trade: International Sources of U.S. Commercial Strategy, 1887–1939.* Ithaca: Cornell University Press, 1988.

————. "Powerful Pacifists: Democratic States and War." *American Political Science Review* 86 (1992): 24–37.

Lampton, David M. "America's China Policy in the Age of the Finance Minister: Clinton Ends Linkage." *China Quarterly* 139 (September 1994): 597–621.

————. "Ending the MFN Battle." *NBR Analysis* 8, no. 4 (July 1997): 7–14.

Lardy, Nicholas R. *China in the World Economy.* Washington, DC: Institute for International Economics, 1994.

————. "Permanent Normal Trade Relations for China." Brookings Institution Policy Brief, no. 58, May 2000.

LaRussa, Robert. "AEA Lauds U.S. Move on Trade." *Electronic News,* 35, no. 1762 (June 12, 1989): 4.

Lax, David, and James Sebenius. *The Manager as Negotiator: Bargaining for Cooperation and Competitive Gain.* New York: Free Press, 1986.

Leeds, Ashley. "Domestic Political Institutions, Credible Commitments, and International Cooperation." *American Journal of Political Science* 43, no. 4 (October 1999): 979–1002.

Lehman, Howard P., and Jennifer L. McCoy. "The Dynamics of the Two-Level Bargaining Game: The 1988 Brazilian Debt Negotiations." *World Politics* 44, no. 4 (1992): 600–644.

Levy, Jack. "Domestic Politics and War." *Journal of Interdisciplinary History* 18, no. 4 (Spring 1988): 653–73.

Lewington, Jennifer. "Senators Warn Canada to Chop Lumber Exports." *Globe and Mail,* February 27, 1986, B8.

———. "U.S. Administration Courts Key Senators on Free Trade." *Globe and Mail,* April 18, 1986, B12.

Leyton-Brown, David. *Weathering the Storm: Canadian-U.S. Relations, 1980–83.* Toronto: C.D. Howe Institute, 1985.

Li, Quan, and Dong-Joon Jo. "Trading-Bloc Formation and Influence of Politics: A Dyadic Analysis, 1960–1992." Manuscript, 2001.

Lincoln, Edward J. *Japan's Unequal Trade.* Washington, DC: Brookings Institution Press, 1990.

Locin, Mitchell. "Trade Chief Hints China's Status with U.S. May Not Change in '93." *Chicago Tribune,* May 21, 1993, 6 (sect. 1).

Lohmann, Susanne, and Sharyn O'Halloran. "Divided Government and U.S. Trade Policy." *International Organization* 48, no. 4 (1994): 595–632.

Lu, Yu-sha. "New 'Eight-Character Principle' of China's Policy toward the United States." Hong Kong *Tangtai* 30 (September 15, 1993): 10.

Madison, Christopher. "Textile Talks Will Put Reagan's Free-Trade Stance to a Real Test." *National Journal* 13 (May 1981): 883–87.

Mann, James. "U.S. Firms Lobby for China Trade Benefits." *Los Angeles Times,* July 15, 1991, A15.

———. "U.S. China Averts Clash over Trade." *Los Angeles Times,* October 10, 1992, A1.

———. *About Face: A History of America's Curious Relationship with China, from Nixon to Clinton.* New York: Alfred A. Knopf, 1999.

Mansfield, Edward D., and Rachel Bronson. "The Political Economy of Major-Power Trade Flows." In Edward D. Mansfield and Helen V. Milner, eds., *The Political Economy of Regionalism,* 188–208. New York: Columbia University Press, 1997.

Mansfield, Edward D., and Jack Snyder. "Democratization and the Danger of War." *International Security* 20 (1995): 5–38.

Mansfield, Edward, Helen V. Milner, and B. Peter Rosendorff. "Free to Trade: Democracies, Autocracies, and International Trade." *American Political Science Review* 94, no. 2 (June 2000): 305–21.

———. "Why Democracies Cooperate More: Electoral Control and International Trade Agreements." *International Organization* 56, no. 3 (Summer 2002): 477–513.

Maoz, Zeev, and Nazrin Abdolali. "Regime Type and International Conflict, 1816–1976." *Journal of Conflict Resolution* 33 (March 1989): 3–36.

Maoz, Zeev, and Bruce Russett. "Normative and Structural Causes of Democratic Peace, 1946–1986." *American Political Science Review* 87 (1993): 624–38.

Martin, Lisa L. *Democratic Commitments.* Princeton: Princeton University Press, 2000.

Mastanduno, Michael. "Do Relative Gains Matter? America's Response to Japanese Industrial Policy." *International Security* 16, no. 1 (Summer 1991): 73–113.

———. "Setting Market Access Priorities: The Use of Super 301 in U.S. Trade with Japan." *World Economy* 15, no. 6 (November 1992): 729–53.

Mayer, Frederick W. "Managing Domestic Differences in International Negotiations: The Strategic Use of International Side-Payments." *International Organization* 46, no. 4 (1992): 793–818.

Mayhew, David. *Congress: The Electoral Connection.* New Haven: Yale University Press, 1974.

McMillan, John. "Strategic Bargaining and Section 301." In Jagdish Bhagwati and Hugh T. Patrick, eds., *Aggressive Unilateralism: America's 301 Trade Policy and the World Trading System.* Ann Arbor: University of Michigan Press, 1990.

McMillan, Susan. "Interdependence and Conflict." *Mershon International Studies Review* 41, no. 1 (1997): 33–58.

McCurry, John. "U.S., China Agree on WTO." *Textile World,* December 1999, 17.

Melo, Jaime de, Arvind Panagariya, and Dani Rodrik. "The New Regionalism: A Country Perspective." In Jaime de Melo and Arvind Panagariya, eds., *New Dimensions in Regional Integration,* 159–92. Cambridge: Cambridge University Press, 1995.

Mertha, Andrew C. "Pirates, Politics, and Trade Policy: Structuring the Negotiations and Enforcing the Outcomes of the Sino-U.S. Intellectual Property Dialogue, 1991–1999." Ph.D. diss., University of Michigan, 2001.

Meunier, Sophie. "Europe Divided but United: Institutional Integration and E.C.-U.S. Trade Negotiations since 1962." Ph.D. diss., MIT, 1998.

Milner, Helen V. *Interests, Institutions, and Information: Domestic Politics and International Relations.* Princeton: Princeton University Press, 1997.

Milner, Helen V., and Keiko Kubota. "Why the Rush to Free Trade? Democracy and Trade Liberalization in the LDCs." Manuscript, 1999.

Milner, Helen V., and B. Peter Rosendorff. "Domestic Politics and International Trade Negotiations: Elections and Divided Government as Constraints on Trade Liberalization." *Journal of Conflict Resolution* 41 (February 1997): 117–46.

Mo, Jongryn. "The Logic of Two-Level Games with Endogenous Domestic Coalitions." *Journal of Conflict Resolution* 38 (September 1994): 402–22.

———. "Domestic Institutions and International Bargaining: The Role of Agent Veto in Two-Level Games." *American Political Science Review* 89 (1995): 914–24.

Moffet, George D., III. "Bush, Congress Clash on China." *Christian Science Monitor,* February 27, 1992, 1 (U.S. sect.).

Moravcsik, Andrew. "Introduction: Integrating International and Domestic Explanations of World Politics." In Peter B. Evans, Harold K. Jacobson, and Robert D. Putnam, eds., *Double-Edged Diplomacy: International Bargaining and Domestic Politics.* Berkeley: University of California Press, 1993.

Morrow, James D., Randolph M. Siverson, and Tressa E. Tabares. "The Political Determinants of International Trade: The Major Powers, 1907–1990." *American Political Science Review* 92, no. 3 (September 1998): 649–61.

Nanto, Dick K., and Glenn J. McLoughlin. *Japanese and U.S. Industrial Associations: Their Role in High-Technology Policymaking.* Washington, DC: Congressional Research Service Report, Library of Congress, June 6, 1991.

Noland, Marcus. "Chasing Phantoms: The Political Economy of USTR." *International Organization* 51, no. 3 (Summer 1997): 365–87.

Odell, John S. "Latin American Trade Negotiations with the U.S." *International Organization* 34 (Spring 1980): 207–28.

———. "The Outcome of International Trade Conflicts: The U.S. and South Korea, 1960–1981." *International Studies Quarterly* 29 (September 1985): 263–86.

———. "International Threats and Internal Politics: Brazil, the European Community, and the United States, 1985–1987." In Peter B. Evans, Harold K. Jacobson, and Robert D. Putnam, eds., *Double-Edged Diplomacy: International Bargaining and Domestic Politics.* Berkeley: University of California Press, 1993.

Odell, John S., and Anne Dibble. *Brazilian Informatics and the United States: Defending Infant Industry versus Opening Foreign Markets.* Washington, DC: Institute for the Study of Diplomacy, Georgetown University, 1992.

Odell, John, and Margit Matzinger-Tchakerian. "European Community Enlargement and the United States." In Robert S. Walters, ed., *Talking Trade: U.S. Policy in International Perspective.* Boulder: Westview, 1993.

O'Halloran, Sharyn S. *Politics, Process, and American Trade Policy.* Ann Arbor: University of Michigan Press, 1994.

Okimoto, Daniel I., Takuo Sugano, and Franklin B. Weinstein. *Competitive Edge: The Semiconductor Industry in the U.S. and Japan.* Stanford: Stanford University Press, 1984.

Oneal, John, and Bruce Russett. "The Classical Liberals Were Right: Democracy, Interdependence, and Conflict, 1950–1985." *International Studies Quarterly* 41 (1997): 267–93.

Organization for Economic Co-operation and Development (OECD). *Global-ization of Industrial Activities, Four Case Studies: Auto Parts, Chemicals, Construction, and Semiconductors*. Paris: OECD, 1992.

O'Shea, Timothy J. C. "The U.S.-Japan Semiconductor Problem." In Robert S. Walters, ed., *Talking Trade: U.S. Policy in International Perspective*. Boulder: Westview, 1993.

Owen, John. "How Liberalism Produces Democratic Peace." *International Security* 19 (1994): 87–125.

Paalberg, Robert L. *Fixing Farm Trade: Policy Options for the United States*. Cambridge, MA: Ballinger, 1988.

Pahre, Robert. "Endogenous Domestic Institutions in Two-Level Games and Parliamentary Oversight of the European Union." *Journal of Conflict Resolution* 41 (February 1997): 147–74.

———. "Divided Government and International Cooperation in Austria-Hungary, Sweden-Norway, and the European Union." *European Union Politics* 2 (2001): 131–62.

Pear, Robert. "Far-off Silver Lining in Dispute with Japan." *New York Times*, May 27, 1989, 29.

Percy, Michael, and Christian G. Yoder. *The Softwood Lumber Dispute and Canada-U.S. Trade in Natural Resources*. Halifax, Nova Scotia: Institute for Research on Public Policy, 1987.

Polachek, Solomon. "Conflict and Trade: An Economic Approach to Political International Interactions." In Walter Isard and Charles Anderton, eds., *Economics of Arms Reduction and the Peace Process*, 89–120. Amsterdam: Elsevier, 1992.

Prestowitz, Clyde V., Jr. *Trading Places: How We Allowed Japan to Take the Lead*. New York: Basic Books, 1988.

Powell, Bill, Rich Thomas, and Bradley Martin. "Japan Makes the Hit List." *Newsweek*, June 5, 1989, 48–49.

Putnam, Robert D. "Diplomacy and Domestic Politics: The Logic of Two-Level Games." *International Organization* 42 (Summer 1988): 427–60.

Raiffa, Howard. *The Art and Science of Negotiation*. Cambridge, MA: Harvard University Press, 1982.

Ray, James L. *Democracy and International Conflict: An Evaluation of the Democratic Peace Proposition*. Columbia: University of South Carolina Press, 1995.

Raymond, Gregory A. "Democracies, Disputes, and Third-Party Intermediaries." *Journal of Conflict Resolution* 38 (March 1994): 24–42.

Reinhardt, Eric. "Posturing Parliaments: Ratification, Uncertainty, and International Bargaining." Ph.D. diss., 1996.

———. "Aggressive Multilateralism: The Determinants of GATT/WTO Dispute Initiation, 1948–1998." Paper presented at the annual meeting of the International Studies Association, Washington, DC, 1999.

Remmer, Karen L. "Does Democracy Promote Interstate Cooperation?

Lessons from the Mercosur Region." *International Studies Quarterly* 42, no. 1 (March 1998): 25–52.

Reuveny, Rafael. "The Trade and Conflict Debate: A Survey of Theory, Evidence, and Future Research." *Peace Economics, Peace Science, and Public Policy* 6, no. 1 (2000): 23–49.

———. "Disaggregated Bilateral Trade and Conflict: Exploring Propositions in a Simultaneous Framework." *International Politics* 38 (2001): 401–28.

Rondinelli, Dennis A. "Resolving U.S.-China Trade Conflicts: Conditions for Trade and Investment Expansion in the 1990s." *Columbia Journal of World Business* 28, no. 2 (Summer 1993): 66–79.

Rosecrance, Richard. *The Rise of the Trading State.* New York: Basic Books, 1986.

Rosendorff, B. Peter, and Helen V. Milner, "The Optimal Design of International Trade Institutions: Uncertainty and Escape." *International Organization* 55, no. 4 (Autumn 2001): 829–57.

Russett, Bruce. *Grasping the Democratic Peace: Principles for a Post-Cold War World.* Princeton: Princeton University Press, 1993.

Ruzicka, Milan. "U.S.-China Tension Building over Piracy." *Journal of Commerce,* February 1, 1995, 1A.

Ryan, Michael P. *Playing by the Rules: American Trade Power and Diplomacy in the Pacific.* Washington, DC: Georgetown University Press, 1995.

———. *Knowledge Diplomacy: Global Competition and the Politics of Intellectual Property.* Washington, DC: Brookings Institution Press, 1998.

Sandholtz, Wayne, Michael Borrus, John Zysman, Ken Conca, Jay Stowsky, Steven Vogel, and Steve Weber, eds., *The Highest Stakes: The Economic Foundations of the Next Security System.* London and New York: Oxford University Press, 1992.

Sands, Lee M., and Deborah Lehr. "IPR Watchdogs." *China Business Review* 21, no. 6 (November–December 1994): 16–18.

Sanger, David E., and Steven Erlanger. "U.S. Warns China over Violations of Trade Accord." *New York Times,* February 4, 1996, 1 (sect. 1).

Scharpf, Fritz. "Economic Integration, Democracy, and the Welfare State." *Journal of European Public Policy* 4, no. 1 (1997): 18–36.

Schatz, Willie. "Who's Winning the Supercomputer Race?" *Datamation* 35, no. 14 (July 15, 1989): 18–21.

Schelling, Thomas. *The Strategy of Conflict.* Cambridge, MA: Harvard University Press, 1960.

———. *Arms and Influence.* New Haven: Yale University Press, 1966.

Schoenberger, Susumu. "Question of Conscience: Human Rights in China or Jobs in California?" *Los Angeles Times,* May 15, 1994, D3.

Schoppa, Leonard J. "Two-Level Games and Bargaining Outcomes: Why Gaiatsu Succeeds in Japan in Some Cases but Not Others." *International Organization* 47, no. 3 (1993): 353–86.

————. *Bargaining with Japan: What American Pressure Can and Cannot Do.* New York: Columbia University Press, 1997.

Schloss, Peter A. "China's Long-Awaited Copyright Law." *China Business Review* (September–October 1990): 24–28.

Schmidt, Vivien. "European Integration and Democracy: The Differences among Member States." *Journal of European Public Policy* 4, no. 1 (1997): 128–45.

Schultz, Kenneth A. "Domestic Opposition and Signaling in International Crises." *American Political Science Review* 92, no. 4 (1998): 829–44.

Schweller, Randall L. "Domestic Structure and Preventive War: Are Democracies More Pacific?" *World Politics* 44 (1992): 235–69.

Sebenius, James K. *Negotiating the Law of the Sea: Lessons in the Art and Science of Reaching Agreement.* Cambridge, MA: Harvard University Press, 1984.

Sherman, Richard. "Democracy and Trade Conflict." *International Interactions* 27 (June 2001): 1–28.

————. "Targeting Democracies: Regime Type and America's 'Aggressively Unilateral' Trade Policy." *Social Science Quarterly* 83, no. 4 (December 2002): 1063–78.

Silk, Leonard. "Japan Tops Sanction 'Hit List'." *St. Louis-Dispatch,* June 3, 1989, 9A.

Smith, Craig S., and Kathy Chen. "U.S. Business Concerned by China Tiff but Then, They've Seen It All Before." *Wall Street Journal,* May 17, 1996, A10.

Snyder, Glenn H. "The Security Dilemma in Alliance Politics." *World Politics* 36, no. 4 (1984): 461–95.

Snyder, Glenn H., and Paul Diesing. *Conflict among Nations: Bargaining, Decision Making, and System Structure in International Crises.* Princeton: Princeton University Press, 1977.

Soh, Felix. "To Earn Respect, China Must Respect Global Rules." *Strait Times,* May 17, 1996, 50.

Sparks, Samantha. "Inter Trade: U.S. Businesses Battle Looming Trade War with Brazil." *Inter Press Service,* December 28, 1987.

Stein, Arthur A. "Governments, Economic Interdependence, and International Cooperation." In Philip Tetlock, Jo L. Husbands, Robert Jervis, P. C. Stern, and Charles Tilly, eds., *Behavior, Society, and International Conflict,* 3:241–321. New York: Oxford University Press, 1993.

Stern, Robert M. "U.S.-Japan Trade Policy and FDI Issues." Paper presented at the Conference on Issues and Options for the Multilateral, Regional, and Bilateral Trade Policies of the United States and Japan, Ann Arbor, MI, 2000.

Stevenson, Richard W. "Tread Carefully with China, Business Leaders Urge U.S." *New York Times,* May 11, 1996, 5 (sect. 1).

Strokes, Bruce. "Trade Disputes Are Straining the Ties That Bind America and Western Europe." *National Journal* 17, no. 33–34 (August 1985): 1894–97.

Sun, Lena H. "China Detains Dissident as French Premier Tries to Mend Relations." *Washington Post,* April 9, 1994, A22.

Sun Zi. *The Art of War* (Sunzi Bing Fa). Translated and with an introduction by Samuel B. Griffith. New York: Oxford University Press, 1963.

Sutter, Robert G. "American Policy toward Beijing, 1989–1990: The Role of President Bush and the White House Staff." *Journal of Northeast Asian Studies* 9, no. 4 (Winter 1990): 3–14.

———. *U.S. Policy toward China: An Introduction to the Role of Interest Groups.* Lanham: Rowman & Littlefield, 1998.

Sykes, Alan O. "Constructive Unilateral Threats in International Commercial Relations: The Limited Case for Section 301." *Law and Policy in International Business* 23 (Spring 1992): 263–330.

Tanaka, H. William, et al. "Reply of the Electronics Industries Association of Japan." Tanaka, Walders and Ritgers. Washington, DC, November 1995.

Tefft, Sheila. "China Sends Huge Trade Vanguard to the U.S." *Christian Science Monitor,* April 8, 1994 (economy sect.).

Tobin, Glenn. "U.S.-Canada Free Trade Negotiations: Gaining Approval to Proceed." Case Program, no. c16–87–785, Appendix G. John F. Kennedy School of Government, Harvard University, 1987.

Tougas, Francois. "Softwood Lumber from Canada: Natural Resources and the Search for a Definition of Countervailable Domestic Subsidy." *Gonzala Law Review* 24 (1988–89): 135–65.

Tsebelis, George. *Nested Games: Rational Choice in Comparative Politics.* Berkeley: University of California Press, 1990.

Tyler, Patrick E. "Beijing Says It Could Live Well Even if U.S. Trade Was Cut Off." *New York Times,* March 21, 1994, A1.

Tyson, Laura D'Andrea. *Who's Bashing Whom? Trade Conflict in High-Technology Industries.* Washington, DC: Institute for International Economics, 1992.

U.S. Department of Commerce. *The Japanese Solid Wood Products Market.* Washington, DC: U.S. Government Printing Office, 1989.

———. *U.S. Industry Output 1992.* Washington, DC: U.S. Government Printing Office, 1992.

U.S. Department of Commerce, International Trade Administration. *Preliminary Negative Countervailing Duty Determination, Certain Softwood Products from Canada.* Washington, DC: Government Printing Office, 1983.

———. *U.S. Foreign Trade Highlights.* Washington, DC: Government Printing Office, various years.

U.S. House. *Omnibus Trade and Competitiveness Act of 1988, Conference Report to Accompany HR3.* Report 100–576. 100th Cong., 2d sess., April 20, 1988.

U.S. House Committee on Finance. *Japanese Trade Barriers to Forest Products.* Hearing before the Subcommittee on International Trade of the Committee on Finance. 101st Cong., 2d sess., June 22, 1989.

U.S. House Committee on Foreign Relations. *United States-European Com-*

munity Trade Relations: Problems and Prospects for Resolution. 99th Cong., 2d sess., July 24, 1986.

U.S. House Committee on Government Operations. *Is the Administration Giving away the U.S. Supercomputer Industry?* Hearings before the Legislation and National Security Subcommittee. Washington, DC: U.S. Government Printing Office, 102d Cong., 2d sess., July 1 and 8, 1992.

U.S. House Committee on Ways and Means. *Disapproval of Extension of Most-Favored-Nation Treatment to the Products of the People's Republic of China.* House Report 102–632. Washington, DC: Government Printing Office, 102d Cong., 2d sess., June 30, 1992.

———. *United States-People's Republic of China Trade Relations, Including Most-Favored-Nation Trade Status for China:* Hearing before the Subcommittee on Trade of the Committee on Ways and Means. 102d Cong., 1st sess., June 12, 1991.

———. *USTR Identification of Priority Practices and Countries under Super 301 and Special 301 Provisions of the Omnibus Trade and Competitiveness Act of 1988.* 101st Cong., 1st sess., June 8, 1989.

U.S. House Office of Technology Assessment. *Competing Economies: America, Europe, and the Pacific Rim.* OTA-ITE-498. Washington, DC: U.S. Government Printing Office, 1991.

U.S. International Trade Commission. *Conditions Relating to the Importation of Softwood Lumber into the United States. Report to the President on Investigation no. 332–210 under Section 332 of the Tariff Act of 1930.* USITC publication 1765, 1985.

U.S. Senate Committee on Commerce. *Japanese Space Industry—An American Challenge.* Hearing before the Committee on Foreign Commerce and Tourism. 101st Cong., 1st sess., October 4, 1989.

U.S. Senate Committee on Finance. *Super 301: Effectiveness in Opening Foreign Markets.* Hearing before the Subcommittee on International Trade of the Committee on Finance. 101st Cong., 2d sess., April 27, 1990.

U.S. Trade Representative. "Intellectual Property Rights Enforcement in China." USTR press release (last modified May 16, 1996).

———. "Statement by Ambassador Barshefsky." Press release 96–53, June 17, 1996.

———. *National Trade Estimate Report on Foreign Trade Barriers.* Various years. Washington, DC: Government Printing Office.

Verdier, Daniel. *Democracy and International Trade: Britain, France, and the United States, 1860–1990.* Princeton: Princeton University Press, 1994.

———. "Democratic Convergence and Free Trade." *International Studies Quarterly* 42, no. 1 (March 1998): 1–24.

Vernon, Raymond, Deborah L. Spar, and Glenn Tobin. *From Triangles and Revolving Doors: Cases in U.S. Foreign Economic Policy Making.* New York: Praeger, 1991.

Wallerstein, Immanuel. *The Modern World-System: Capitalist Agriculture and the Origins of the European World Economy in the Sixteenth Century.* New York: Academic Press, 1976.

Walsh, Edward. "Clinton Indicts Bush's World Leadership." *Washington Post,* October 2, 1992, A12.

Walter, Donna. "Firms Unshaken by U.S. Terms for China." *Los Angeles Times,* June 7, 1993, D3.

Waltz, Kenneth. "The Myth of National Interdependence." In Charles P. Kindleberger, ed., *The Multinational Corporation.* Cambridge, MA: MIT Press, 1970.

———. *Theory of International Politics.* Reading, MA: Addison-Wesley, 1979.

Weart, Spencer R. "Peace among Democratic and Oligarchic Republics." *Journal of Peace Research* 31 (1994): 299–316.

Wolff, Alan W. *Identification of Japan's Failure to Abide by the Semiconductor Agreement, Submission before the United States Trade Representative.* Dewey, Ballantine. Washington, DC. March 1989.

———. *Petition of the Semiconductor Industry Association: Pursuant to Section 301 of the Trade Act of 1974, as amended, for relief from the Effects of Japanese Market Barriers in Semiconductors.* San José: Semiconductor Industry Association, 1985.

Woodall, Brian. *Japan under Construction: Corruption, Politics, and Public Works.* Berkeley: University of California Press, 1996.

World Bank. *World Tables.* Baltimore: Published for the World Bank by the Johns Hopkins University Press. Various years.

Wray, William D. "Japanese Space Enterprise: The Problem of Autonomous Development." *Pacific Affairs* 64, no. 4 (Winter 1991–92): 463–88.

Wriggins, W. Howard. "Up for Auction: Malta Bargains with Great Britain, 1971." In I. William Zartman, ed., *The 50% Solution: How to Bargain Successfully with Hijackers, Strikers, Bosses, Oil Magnates, Arabs, Russians, and Other Worthy Opponents in This Modern World,* 208–34. New York: Anchor Books, 1976.

Wu, Pei-tsu. "U.S.-China Tensions Frighten Importers." *Journal of Commerce,* February 10, 1992, 1A.

Yabunaka, Mitoji. *Taibei keizai kosho: masatsu no jitsuzo* (Economic negotiations with the United States: Views from the negotiating table). Tokyo: Saimaru Shuppankai, 1991.

Yannopoulos, G. N. *Customs Unions and Trade Conflicts.* London: Routledge, 1988.

Yeutter, Clayton. "Preserving the Atlantic Peace: EEC Tariffs." *Financial Times,* January 23, 1987, 23.

Yoffie, David B. *Power and Protectionism: Strategies of the Newly Industrialized Countries.* New York: Columbia University Press, 1983.

———. "How an Industry Builds Political Advantage." *Harvard Business Review* 66, no. 3 (May–June 1988): 82–89.

Yoffie, David B., and John J. Coleman. "The Semiconductor Industry Association and the Trade Dispute with Japan (A)." Cambridge, MA: Harvard Business School case no 9–387–205, Harvard College, 1987.

Yuan, Jing-dong. "Sanctions, Domestic Politics, and U.S. China Policy." *Issues and Studies* 33, no. 10 (1997): 90–123.

Zartman, William. *The Politics of Trade Negotiations between Africa and the European Economic Community.* Princeton: Princeton University Press, 1971.

Zhang, Jia-ling. "Maoyi Baohu Zhuyi Dui Zhongmei Liangguo de Weihai" (The negative impact of trade protectionism on the United States and China: An analysis of U.S. textile trade policies). In Wang Xi and Charles H. Holton, eds., *Zhongmei Jingji Guangxi: Xianzhuang Yu Qianjing* (China-U.S. economic relations: Present and future). Shanghai: Fudan University Press, 1989.

Zhou, Xiao-lin. "U.S.-China Trade Dispute and China's Intellectual Property Protection." *New York University Journal of International Law and Politics* 24, no. 3 (1992): 1115–29.

Index